Till There Was No Remedy

The Story of the Divided Kingdom

And the Prophets of the Period

By

Bob and Sandra Waldron

"Jehovah Hath Declared His Salvation"
Bible Narrative Cycle From Genesis to Revelation
By Bob and Sandra Waldron

Teacher resource books. The Bible narrative retold in easily understood language. More than a Bible story book; easier to read than a commentary. Each book can stand alone as a study help for a particular period of Bible history, or used in sequence for a careful survey study of the whole Bible. Individual or classroom use. High school or adult level.

In the Beginning, The Book of Genesis. . . . . $ 7.95
You Shall Be My People, From Egypt to Canaan $11.95
In the Days of the Judges, Conquest of the Land and the Period of the Judges . . . . $ 8.95
Give Us A King, The United Kingdom and the Wisdom Literature . . . . $ 9.95
Till There Was No Remedy, The Divided Kingdom and the Prophets . . . . $ 8.95
A Remnant Shall Return, Captivity, Return, Years of Silence $10.95
"Sir, We Would See Jesus," The Life of Christ in chronological order. . . . . $ 9.95
Go Tell the Good News, The Early Church, Acts through Paul's Epistles $11.95
"How Long, O Lord?" Hebrews through Revelation . . . . $ 8.95

Other Products Available by Bob and Sandra Waldron

A Generation That Knows Not God, A Teacher Training Manual. A practical book calling for teachers
    everywhere to come back to teaching exactly what the Bible *says.* Individual study or classroom use . . . $ 8.95
The History and Geography of the Bible Story, A Study Manual. Tells the complete story of the Bible
    with an emphasis on where the events happened. 52 lessons. Individual or classroom use $12.99

Maps:

Waldron Publications: Bible Study Maps. Keyed to all of our books; appropriate for all Bible study.
    CD (Windows, Mac OS) $44.95
    Transparencies $118.50

Revised Edition:

Christ In You, The Hope of Glory, A textbook/workbook format. Explores the basic relationship God wants
    with men. 13 lessons. Individual or class study. Adult level. . . . . $ 7.95

Tracts:

    Human Suffering . . . . $ 0.75
    The Unfolding of God's Plan . . . . $ 0.75
    The 3 Cycle Approach . . . . $ 1.25

Video:

    Three Cycle Approach to learning Bible Chronology. An informal video of Bob teaching the material
    as if he were teaching it in a class $18.00

Order From:
Bob Waldron
108 French Way
Athens, Alabama 35611
bwaldron@HiWaay.net
(256) 232-4666

These books are also available at your favorite bookstore.
Prices subject to change without notice.

Table of Contents

The Divided Kingdom *(921 B.C. — 721 B.C.)*
Judah Alone *(721 B.C. — 586 B.C.)*

Israel reached its peak in size and in splendor during the reign of Solomon. Riches were so plentiful in Israel, silver was counted as no more value than stones in the street (1 Kings 10:27). Solomon controlled at least the trade routes all the way from the tip of the Gulf of Aqaba in the south, to the Euphrates River in the north. God had blessed Solomon in so many ways.

But Solomon turned away from Jehovah in his last years. He had built places for his foreign wives to worship their gods — and had even gone with them to participate in their worship. Therefore, the Lord appeared to him one more time, and told him that the kingdom would be torn away from his family. Only a small portion of the kingdom would be left in the family of David, in order to fulfill the promise God had made to David. (1 Kings 11:1-13.)

The outer fringes of Solomon's kingdom began to erode away even before his death. Rezon set up a stronghold in Damascus as the beginning of the kingdom we will soon meet as Syria (1 Kings 11:23-25). Hadad from Edom returned home from his time of exile in Egypt, so that he could be in position to take control of his homeland if possible (1 Kings 11:14-22). Ahijah the prophet predicted that Jeroboam of the tribe of Ephraim would be named king of ten of the tribes of Israel — and Jeroboam had to flee to Egypt to save his life from Solomon (1 Kings 11:26-40).

The United Kingdom is about to fall apart!

The Divided Kingdom began within a few weeks of Solomon's death. Usually a period of mourning followed a king's death, but the length of such a period varied from one circumstance to another. Three days, however, after Rehoboam the son of Solomon took over the kingdom, Israel divided into the north and the south. The northern kingdom continued to be called Israel and the southern kingdom was called Judah.

The Divided Kingdom lasted until 721 B.C., when the northern kingdom of Israel fell to Assyria. After that, only the very small kingdom of Judah remained, until 586 B.C., when it fell to the Babylonians. This book will cover the history all the way from the division of Solomon's kingdom, through the fall of the kingdom of Israel, and on through the fall of Jerusalem and Judah. Therefore, we have both the Divided Kingdom and Judah Alone highlighted in our outline of Bible history.

The history of the Divided Kingdom is a study of the blessings of obedience and the curses of sin. The lesson is pounded home relentlessly. The king who led his people in righteousness was blessed, and, in his time, his kingdom would prosper. It would be spared against impossible odds. The kings who were evil were sorely punished, and the kingdom suffered as well. Israel had *no* good kings, so its plunge into wickedness was very fast. Judah had some good kings, so its course, although generally downward, had some ups to counter the downs. The contrast in the history of the two kingdoms emphasizes the lesson of the blessings of righteousness and the chastisements of wickedness.

Since this material takes us all the way through 721 B.C. and the fall of Israel, on through 586 B.C. and the fall of Judah, allow two full quarters (Sunday morning and Wednesday night classes) to study the whole material. Our format is different for this period of history. Because of the two kingdoms that must be studied at once, we have put all the information about the kingdom of Judah in the left hand column, and all the information about Israel in the right hand column. When we come to accounts where the two kingdoms are both involved in an event — such as a battle against each other, or a united effort to fight an enemy — we have put the account into a column down the center of the page. The two-column format is briefly interrupted when we come to the stories of Elijah and Elisha, because the history of Judah fades into the background for a time, while the mighty effort of God to bring the kingdom of Israel back to Him is told through the description of the work of His mighty prophets Elijah and Elisha. When we come to the writing prophets, we include a summary of their message in place where they fit into the history. It will be made clear to which kingdom each prophet came. The writing prophets are introduced with the name of the prophet centered and underlined above his message.

As you study the period of history, notice that the books of 1 and 2 Kings emphasize the events taking place in the kingdom of Israel, with only some details about the kingdom of Judah. On the other hand, the book of 2 Chronicles emphasizes the events taking place in the kingdom of Judah, with only the details about Israel that fit directly with some king of Judah. Do not leave 2 Chronicles out of your study.

This is a complicated period of Bible history because there are so many names and so many events involved. But do not let that discourage you from studying the period. It is a fascinating period of history, and a very important one in understanding the whole story of God's people, and what happened to them. There will be a vast gap in your Bible knowledge if you let this period stay blank. Even the younger children can learn fascinating stories from the period of the kings. Do not deprive them of the beloved stories.

The following chart shows the list of the kings that ruled in each kingdom. It shows the name the king is called most often, plus other spellings of the name, or other names the king is called. It includes how long each king reigned, and whether he was good or evil. The chart also shows how the kings overlapped. The asterisks in the list of kings of Israel indicate changes in the ruling family (dynasty). Study the chart carefully, and continue to refer back to it as you study the period of history.

Kings of the Divided Kingdom

Judah

Rehoboam - 17 years - Evil *married Maacah daughter of absalom*
  1 Kings 12:1-24; 14:21-31; 15:6;
  2 Chron. 10:1-12:16
Abijam (Abijah) - 3 years - Evil *son of Maacah*
  1 Kings 15:1-8;
  2 Chron. 13
Asa - 41 years - Good
  1 Kings 15:9-24;
  2 Chron. 14:1-16:14

Jehoshaphat - 25 years - Good
  1 Kings 22:41-50; 22:2-36;
  2 Chron. 17:1-21:1

Jehoram (Joram) - 8 years - Evil
  2 Kings 8:16-24;
  2 Chron. 21

Israel

Jeroboam - 22 years - Evil
  1 Kings 11:26-40; 12:1-14:20;
  2 Chron. 10:1-17; 13:1-20

Nadab - 2 years- Evil
  1 Kings 15:25-32

****

Baasha - 24 years - Evil
  1 Kings 15:16-22; 15:33-16:7;
  2 Chron. 16:1-6
Elah - 2 years - Evil
  1 Kings 16:8-14

****

Zimri - 1 week - Evil
  1 Kings 16:15-20

****

Omri - 12 years - Evil
  1 Kings 16:21-28
Ahab - 22 years - Evil
  1 Kings 16:29-22:40;
  2 Chron. 18:1-34

Ahaziah - 2 years -Evil
  1 Kings 22:51 - 2 Kings 1:17;
  2 Chron. 20:35-37
Jehoram (Joram) - 12 years - Evil
  2 Kings 3:1-8:24

Ahaziah - 1 year - Evil
  (Jehoahaz, Azariah)
  2 Kings 8:25-9:28;
  2 Chron. 22:1-9

*Athaliah - 6 years - Evil
  2 Kings 11:1-20;
  2 Chron. 22:10-23:21
Joash (Jehoash) - 40 years - Evil
  2 Kings 11:21-12:21;
  2 Chron. 24:1-27

Amaziah - 29 years - Good
  2 Kings 14:1-20;
  2 Chron. 25:1-28

Uzziah (Azariah) - 52 years - Good
  2 Kings 15:1-7;
  2 Chron. 26:1-23

****

Jehu - 28 years - Evil
  2 Kings 9:1-10:36

Jehoahaz - 17 years - Evil
  2 Kings 13:1-9
Joash (Jehoash) - 16 years - Evil
  2 Kings 13:9-14:16;
  2 Chron. 25:17-25

Jeroboam II - 41 years - Evil
  2 Kings 14:23-29

Zechariah - 6 months - Evil
  2 Kings 15:8-12

****

Shallum - 1 month - Evil
  2 Kings 15:13-15

****

Menahem - 10 years - Evil
  2 Kings 15:16-22
Pekahiah - 2 years - Evil
  2 Kings 15:23-26

****

Pekah - 20 years - Evil
  2 Kings 15:27-31; 16:1-5;
  2 Chron. 28:5-15

Jotham - 16 years - Good
  2 Kings 15:32-38;
  2 Chron. 27:1-9
Ahaz - 16 years - Evil
  2 Kings 16:1-20;
  2 Chron. 28:1-27

****

Hezekiah - 29 years - Good
  2 Kings 18:1-20:21;
  2 Chron. 29:1-32:33

Hoshea - 9 years - Evil
  2 Kings 17:1-18:12

Fall of Samaria — 721 B.C.
  2 Kings 17:5, 6; 18:9-12
  ****

Manasseh - 55 years - Evil
  2 Kings 21:1-18;
  2 Chron. 33:1-20
Amon - 2 years - Evil
  2 Kings 21:18-26;
  2 Chron. 33:21-25
Josiah - 31 years - Good
  2 Kings 22:1-23:30;
  2 Chron. 34:1-35:27)
Jehoahaz (Shallum) - 3 months - Evil
  2 Kings 23:31-34;
  2 Chron. 36:1-3
Jehoiakim (Eliakim) - 11 years - Evil
  2 Kings 23:34-24:6;
  2 Chron. 36:4-8
Jehoiachin - 3 months - Evil
  (Coniah, Jeconiah)
  2 Kings 24:6-16;
  2 Chron. 36:8-10
Zedekiah (Mattaniah) - 11 years - Evil
  2 Kings 24:17-25:7;
  2 Chron. 36:10-23

Fall of Jerusalem - 586 B.C.
  2 Kings 24:20- 25:21;
  2 Chron. 36:13-21

****

Gedaliah is Appointed Governor
  2 Kings 25:22-26;
  Jeremiah 40:5-44:30

The Kingdom Divides
(1 Kings 12:1-20; 2 Chronicles 10:1-19)

After Solomon's death, when Rehoboam was ready to take up the reins of government, he called the people to meet him at Shechem. Possibly Shechem was chosen for the site of this meeting because it was there God promised to give the land of Canaan to Abraham's descendants (Gen. 12:6-7); and it was there that Israel staked her claim upon the land as Moses had commanded in the law (Josh. 8:30-35).

Do you remember that Jeroboam the son of Nebat, of the tribe of Ephraim, had been told by Ahijah the prophet that he would be given rule over ten of the tribes? And, do you remember, Jeroboam had to flee to Egypt to escape Solomon's wrath? (See 1 Kings 11:26-40.) When Jeroboam heard of Solomon's death, he returned to Israel and he acted as spokesman for the people when they assembled before Rehoboam at Shechem.

The people told Rehoboam, "Your father put a heavy yoke on us. Lighten the harsh labor we are required to do and the heavy yoke he put on us, and we will serve you."

Rehoboam replied, "Come again in three days, and I will give you my answer."

During the three days, Rehoboam counselled with his advisers. His older advisers said, "Listen to the people. Show them you have their interest at heart and help them in their distress, and they will serve you."

The king's younger men, however, seemed to think that any concession would be taken as a sign of weakness. They advised, "Tell them, 'My little finger will be thicker than my father's thigh. My father chastised you with whips; I will scourge you with scorpions.'" Unfortunately, the advice to be harsh and to sound tough appealed to Rehoboam.

When the people returned to Shechem, Rehoboam went out and repeated these harsh words to his subjects. When the Israelites heard Rehoboam's words, they replied: "What share do we have in David? Everyone go home. You can have your kingdom, O David."

The situation was fraught with danger. Rehoboam sent Adoniram, the officer in charge of all taskwork, to try to quell the rising tide of rebellion. Rehoboam could not have picked a worse one to send because Adoniram represented all the task work they had been required to do. The Israelites were angry and they stoned him to death with stones. Rehoboam managed to escape in his chariot and he fled to Jerusalem.

JUDAH	ISRAEL
Rehoboam—17 years (evil)	**Jeroboam—22 years (evil)**
(1 Kings 12:1-24; 14:21-31; 2 Chron. 10:1-12:16):	(1 Kings 11:26-40; 12:1-14:20; 2 Chron. 10:1-17; 13:1-20):
Just as God had foretold to both Solomon and Jeroboam, a portion of the kingdom was left in the control of Rehoboam and the house	Just as Ahijah the prophet had foretold, the other ten tribes made Jeroboam their king. He set up headquarters at the city of

Judah

of David, not because Rehoboam was righteous, but because of God's promise to David (see 1 Kings 11:11-13; 2 Sam. 7:11-16). Rehoboam's own tribe of Judah and the tribe of Benjamin remained loyal. Judah was, by far, the larger of the two tribes; therefore Benjamin is sometimes named with Judah, sometimes not.

Rehoboam took the name of Judah as the name for his kingdom. They kept the capital city of Jerusalem which was located very near the border of Benjamin and Judah's ancestral territory, though barely inside Benjamin's portion. Jerusalem was the site of the palace and, more importantly, the temple of Jehovah.

Israel

Shechem, likely as an effort to establish the legitimacy of his rule because of the historical significance of Shechem.

They kept the name of Israel that the people had used for generations. Since there were ten tribes in this group, in contrast to two tribes in Judah, Israel was the larger of the kingdoms.

Look at the maps included with this material. All maps are together in the back of the book. The grey-tone ones have the places named on them. Use them as a guide to do your study maps. You will understand each map better if you take time to fill in one of your own. First look at the map showing the kingdom as it was in Solomon's day. Color and label your map like it. Now look at the map of Canaan showing the land divided into the little kingdoms of Israel and Judah. Do you see the contrast? The kingdom of Israel continued to hold the little nation of Moab for a few more years, while the kingdom of Judah held Edom for a little longer. The rest of the territory that had been at least under Solomon's economic control was lost immediately. Color your first map of Canaan showing the two little kingdoms as they were at this point in history.

Let us make some more comparisons from our maps before we go further in our story. Note that Israel still held a portion of the land on the east side of the Jordan River. That means they could still tax the caravans that moved through the land on the trade route called the Kings Highway. On the other side of the Jordan River, the trade route called the Way of the Sea crossed the Jordan and moved southwest across Israel's territory, thus more taxes available. In contrast, Judah was land-locked. The main trade routes avoided the more difficult roads through the hill country. The Dead Sea was a natural barrier on the east, and the Philistines still held firm control of the southern coastal plain. Sometimes, Judah controlled part of Edom and held access to the riches of Ezion-geber at the tip of the Gulf of Aqaba, but more often either Egypt or Edom took that prize away.

Therefore, Israel tended to be more prosperous with more contact with other peoples. But that prosperity proved to be a mixed blessing. They tended to be at ease and to forget their need for Jehovah. Also, any foreign power who wanted control of the trade routes came into direct conflict with Israel.

Rehoboam is Forbidden to Stop the Rebellion (1 Kings 12:21-24; 2 Chron. 11:1-4):

Rehoboam was enraged, as well as frightened, over the insurrection. He called for the fighting men of Judah and Benjamin to gather — 180,000 of them — to fight against Israel and re-unite the kingdom.

God sent a prophet named Shemaiah to Rehoboam with this message: "Do not go up and fight with your brethren, the Israelites. All of you go home, for this is my doing."

Rehoboam obeyed the voice of God and did not pursue his plans for war.

Rehoboam Fortifies Judah (2 Chron. 11:5-12):

Rehoboam began fortifying cities in his territory very early in his reign. It is interesting to note that the cities named that he fortified were in the Shephelah, south and west of Jerusalem, rather than north of Jerusalem. Obviously, Rehoboam did not consider Jeroboam the worst of the threats against his kingdom.

Solomon had made a treaty of peace with Egypt very soon after he became king, and he sealed that treaty by marrying Pharaoh's daughter (1 Kings 3:1). But years have passed since that treaty. A new Pharaoh named Shishak came to power in Egypt before Solomon died. Solomon's wealth was known far and wide, so Shishak was watching for his chance to invade the land and take part of that wealth. Rehoboam was aware of the danger.

Find the fortified cities on your map. Note how they protected the approaches to Jerusalem from the south and west. Also note that attacks from Egypt would likely reach Judah before Israel.

Jeroboam Sets Up a False Religion (1 Kings 12:25-33; 2 Chron. 11:15):

Jeroboam was afraid that his kingdom would not remain his own, even though God had assured him it would, if he remained faithful. In fact, God had told him that he could establish his family as the reigning dynasty just as David had, if he would only be faithful (1 Kings 11:37-38). But Jeroboam did not have enough faith to trust God's promise.

One thing that added fuel to the king's worries was the continual visits all Israelites would be making back to Jerusalem, the capital of Judah, to the temple to worship Jehovah. He therefore decided on a drastic course of action. He made two golden calves and he built shrines for them: one at Dan on his northern border and one at Bethel on his southern border, a few miles north of Jerusalem.

Jeroboam told his people, "It is too much for you to have to go to Jerusalem."

He showed them the golden calves which he had made and said, "These are your gods, O Israel, the very ones who brought you up out of Egypt."

Jeroboam did not entirely dismiss Jehovah. He wanted the people to associate the reputation of Jehovah with the golden calves. Notice that he said they were still worshiping the very gods who had brought them out of Egypt. In other words, he was saying, "We are still worshiping Jehovah — we are just going to do it our way."

Jeroboam appointed priests from tribes other than Levi. He changed the observance of the annual atonement from the seventh month to the eighth month.

Jeroboam publicly dedicated his shrines of worship with sacrifices.

Since, then as now, most people merely went through the motion of religion, most Israelites accepted these changes with little problem.

The Faithful in Israel Flee to Judah
(2 Chron. 11:13-14, 16-17):

When Jeroboam set up his false worship with his false priests, the Levites and priests living in Israel were without a job. They began moving south; they even left their ancestral fields and homes and moved to Judah. Others who were determined to remain faithful to Jehovah also fled to Judah.

This influx of righteous people strengthened the kingdom of Judah and weakened the kingdom of Jeroboam. For three years the people of Judah served Jehovah faithfully.

Rehoboam's Family (2 Chron. 11:18-23):

Rehoboam married eighteen wives and took sixty concubines. He had twenty-eight sons and sixty daughters. Among his wives were Mahalath, a first cousin; Abihail the daughter of David's brother Eliab; and Maacah the daughter of Absalom. It was one of Maacah's sons, Abijah, who would succeed Rehoboam upon the throne.

Rehoboam appointed Abijah the chief prince among his sons because he intended for him to be king. Rehoboam scattered his sons throughout the land, probably in supervisory capacities, and gave them good salaries and many wives.

The Prophecy of the Man of God
(1 Kings 13:1-32):

On the day of the dedication, Jeroboam was at the shrine in Bethel. Everyone was gathered together. Right in the midst of the ceremonies, a man came up and cried out to the altar. He said:

> Oh altar, altar! Thus saith Jehovah, "A son named Josiah will be born to the house of David. He will burn upon you the bones of the priests who now make offerings here."
>
> This is the sign that these things will come true: the altar will be split apart and the ashes will be poured out on the ground.

Jeroboam shouted, "Seize him!" and he pointed at the man of God. Instantly the stretched out arm was shriveled so that he could not pull it back. Also the altar split and the ashes fell out.

Jeroboam was terror-stricken! He begged the man of God: "Ask the Lord your God for me and pray for my hand to be returned." The man of God did pray, and the king's hand was restored.

Now no kindness was too great for Jeroboam to show the prophet. "Come home and eat with me, and I will give you a gift."

The man of God replied, "Even if you were to give me half of your possessions, I could not go with you. God told me, 'You must not eat bread, or drink water, or return by the way you came.'" The prophet headed home another way.

There was an old prophet living in Bethel. When his sons told him about the man of God, he asked, "Which way did he go?"

When they told him, he said, "Saddle my donkey for me." He rode off after the man of God and found him sitting under an oak tree. He said, "Are you the man of God from Judah?"

"Yes," the man replied.

The old prophet said, "Come home with me and eat."

The man of God said, "Oh I can't do that because the Lord told me not to eat or drink with anyone, or to return home the way I came."

The old prophet then lied. He said, "I am also a prophet, and God spoke to me telling me to bring you to my house to eat and drink." When he heard this, the man of God went home with the prophet.

He did not make any inquiry of God from whom he had personally been given his instructions; nor did he seek any verification that the old prophet was indeed telling him the truth. Since the old prophet flatly contradicted what God Himself had told the man of God, the man of God should have demanded some sort of proof.

Judah Turns to Idolatry (1 Kings 14:22-24; 2 Chron. 12:1, 14):

When Rehoboam felt that he was secure in his kingdom, he and Judah abandoned Jehovah. They were faithful only for about three years. It seems that they still offered sacrifices at the temple and had their feast days, but it was only a ritual of worship with many of the people. They also set up the Asherim on every hill. There were even male shrine prostitutes in the land. Soon the people were practicing every abomination which the Canaanites had done, for which the Lord had driven them out of the land. (See Lev. 18:24-28.)

How could Rehoboam turn his back upon Jehovah so quickly? Look in 1 Kings 14:21. Do you see that he was the son of Naamah, an Ammonite? That means he was the son of one of the foreign wives Solomon married. He grew up seeing his mother worship idols regularly.

As they were eating together, God really did speak to the old prophet. The old prophet told the man of God, "This is what the Lord says: 'You have defied the command of God. You came back and ate bread and drank water in the place where you were forbidden to do so. Therefore your body will not be buried in the tomb of your fathers.'"

After the meal, the prophet brought the man's donkey for him and he rode away. As he went along, a lion met him on the road and killed him; but the lion did not devour the body nor kill the donkey. People passing by saw the lion still standing there beside the man it had killed. They went into Bethel and reported it.

When he heard it, the old prophet said, "It is the man of God who disobeyed God's word. The lion has killed him as the Lord spoke."

The prophet went out and put the man's body on his donkey, brought it back to the city, and buried it. The old prophet told his sons, "When I die, bury me in the grave where the man of God is buried; lay my bones by his

Shishak, Pharaoh of Egypt, invades Judah (1 Kings 14:25-28; 2 Chron. 12:2-12):

Because of Judah's unfaithfulness, God delivered them into the hand of Shishak. This was the Pharaoh who had given Jeroboam refuge in the last days of Solomon (1 Kings

11:40).

Pharaoh Shishak invaded in the fifth year of Rehoboam. He came with a vast army, 1200 chariots and 60,000 cavalrymen. He took Rehoboam's fortified cities and came to Jerusalem itself.

The Lord sent the prophet Shemaiah to Rehoboam and to the leaders of Judah who had gathered in Jerusalem for fear of Shishak. He said, "The Lord sent me to tell you, 'You abandoned me, so I have abandoned you to Shishak.'"

Rehoboam and the other rulers were very humble and said, "Jehovah is just."

When God saw that they humbled themselves, He said to Shemaiah, "Since they have humbled themselves, I will not destroy them. But I will deliver them into Shishak's hand so that they may learn the difference between serving me and serving the kings of other lands."

Shishak entered Jerusalem and carried away the temple treasures, including the golden shields Solomon had made for ceremonial occasions. Rehoboam made bronze shields to replace them. Do you see that the wealth Solomon left is now gone from Judah?

Because Rehoboam humbled himself, God did not totally destroy him. There was some good still left in Judah.

bones because the word which he said against the altar in Bethel will definitely come true."

Historical Note —Shishak Invades Israel Also:

Even though the Bible does not tell of it, Shishak's own inscriptions tell that he invaded Israel as well as Judah. Both kingdoms were mauled by this man who had been Jeroboam's former protector. The Egyptian records of Shishak list 150 cities in Canaan that he attacked.

Jeroboam Continues His idolatry
(1 Kings 13:33-34):

Jeroboam never drew back or hesitated in choosing the course of idolatry. This was the sin that led to the downfall of Jeroboam's house. Ever after, this sin of Jeroboam in introducing the golden calf worship is referred to as "the sin of Jeroboam the son of Nebat."

The Death of Jeroboam's Son (1 Kings 14:1-18):

Jeroboam had a young son named Abijah. The boy fell ill and Jeroboam wanted to know if he would live or die. He told his wife, "Disguise yourself so that you will not be recognized as my wife. Then go to Shiloh. Ahijah the prophet is there, the same one who told me I would be king. Take ten loaves of bread, some cakes, and a jar of honey with you. Go to him and he will tell you what will happen to the boy."

Jeroboam's wife set out on her way. Some years had passed since Ahijah had told Jeroboam he would be given a portion of the kingdom. By now, Ahijah was old and blind.

While Jeroboam's wife was on her way, God spoke to Ahijah, saying, "Jeroboam's wife is coming to ask about her son because he is ill.When she arrives, she will be disguised as someone else."

When Ahijah heard footsteps at the door, he calmly said, "Come in, O wife of Jeroboam. Why are you pretending to be someone else? I have been given bad news to tell you. Go tell Jeroboam that this is what Jehovah the God of Israel says:

> I made you leader of my people Israel. I took the kingdom away from the house of David and gave it to you. But you have not been like my servant David who kept my commands. You have done more evil than all who have come before you. You have made yourself other gods. You have provoked me to anger and thrust me behind your back.

> Therefore I will bring disaster upon the house of Jeroboam. I will cut off every male of Jeroboam, slave or free. I will burn up the house of Jeroboam as one burns up dung until it is gone. Dogs will eat those who die in the city and vultures will eat those who die in the country. This is what God has said.

Rehoboam's Reign as King (1 Kings 14:21, 29, 30; 15:6; 2 Chron. 12:13, 15):

Rehoboam was forty-one when he began to rule and he ruled for seventeen years. The records of Rehoboam's rule were written in the chronicles of Shemaiah the prophet and of Iddo the seer.

A similar note will be given in the Bible text about each king. There were records kept of the history of the kings that we do not have. The

Ahijah continued:
As for you, go back home. When you set foot in the city, your son will die, and all Israel will mourn for him and bury him. But he is the only one of Jeroboam's family who will be buried for he is the only one in whom the Lord has found anything good.

God will raise up another king who will cut off the family of Jeroboam, and it will be soon.

Judah	Israel

information we have is a <u>religious</u> history of the period. Over and over, we are told that a king prospered, or that he suffered <u>because</u> he did or did not serve God.

Then, by the Spirit of God, Ahijah's blind eyes saw far into the future and he said, "God will uproot Israel from this good land which He gave to their forefathers and will scatter them beyond the Euphrates River *[in the lands of Assyria and Babylon]*. He will give Israel up because of the sins Jeroboam has committed and has caused Israel to commit."

There was constant war between Rehoboam and Jeroboam all their days. In other words, not that they had open battles, but they never reconciled their differences, or made peace. Finally Rehoboam died and was buried in the City of David.

Jeroboam's wife returned to Tirzah where Jeroboam had established headquarters. As soon as she stepped over the threshold of the house, her son died and all Israel mourned for him and buried him, as Ahijah had said.

Abijah (Abijam) — 3 years (evil)
(1 Kings 15:1-8; 2 Chron. 13):

18th year of Jeroboam

Abijah's mother was Maacah, the daughter of Absalom (or Abishalom, a slightly longer spelling). Abijah followed the ways of Rehoboam his father, and did not live as David did who served Jehovah faithfully, except in the matter of Uriah the Hittite.

Abijah's War With Jeroboam
(2 Chron. 13)

The only story given about Abijah's reign is of a war he fought with Jeroboam. They went into battle with large armies, but Abijah was outnumbered two to one. While the armies were drawn up in array for battle, before the battle began, Abijah stood on Mount Zemaraim in the hill country of Ephraim and spoke to Jeroboam and his men. He said:

Jeroboam and ye men of Israel, listen to me. Do you not know that God gave the kingdom of Israel to David and his descendants forever? Yet Jeroboam, the son of Nebat, who was an official of Solomon, rebelled against his master. He gathered together some scoundrels, and they opposed Rehoboam the son of Solomon when he was young and inexperienced and unable to resist them.

And you still resist the kingdom of Jehovah which is in the hands of David's descendants. You have a very strong army and the golden calves which Jeroboam made. But didn't you drive out the priests of God and the Levites and make priests of your own like the people of other lands? Anybody can be a priest for you if he brings a nice offering.

As for us, we are still serving the Lord. We have not forsaken Him. Our priests are the sons of Aaron as they are supposed to be, and the daily offerings are given as Jehovah has ordained. We are observing God's statutes, and you are not. Men of Israel, do not fight against the Lord, the God of your fathers, for you cannot succeed.

Jeroboam's men appeared to be listening, but while Abijah was delivering his warning, the men of Jeroboam were quietly encircling Abijah's army. Even as he talked, Jeroboam's men attacked. The men of Judah saw that they were being attacked before and behind. They cried to Jehovah, the priests blew their trumpets (see Num. 10:8-9), and Judah sounded the battle cry.

God delivered Israel into the hands of Judah, and Jeroboam's forces suffered the loss of many men. The men of Judah were victorious *because they relied on Jehovah*. Abijah pursued Jeroboam and took Bethel and some other towns from him. Jeroboam did not regain power during the remainder of Abijah's reign.

<u>**JUDAH**</u>	<u>**ISRAEL**</u>

Abijah died and was buried in the City of David.

Asa — 41 years (good)
(1 Kings 15:9-24; 2 Chron. 14:1-16:14):

20th year of Jeroboam

The Early Years of Asa (1 Kings 15:11-15; 2 Chron. 14:1-8):

Asa was a righteous man, so Judah enjoyed peace for the first ten years of his reign. Asa used the time to good advantage.

First he reformed Judah by destroying the idols which had been built during the years of Rehoboam and Abijah. He commanded the people of Judah to serve Jehovah. It is amazing that within twenty years of Solomon's death and only sixty years since David's death, every town in Judah had its own high place where incense was burned and offerings were made to false gods. Asa destroyed those. Therefore, the kingdom enjoyed peaceful times.

2nd year of Asa

Asa continued to use the years of peace wisely by fortifying the cities of Judah. Remember that Rehoboam fortified a belt of cities that extended from the Dead Sea west to the Shephelah and then north to the border between Israel and Judah. Shishak of Egypt captured those cities when he entered the land. These were the same cities Asa fortified

Nadab — 2 years (evil)
(1 Kings 15:25-32):

After a rule of 22 years, Jeroboam died and his son Nadab succeeded to the throne. But God no longer planned to establish Jeroboam's dynasty because of the idolatry he had introduced as the official religion of Israel.

Nadab was very wicked and was rejected after a portion of only two years. He was struck down by Baasha during the siege of the again. He also fortified others of the cities. Asa encouraged the people by saying, "The land is still ours because we have sought the Lord."

As part of his defenses, Asa put together a well equipped army of 300,000 men of Judah and 280,000 men of Benjamin.

3rd year of Asa

Asa and Judah are Delivered from the Ethiopians (2 Chron. 14:9-15):

After the ten years of peace, the calm was broken by the invasion of a fearsome army led by Zera the Cushite (or Ethiopian). The figure given in Hebrew is usually taken to mean an innumerable army rather than a literal count. It was clear that the Ethiopian army was many times more powerful than that of Judah.

The army of Judah went out to resist the invasion and took their stand at Mareshah southwest of Jerusalem, only a few miles from Lachish.

Asa prayed to God for help. He said, "Lord, there is no one like you to help the weak against the mighty. We are counting on you, and in your name we have come out against this vast army. O Jehovah, you are God. Do not let men prevail against you."

God gave Asa and his army a great victory. The Cushites were destroyed in great numbers. They were crushed before the Lord and His forces. Asa's men pursued the Cushites as far as Gerar, about 30 or 35 miles southwest of Mareshah. The Cushites were obviously fleeing back to Egypt.

The men of Judah took an enormous amount of booty from the fleeing army. They destroyed all the villages around Gerar and took booty from those Philistine villages. A

Philistine city of Gibbethon. Baasha left none of the house of Jeroboam alive, just as God had predicted through Ahijah the Shilonite, because of the sins Jeroboam had committed.

****

Baasha — 24 years (evil)
(1 Kings 15:16-22; 15:33-16:7; 2 Chron. 16:1-6):

Baasha, the murderer of Jeroboam's family, became the next king in Israel. He could have established his family upon the throne of Israel, but he was wicked and followed in the same ways as Jeroboam, worshiping the golden calves.

This lets us know that he did not kill Jeroboam's family in order to purge Israel of the sin that had been introduced, but rather because of his own lust for power.

Many Faithful Move From Israel to Judah (2 Chron. 15:9):

Do you remember that when Jeroboam first set up the golden calves and his new priests, the Levites and the most faithful people in Israel moved south to Judah? Now years have passed, but conditions have not improved in Israel. Baasha is just as wicked as his predecessor.

Meanwhile, Judah is at peace. They have a righteous king who is bringing about reforms in the land. As the faithful people still living in Israel saw that God was with Judah, they began moving south. The Bible says "large numbers" from Israel joined Asa and his kingdom at this point.

Do you see that the population in the two kingdoms was by now much nearer the same than it was at the beginning? Do you also see

great deal of the plunder consisted of flocks of sheep and herds of goats and camels.

The Message of Azariah the Prophet
(2 Chron. 15:1-7):

God sent word to Asa by Azariah the son of Oded. Azariah met Asa and he said, "Listen to me, Asa and all Judah and Benjamin. The Lord has been with you because you have been faithful. If you continue to seek Jehovah, He will be with you. But if you turn away from God, He will turn away from you."

Azariah reminded the people of the turmoil and strife which had been in the land in recent years. He said, "For a long time" [*including the later years of Solomon's reign, most of the reign of Rehoboam, and Abijah's reign*] "Israel was without God. There was no priest who taught the law of God to the people. In those days it was not safe to travel. But if you will be strong and faithful, you will be rewarded."

Asa Renews the Covenant with God
(1 Kings 15:9-15; 2 Chron. 15:8-19):

Encouraged by the astonishing victory God had given Judah over the Ethiopians and by Azariah's message, Asa continued his efforts to reform Judah spiritually. He removed idols from the towns of Judah and Benjamin and also from towns he had captured from Israel. He repaired the bronze altar of burnt offering which was in the courtyard of the temple of God.

One of the fascinating things he did was to confront his grandmother about her idolatry. She had set up a pole which was the symbol associated with the Asherah worship. The Asherah (or the plural form Asherim) was the female counterpart to the false god Baal. It was a crude and despicable worship. Asa cut down the pole, burned it in the Kidron Valley, and removed Maacah from her position as Queen Mother.

that the kingdom of Judah was strengthened each time a faithful family moved south, but that Israel was weakened — not only in number, but more importantly, in spiritual strength? Each time a faithful family left Israel, there was one less family to protest the introduction of more wickedness.

Chronological Note:
Baasha came to power in Asa's third year and he ruled for 24 years. He died in Asa's 26th year. The first thing that must be understood is that if Baasha ruled any part of Asa's third year and from then to any part of Asa's 26th year, that would be counted by the Jews as 24 years of rule.

The second thing we must note is that Asa's rule began with ten years of peace. Then came the battle with Zerah and the Ethiopians. Then, it says there was no more war until the 35th year of Asa and the war at that time was with Baa-

16

| Judah | Israel |

Judah

Remember that Maacah was the daughter of Absalom, the wife of Rehoboam, the mother of Abijah, and therefore the grandmother of Asa.

Asa realized that in Judah's departure from God, the people had forsaken their covenant with God. The king gathered the people together, including those who had recently joined his kingdom from Israel, and renewed their covenant to seek Jehovah, the God of their fathers, with all their heart and soul. All those who would not do so were to be put to death.

Though the day was a great day and Asa was certainly to be commended, later events show that Asa reformed everything except the hearts of the people. As time goes by, we will see that the kings of Judah had tremendous influence upon events that happened to the kingdom and upon the public character, but little or no influence upon the individual hearts and lives of the people. Nevertheless, the efforts of the people of Judah seemed to be sincere for the moment, even if the condition did not endure.

Israel

sha. Yet Baasha died in Asa's 26th year. Obviously there is a discrepancy in the numbers. How this discrepancy came about is not known for sure, but the most reasonable explanation is that in copying the manuscript, at some time, a scribe made an error and wrote down one thing when he meant another. Virtually all discrepancies in the Old Testament are matters of chronology and numbers. Yet enough accounts are given for it to be possible for us to find those discrepancies and take them into account. Therefore, instead of the war told about in the next section being in the 35th year of Asa, it was in his 25th year.

All of the chronological problems in the Divided Kingdom are not as obvious as this one. We will deal with only the most obvious ones.

Remember that these numbers concerning when a man began to rule, or when some particular battle was fought, or exactly how many men died do not effect our soul's salvation. Do not spend long in class discussing such matters.

Asa's War With Baasha
(1 Kings 15:16-22; 2 Chron. 16:1-6)

There were about fourteen more years of peace in Judah after the battle with the Ethiopians. Then Baasha moved against Judah. He took his forces to Ramah to build a fort between Israel and Judah. This was an effort to keep his subjects from moving south to Judah.

Asa did not want the fort on his northern border, so he took silver and gold from the temple treasures and sent it to Ben-hadad the king who ruled the little kingdom of Syria on Baasha's northern border. He asked Ben-hadad to attack Baasha in the north. The Syrian king was happy to do so, and he attacked several cities north and west of the Sea of Galilee. Baasha was forced to withdraw his men from Ramah and go fight Ben-hadad. While he was gone, Asa took his own men to Ramah and stole Baasha's building materials. He used the supplies to fortify his own cities of Geba and Mizpeh in Benjamin. These cities, like Ramah, were border cities, but they were fortified under Asa's control rather than Baasha's control.

Historical Note:

   Label the kingdom of Syria on your map. Label the city of Damascus as the capital of Syria. Look back to 1 Kings 11:23-25. A man named Rezon took control of the city of Damascus before Solomon died. He was hostile toward Solomon and Israel, adding to the trouble Solomon was facing in his last years. The kingdom of Syria was quietly growing in strength during these years we have been following the history of Israel and Judah. This is the first open warfare between Israel and Syria so far as the record goes. Syria will continue to be a problem to Israel as the years pass.

JUDAH

Hanani the Prophet Rebukes Asa
(2 Chron. 16:7-10):

   Many have admired the "strategy" of Asa in dealing with Baasha. God did not admire it at all. He sent His prophet to say:

   "Asa, do you remember the huge army of the Cushites, and do you remember how I delivered you from their hand? You relied upon me and I saved you. Jehovah looks to and fro throughout the earth to see those whose hearts are truly devoted to Him. Why have you relied upon the king of Syria this time instead of upon the Lord? Therefore, you will have war from now on."

   Sadly, Asa became very angry with Hanani and cast him into prison. At the same time he afflicted certain others of the people of Judah, likely others who did not approve of his actions.

26th year of Asa

ISRAEL

The Prophet Jehu Reproves Baasha
(1 Kings 16:1-6):

   God sent Jehu, the son of Hanani, to Baasha to say, "I chose you to be leader in Israel in the place of Jeroboam. Yet you have continued in the ways of Jeroboam. Therefore I am going to consume Baasha and his house."

   Baasha died and was succeeded by his son Elah.

Elah — 2 years (evil)
(1 Kings 16:8-14):

   Elah ruled for portions of two years (*therefore listed as two years according to the Jews' way of recording time*). He was killed by an official of his army named Zimri. Elah was drinking himself drunk in the home of Arza the chief steward of the royal house in Tirzah.

   Zimri also killed every member of the family of Baasha. Not one was left alive, either family or friend. Thus was fulfilled the word of the Lord which had been spoken by Jehu the prophet.

Judah	Israel

Israel

****

27th year of Asa

Zimri — 1 week (evil)
(1 Kings 16:15-20):

While Zimri was killing Elah and the other members of Baasha's family, the army of Israel was besieging the Philistine city of Gibbethon. When word came to the army that Zimri had killed Elah and had proclaimed himself king, the soldiers appointed Omri, the captain of the host, king over Israel. Omri took the army from Gibbethon and besieged the palace in Tirzah. Zimri saw that his case was hopeless, so he burned the palace down over himself.

****

31st year of Asa

Omri — 12 years (evil)
(1 Kings 16:21-28):

After Zimri committed suicide, there was a time of civil war. Some in the land wanted a man named Tibni to be king, while others supported Omri. Omri finally gained full power and became the undisputed king.

Omri reigned a total of twelve years. This figure includes all the time from the death of Zimri to the death of Omri. He had undisputed control of the kingdom for eight years, from the 31st year of Asa to the 38th year of Asa. That means the strife between Omri and Tibni went on during the first four years after Zimri's death.

Omri remained in Tirzah two more years after Tibni's death. Then he bought the hill of Samaria from a man named Shemer and built a new capital for Israel on it. The name Samaria reflects the name of the man from whom it was bought. Samaria remained the capital of Israel from this point until the land was conquered.

Omri was very wicked. He continued in the sins of Jeroboam, worshiping the golden calves. We are told he sinned "more than all those who had gone before him."

The Bible does not contain much informa-tion about Omri, but he must have been a strong king politically. Remember, the Bible record is a religious history of the period rather than the normal relating of events within a kingdom. According to secular history, Omri made a powerful impression upon the history of the land. Years later, after Omri's house no longer ruled in Israel, the Assyrian records refer to Israel as "the house of Omri."

38th year of Asa

Ahab — 22 years (evil)
(1 Kings 16:29-22:40; 2 Chron. 18:1-34):

Asa's Diseased Feet (2 Chron. 16:12):

When Asa was old he was afflicted with a disease in his feet. Though he could have sought the help of God, he did not. He ig-nored the Lord and sought help only from the physicians.

Asa is described as a righteous king and God blessed Judah in his day. Yet he was rebuked on occasion for not relying upon God as he should have, for example, in his conflict with Baasha over the city of Ramah, and now in his last sickness. Asa did not turn away from God to serve idols, but he did not rely upon Him in all circumstances as he should have.

We can learn lessons from his story about our own reliance upon God.

Character of Ahab (1 Kings 16:29-33):

The Bible uses the very strongest language to condemn the actions of Ahab. According to the text, one of the worst things he did was to marry Jezebel, the daughter of Ethbaal the king of the Sidonians. This act would result in severe misery for both Israel and Judah.

Urged on by his pagan wife Jezebel, Ahab made Baal worship the official religion of Israel. He also made an Asherah pole, and he had a temple built for Baal in Samaria. Thus Ahab provoked Jehovah to anger more than all the kings of Israel before him.

Historical Note:
Jezebel was the daughter of Ethbaal, the king of the Sidonians. The names Jezebel and Ethbaal include the name of the false god Baal in them. That gives the first indication of how bad this marriage was for Ahab. Beyond that, Jezebel was another of the foreign wives a king of Israel married. Of course, the law of Moses repeatedly forbade such marriages.

Sidon was one of the main cities of the Phoenicians. The Phoenicians were a branch of the Canaanites who lived in the land when the Israelites entered it. This branch of Canaanites lived on the narrow coastal plain north of Mt. Carmel. There was a treaty of peace with Phoe-

nicia from the days of King David (1 Chron. 14:1). The Phoenicians helped both David and Solomon in their building projects.

Now the treaty of peace continues with Israel, sealed with the marriage of Jezebel and Ahab. Though there was peace with Phoenicia, their wicked influence did more harm to Israel than all the armies of enemies around.

Baal worship and the golden calf worship were both wrong. Both included idols. Baal worship was worse in its consequences, however, because the rituals involved in the worship were so degrading. Baal and Asherah were gods of fertility. Therefore, fornication was part of the ritual of worship. The priests and priestesses were male and female prostitutes. The morals of the people would plummet to the depths when they would turn to Baal worship.

On the other hand, the golden calves were theoretically representative of Jehovah. They still had their priests whose function was to offer animals upon an altar; they still had their feast days and special occasions similar to those found in the law of Moses. God did not accept the worship from the golden calves, because it was not in harmony with any part of the law of Moses, but the worship was not as destructive to the morals of the people involved.

Asa's Death (1 Kings 15:23-24; 2 Chron. 16:11-14):

After a rule of 41 years, Asa died and was buried in the City of David. The people burned an enormous quantity of spices and blended perfumes in his honor.

4th year of Ahab

Jehoshaphat — 25 years (good)
(1 Kings 22:41-50; 22:2-36; 2 Chron. 17:1-21:1):

Jehoshaphat was truly a good and righteous man: he followed in the ways of his father Asa; he continued the reforms his father had begun; and he removed the male shrine prostitutes (sodomites) that had reappeared in the land during his father's last years.

The people of the land were not, however, truly devoted to Jehovah. They kept their high places to worship whom they would.

Jericho is Rebuilt (1 Kings 16:34):

In Ahab's day a man named Hiel from Bethel rebuilt the fortress part of the city of Jericho. When he laid the foundations his oldest son Abiram died. When he set up the gates, his youngest son Segub died. This fulfilled the prophecy spoken by Joshua in the days when Jericho was destroyed by the Lord (Josh. 6:26).

God always keeps His word. His prophecies come true — whether for good or evil. It was an

Judah	Israel

Jehoshaphat Strengthens His Kingdom (2 Chron. 17:1-6):

Edom was under the control of Judah at this time. A deputy administered the territory of Edom for Jehoshaphat.

Jehoshaphat stationed his troops in garrisons throughout the land of Judah and in certain cities of Ephraim which Asa had taken from Israel. He sought the Lord instead of Baal, so God strengthened his hand and brought him riches and honor in abundance.

Jehoshaphat sends out the Princes, Levites, and Priests (2 Chron. 17:7-9):

Jehoshaphat realized that Judah was not serving the Lord faithfully and that they were ignorant of Jehovah. He sent out the princes, the Levites, and the priests to teach the people the law. They went out and taught among all the cities of Judah. This was in the third year of Jehoshaphat's reign.

Jehoshaphat Grows in Power (2 Chron. 17:10-19):

God gave Jehoshaphat peace. His neighbors, the Philistines and the Arabians, brought him great gifts. He built forts and cities with warehouses for all his goods. His army grew to be exceeding mighty. He had at his disposal an army of 1,160,000 besides those on garrison duty.

act of defiance and unbelief for Hiel to undertake the project of rebuilding Jericho.

A Treaty of Peace

Jehoshaphat and Ahab made a treaty of peace (see 1 Kings 22:44). This was the first time since the kingdoms had separated that official peace was made between them, even though there had been very little open warfare. At first glance, this would seem to be a good move for the kingdoms, but it was not. Look at the contrast between the two little kingdoms. None of the kings that Judah had had up until this point were extremely wicked. Rehoboam and Abijah did not serve God as faithfully as they should have, but they still offered the sacrifices at the temple and, at least, did not discourage the faithfulness of those who wanted to worship correctly. Asa and Jehoshaphat both sought to bring the people closer to Jehovah. As a result, God was with the kingdom of Judah and they were prospering. On the other hand, Israel had gone down spiritually from the day it began. Jeroboam had introduced the golden calves at the very beginning of his *reign and they had never been rejected; the righteous people living in Israel had migrated to Judah; and now Ahab not only <u>allows</u> Baal worship in his land, he has made it the official religion.*

Any contact between Judah and Israel could only prove to be a corrupting influence to Judah. That indeed proved to be the case. It is one of the mysteries of the centuries how Jehoshaphat, one of the best kings of Judah, could ally himself with Ahab, one of the worst kings of Israel. The association caused great damage to the house of David and to Judah.

As was so often true, the treaty of peace was sealed with the marriage of Jehoshaphat's son Jehoram and Ahab's daughter Athaliah (2 Chron. 21:6).

An Interruption in our two Column Style

Only 27 years pass from the time Ahab ascended to the throne (1 Kings 16:29), until the deaths of Ahaziah king of Judah and Jehoram king of Israel at the hand of Jehu (2 Kings 9:14-29). Yet so much attention is given to the period in the divine record, it is easy to think it was much longer.

During this period, God strove mightily to bring Israel back to His side. During the darkest hour Israel had seen as a nation, two great prophets came from the Lord to stand against the efforts of Ahab and Jezebel and their descendants. Most of the record of this period involves the lives of Elijah the Tishbite and Elisha the son of Shaphat.

In Israel there was a fierce conflict between the prophets of Jehovah and Ahab. Baal worship was finally destroyed, but the worship of Jehovah was not restored as it should have been. Instead, the golden calves were brought back into supremacy. Therefore, this period of conflict was not followed by any period of permanent blessing to the kingdom.

The history of Judah during this period fades very much into the background. Through the alliance between Jehoshaphat and Ahab, and the marriage between Jehoram and Athaliah that resulted, the welfare of Judah became linked with Israel. Therefore the blessings that should have come from the reign of such a righteous king as Jehoshaphat were not as many, nor as long lasting, as they could have been. The blessings that were given were soon destroyed as the result of the wickedness of Jehoram and Athaliah.

As part of the effort God made to bring Israel back to Him, there was an outpouring of miracles. It should be understood that miracles were very rare even in Bible days. It was only at times when God was trying to impress certain lessons upon His people that there were miracles. For example, during the period of the exodus from Egypt, there were many miracles. At that time, God was making this group of Hebrew slaves into His chosen people. He was giving them the law they were to live by for all the centuries until Christ should come. Now, here in the days of Ahab, the kingdom of Israel is in distress. Ahab was the sixth wicked king on the throne. But God still saw some chance for the kingdom to yet be what He wanted it to be. Therefore, He demonstrated His power and might through miracles and through the word of His prophets Elijah and Elisha. Later, during the period of the fall of Judah and during the Babylonian captivity, there was another outpouring of miracles. God was demonstrating the reason why the people were being punished at that time and He was trying to bring a remnant of them back to Him. Of course, the greatest outpouring of miracles was in the days of the New Testament when Jesus came into the world as a man and showed Himself to be the Divine Son of God. He gave His apostles and prophets power to do miracles also to prove that they were indeed His messengers and to guide them into all truth as they recorded the new law for all generations that followed them.

Most of our attention through the remainder of 1 Kings will, therefore, be devoted to Israel and the stories of Ahab and Elijah. Remember that Jehoshaphat was upon the throne in Judah, and that kingdom was prospering because of Jehoshaphat's reforms. Instead of having two columns at this point, however, we will use only one as we tell the story of Elijah. We will go back to the two column arrangement when we get back to a point where the history of both kingdoms is told at once.

Elijah the Tishbite

At this dark moment in Israel, the man Elijah appears on the stage of history. Elijah virtually lived in the mouth of a lion, in the very jaws of death, yet not a hand of his vicious enemies was ever laid upon him. He was sustained through all his trials by the hand of God. Greater power was given to Elijah, and to Elisha after him, than was given to any other Old Testament prophet except Moses.

Not much is known about Elijah. He was a plain, courageous man of faith. He was an implacable foe of Ahab and Jezebel. His message burned with the flame of God's judgment. He was, perhaps, the greatest of the Old Testament prophets, yet he left no writings for us. Sometimes he seems almost superhuman in his courage until we follow him to Mt. Horeb and look into his noble, but still mortal, human heart.

Elijah was a Tishbite, a sojourner of Gilead. The location of Tishbe or Tishbeh is unknown. Some think it was in Galilee, but that Elijah had moved from there and was living in Gilead, hence a sojourner in Gilead, when the Lord called him. Others think the village was located in northern Gilead — but no one knows.

Elijah Predicts a Drought
(1 Kings 17:1-24)

With a simple, rather abrupt, introduction, Elijah steps onto the stage of Bible history. He told Ahab, "As Jehovah, the God of Israel lives, there will be neither dew nor rain again until I say so." Then Elijah turned away from Ahab and left.

Not only did Elijah predict a drought, the book of James tells us he had prayed fervently that it come to pass (see James 5:17). Since Baal was a fertility god who was supposed to make the land beautiful, this drought at the hand of Jehovah showed the impotence of Baal.

When Elijah had delivered his message to Ahab, God told him, "Leave here. Go and hide in the ravine of Kerith, east of the Jordan. You will drink from the brook, and I have commanded the ravens to feed you there."

No one knows the location of the brook Kerith. Some say it was the Wadi Qelt a few miles south of Jericho. Obviously it was a place away from people, because God was providing a safe hiding place for His servant.

Elijah stayed at Kerith with the birds feeding him regularly until the drought caused the brook to run dry. Then God said, "Get up and go to Zarephath, near Sidon, and live there for a time. I have appointed a widow there to care for you." God had not actually spoken to the widow, but He had arranged in His own plan for her to do this.

Zarephath was a town on the Mediterranean coast situated between Tyre and Sidon. It lay in Phoenician territory. When Elijah got there, he found the widow in question out gathering sticks for a fire.

Elijah said, "Would you please give me a cup of water to drink?" As she went to get the water, Elijah said, "Would you also bring me a piece of bread?"

The widow stopped; she could not grant this request because she had no bread. Widows in those days were desolate and, in hard times, were the first to suffer. She replied, "As Jehovah your God lives, I don't have any bread. I have only a handful of flour in a jar and a little oil in a bottle. I was gathering a few sticks to cook the bread for me and my son that we may eat it and die."

Elijah said, "Do not be afraid. Go and do as you planned, but first make a cake for me and bring it to me. Then make a meal for you and your son, because Jehovah, the God of Israel, says the jar of flour will not be used up nor the bottle of oil run out until the day He sends rain upon the land."

One can only wonder what thoughts went through the widow's mind as she went to do as Elijah said. But trusting in Elijah's God, she went and baked the bread for Elijah, and then for herself and her son. There was still flour left. So the miracle continued: for many days there was always flour in the jar and oil in the bottle.

Some time passed, and then a very sad day came. The widow's son became sick. He grew worse and died. The poor widow was distraught. She had been caring for God's prophet and now her son was dead. She cried out to Elijah, "Did God send you to remind me of my sins by killing my son?"

Elijah only said, "Give me your son."

Elijah took the child's body from his mother's arms and carried it up to the room where he stayed. He laid the little body on his bed and he prayed to God: "Have you brought tragedy upon the widow I am staying with by killing her son?" Elijah stretched himself upon the boy three times, praying, "O Lord, let this child's soul come into him again."

God heard Elijah's prayer and did as he asked. The child's life came back into him. With joy, Elijah took up the child, brought him to his mother, and said, "Look, your son lives."

Now the widow was filled with joy. She said, "Now I know that you are indeed a man of God, and that the word in your mouth is true."

Elijah Challenges Ahab and Baal
(1 Kings 18:1-46)

Finally, after three years and six months (see James 5:17), God told Elijah, "Go, show yourself to Ahab and I will send rain upon the land." Elijah left the widow's house and headed back to Israel.

Israel had been severely afflicted by the drought. Ahab and his palace steward named Obadiah went out to search for grass and water so that they could save a few of the horses and mules still left. Ahab went one way and Obadiah another.

Now Obadiah feared Jehovah. When Jezebel had slaughtered the prophets of God, Obadiah had hidden a hundred of them in two caves and had supplied them with food and water. Therefore, it was to Obadiah that Elijah went. When Obadiah saw him, he said, "Is it really you, my lord Elijah?"

"Yes," Elijah replied. "Go tell your master that Elijah is here."

Obadiah was afraid. He said, "What have I done wrong? Why would you give me into the hand of Ahab to kill? My master has looked high and low for you. There is no nation or kingdom he has not asked about you. He even made them swear that you were not there. And now you calmly say, 'Go tell Ahab that Elijah is here.' Just as soon as I am gone, the Spirit of God will carry you away to who knows where. Then I will tell Ahab what you have said, he will come and not be able to find you, and he will kill me. But I have feared Jehovah from my youth up. Did you not hear how I hid a hundred of the prophets of Jehovah by fifty in a cave and fed them bread and gave them water?"

Elijah assured Obadiah, saying, "As surely as God lives, I will be here and I will show myself to Ahab today." So Obadiah went and told Ahab.

When Ahab saw Elijah, he spat out the words, "Is it you, you troublemaker?"

Elijah answered, "I am not the troublemaker in Israel, but you and your father's house are because you have forsaken Jehovah and have followed the Baalim [*plural form of Baal*]. Go now and gather all Israel to meet me at Mount Carmel. Bring with you the 450 prophets of Baal and the 400 prophets of the Asherah whom Jezebel feeds."

Ahab went to do Elijah's bidding, and soon all the people came together upon the mountain. Elijah stood before them and said: "How long are you going to flop from one side to the other? If Jehovah be God, follow Him; but if Baal is god, then follow him." The people made no answer at all.

Elijah said, "I am the only prophet of Jehovah left, but there are 450 prophets of Baal. Get two bullocks for us. Let them choose a bullock, cut it in pieces, and lay it upon the wood, but do not set fire to it. I will do the same. Then call upon your god and I will call upon the name of the Lord, and the god who answers by fire, He is the true God."

The people said, "It is a good idea."

Elijah told the prophets of Baal, "Since there are many of you, you go first. Prepare your sacrifice, but do not set fire to it, and then call upon the name of your god."

The prophets of Baal did as Elijah had said. They prepared their sacrifice and began praying to Baal. When nothing happened, they began to leap and dance around the altar. Hours passed, and they continued to leap and dance. Baal made no response.

At noon Elijah began to taunt them. He knew that Baal must be discredited in the eyes of the people. Elijah said, "Shout louder. Surely he is a god. Maybe he is thinking about something. He may be busy, or on a trip somewhere. Why, he may even be asleep and will have to be awakened."

This goaded the Baal prophets into a frenzy, so they shouted louder and slashed themselves with swords and spears, as was customary not only with Baal worship, but also with the worship of other pagan gods. They continued their frantic efforts until time for the evening sacrifice.

Then Elijah gathered the people together. He repaired an altar of unhewn stones such as Abraham would have used. He took twelve stones, one for each tribe, and built an altar in the name of Jehovah. Then he dug a trench around the altar that would hold a little over three gallons of water. He arranged the wood, cut the bull into pieces, and laid it on the wood. Then Elijah commanded that four large jars of water be brought and poured over the sacrifice.

Where did they get the water? They were in the midst of a severe drought, but the Mediterranean Sea was very near the foot of the mountain even if the large cistern on top of Mt. Carmel were dry. As we will see in a moment, the Kishon River at the foot of the mountain was not completely dry, so it could also have been the source for the water.

When they had poured the water from the four jars on the sacrifice, Elijah said, "Do it again." Then he said, "Do it a third time."

By now the flesh of the bullock was soaked, and so was the wood under it. The ground around the altar was wet and water stood in the ditch. It would have been impossible for anyone to set fire to Elijah's sacrifice by ordinary means.

At the time of sacrifice, Elijah prayed aloud to God. He said, "O Lord, God of Abraham, Isaac, and Israel, let it be known today that you are God in Israel, and that I am your servant, and have done all these things at your command. Answer me, O Lord, so that this people may know that you are God and that you are turning their hearts back again."

Instantly fire came down from heaven and consumed everything standing on the spot — the sacrifice, the wood, the stones, the soil that had been dug out of the ditch, and the water standing in the ditch. This was not lightning. No cloud had yet arisen (1 Kings 18:42-44). Even lightning could not have vaporized twelve large stones. A mighty miracle had been done by the hand of Jehovah.

The people fell on their faces and said, "Jehovah — He is God! Jehovah — He is God!"

Elijah commanded: "Seize the prophets of Baal. Do not let anyone get away." The people took the prophets down to the River Kishon and slew them there. Thus Elijah used this temporary enthusiasm of the people to strike a blow against Baal worship.

In killing the false prophets, Elijah was carrying out the instructions in the law (Deut. 13:12-17; 17:2-7). Ordinarily the properly constituted authorities were to do this. But in this case, since the authorities were protecting the false prophets instead of killing them, Elijah, the emphatically declared representative of Jehovah, did what God required.

Elijah told Ahab to go where a meal was being prepared and to eat and drink because there was the sound of a great rain. Literally, he said, "For sound of great rain." He did not say that there was such a sound at that moment. As a prophet he could hear such a sound, because he anticipated the Lord's response to the prayer he was about to utter.

Ahab went to eat, but Elijah went back to the top of Mt. Carmel. He bowed himself to the ground with his face to his knees. Elijah was praying for rain (see James 5:18). He sent a servant to look toward the sea. The servant returned and said, "There is nothing."

Elijah prayed again and said, "Go back." This happened seven times.

Then the servant came back, saying, "Behold, a cloud as small as a man's hand is rising from the sea." Elijah knew his prayer was answered.

Elijah told his servant to tell Ahab, "Hitch up your chariot and go before the rain stops you." Ahab's destination was the city of Jezreel. The kind of rain that was about to fall would turn the plain of Jezreel into a flood and a quagmire of mud.

Meanwhile, the sky grew black with clouds, a strong wind began to blow, and a heavy rain headed their way. Ahab rode off toward Jezreel. The Spirit of God came upon Elijah and he ran ahead of Ahab's chariot all the way to the city.

It had been a day of great victory for the cause of Jehovah. Elijah and all other faithful people could go to bed happy that night in the hope that the kingdom had turned back to Jehovah. That was not what lay ahead, however.

Elijah Flees to Mount Horeb
(1 Kings 19:1-18)

Ahab told Jezebel all that had happened on Mount Carmel: the contest between Jehovah and Baal and how her false prophets had been killed. Jezebel was furious. She sent word to Elijah, saying, "May the gods punish me severely if I do not kill you by this time tomorrow."

Elijah was terrified. He would certainly not be the first prophet of God that Jezebel had killed. He ran for his life. When he came to the city of Beersheba in the southern part of Judah, he left his servant there and he went on another day's journey into the desert. Finally he stopped to rest under a juniper tree. He was so discouraged he wanted to die. He prayed: "O Lord, I have had enough. Please take my life. I am no better than my ancestors." Then he lay down under the tree and went to sleep.

Suddenly, an angel touched him and woke him, saying, "Get up and eat." Elijah looked, and there by his head was a cake of bread baked on some hot coals and a jar of water. He ate and drank, and then lay back down and slept again.

After a time, the angel came back. He said, "Get up and eat because you are going on a long journey."

So Elijah ate again. Then he continued his journey south. He was sustained on the strength of the food the angel had given him while he made the trip to Mount Horeb, a forty day journey. The name "Horeb" is another name for Mt. Sinai. When he got to Horeb, he went into a cave and spent the night.

God spoke to Elijah, "What are you doing here, Elijah?"

Elijah answered, "I have been very zealous for your cause, but it has not helped. The Israelites have broken your covenant; they have broken down your altars; and they have killed your prophets. I am the only one left, and they are trying to kill me too."

God said, "Go out and stand on the mountain because the Lord is about to pass by."

Elijah went out to observe, and some startling things happened. First there was a strong, powerful wind that passed by. Even the rocks were shattered. But the Lord was not in the wind. Next there was an earthquake, and then a fire. But the Lord was not in the earthquake, or the fire.

After these demonstrations of God's power, there was a gentle whisper, "Elijah, what are you doing here?"

Elijah had not yet understood God's point. He answered just as he had earlier: "God, it is no use. I have been very zealous for the Lord God Almighty, but it has not helped. The Israelites have rejected your covenant; they have broken down your altars; and they have killed your prophets. I am the only one left and they are trying to kill me too."

God said, "Elijah, get up and go back. There is work to be done. It is not time for you to die yet. Go back and anoint Hazael king of the Syrians; anoint Jehu king of Israel; and anoint Elisha to take your place. These men will bring the judgment upon the wicked ones you are concerned about. But, Elijah, it is not hopeless in Israel. There are still 7,000 in Israel who have not bowed the knee to Baal."

So Elijah got up and went back to Israel.

Find Mt. Horeb (Mt. Sinai) on a map. Do you see it is too far south to be included on your map of the divided kingdom? Label Mt. Carmel, Jezreel, and Beersheba on your map. Elijah had already fled several miles by the time he left his servant at Beersheba.

28

Let us take a moment to look at this story before we move further in the history. Elijah had won a mighty victory on Mt. Carmel against the false prophets of Baal. We see the courage that faith produces on that day. But his efforts did not bring about the lasting reforms he had hoped for. Immediately Jezebel threatened to kill him — and he knew she had the power to do so. He was afraid and fled. The more he thought about the matter, the more discouraged he became. He felt there was no use trying more. Nothing was going to help. We have already noted that the three and a half year drought was in response to Elijah's prayer. On Mt. Carmel, Elijah hoped the people had learned the lesson that Baal was impotent — he could neither send fire to burn his own sacrifice, nor could he produce rain to help the land. Yet, it was obvious, Jezebel had a strangle-hold on the land. The people were not going to reject the Baal worship. Why keep trying?

Now let us look at the story from God's response. Do you notice that forty days passed from the time Elijah left the point a day's journey south of Beersheba until God spoke to him at Mt. Horeb? That means God was allowing time itself to act as a healer for Elijah's discouragement. There was reason to grieve for the nation of Israel, and God allowed time for Elijah to grieve. But grieving alone would not solve Israel's problems. It was not as hopeless as Elijah thought it was.

Notice God's next actions. He spoke to Elijah, asking him why he was there instead of back home in Israel. But, do you notice, He did not <u>rebuke</u> Elijah for his discouragement? Instead He demonstrated His might over nature. He was reminding Elijah that God is in control. He could care for His prophet.

Then God quietly spoke to Elijah again, asking him why he was there. Elijah was still too discouraged to understand. God still did not rebuke him. Instead, God told him to go back and perform the duties God had for him. Then, after all else, God told him it was not really hopeless. It is interesting that God waited until last of all to tell Elijah he was not alone. Even if Elijah had been standing totally alone in Israel, God could still have protected him and Elijah could have performed his assigned tasks.

Another thought is that God was teaching Elijah that God works in different ways. There is a time for fire and earthquakes, when God deals judgment to the wicked as was done on Mount Carmel. But it is as surely God who speaks quietly through His word when He seeks to teach men His will.

This story should be an encouragement to us in our service to God. There are times when we grow discouraged in our efforts to serve God faithfully. Perhaps we, too, have fought some mighty battle against the forces of evil, only to find that we have not had any success that we can see. We may grieve just as Elijah did — but God's message is the same to us today. Grieve over the sin in the world, but do not let that grief cripple you to the point you cannot move forward to the tasks before you. God has asked that we do <u>our</u> part in trying to teach the truth, but He has never demanded that His servants convert all around them.

Elisha, the Successor
(1 Kings 19:19-21)

When Elijah got back to Israel, he went to the field where Elisha the son of Shaphat was plowing. Elisha's yoke of oxen was the twelfth pair of oxen in the field. Elijah walked up to him and threw his cloak around him and, seemingly, turned away without saying anything to Elisha.

Elisha understood the signal that Elijah was asking him to follow him. He hurried after Elijah, saying, "Wait. Let me tell my parents good-by and then I will come with you."

Elijah, testing him, said, "What do you mean? Go back. What have I done to you?"

But Elisha would not be turned aside. He hurried back, took the oxen he had been plowing with, and cooked them for the people in the field with him. This seems to have been his way of expressing his farewell to them. Then he set out to follow Elijah, becoming his attendant.

Samaria is Attacked by the Syrians
(1 Kings 20:1-21)

Remember that Jehoshaphat is still ruling in Judah and that they are prospering because Jehoshaphat is a righteous king. But the divine record continues with stories about Israel during this period. God is still trying to bring the people back to Him. Do you see God's mercy and long-suffering? He wanted the kingdom of Israel to be what it should be.

We met a king named Ben-hadad during the story of Asa and Baasha. Some years have passed since that time. This story is more about Ben-hadad. It would be possible for it to be the same man, but enough years have passed to make it a reasonable assumption that this man was the son of the first Ben-hadad mentioned. Ben-hadad was the title of the king of the Syrian city-state based around the city of Damascus. Modern speech translations of the Bible call the area of Syria "Aram," the people "Arameans," and their language "Aramaic." Be sure you have Syria labeled on your map, with Damascus as its capital. Be sure you have Samaria labeled as the capital of Israel. Syria was a small country about the same size as Israel.

In this story, Ben-hadad comes with thirty-two allied kings to besiege the city of Samaria. Ben-hadad was so sure of his superior strength, he sent messengers into the city with a haughty demand: "Your silver and your gold are mine; so are your wives and your children."

Ahab knew that his forces were out-numbered, so he sent this reply: "Just as you say, my lord the king. I and all I have are yours." In other words, Ahab was saying he was willing to negotiate. He did not have the strength to fight and would, therefore, have to agree to whatever terms Ben-hadad set.

Ben-hadad sent the messengers back with an even haughtier demand: "I sent to tell you that your possessions and your people were mine, but instead of letting you send the payment of my demands out to me, I am coming in to get them. About this time tomorrow I am going to send my officials to search your palace and the houses of your officials. They will pick out your most prized possessions and bring them out to me." Such a demand was an insult to any people.

Ahab called his officials together and laid the matter before them. Ahab was still as out-numbered as he had been when he accepted the first demand, but Ben-hadad had gone too far. He told the officials, "Do you see how this man is looking for trouble? I accepted his terms when he sent first to demand my gold, silver, wives, and children, but I cannot accept these terms."

The officials agreed. They said, "Do not listen to him or agree to his terms."

So Ahab sent the messengers back to Ben-hadad, saying, "Your servant will do all you demanded the first time, but this demand is too much."

Ben-hadad and the thirty-two other kings were drinking together in their tents while this exchange of messages was taking place. The kings were feeling more boastful as the exchange continued. Ben-hadad responded by saying, "Tell Ahab there won't be enough dirt left in Samaria to give each of my men a handful by the time I am finished with the city."

Ahab responded, "Tell Ben-hadad that the one who is putting on his armor to go to battle should not boast about what he will do. Wait until he is ready to take off his armor after the battle, and then boast about what he accomplished."

Ben-hadad said, "Prepare for battle."

Meanwhile, a prophet of God came to Ahab. He said, "Ahab, this is what the Lord says: 'Do you see this vast army? I will give it into your hands today, so that you may know that I am the Lord.'"

This was unusually good news to Ahab. Usually God was not on Ahab's side because of Ahab's wickedness. But God was using another tactic this time to try to get the attention of the people of Israel. Notice that God did not say He was helping Ahab because of Ahab's righteousness, but rather to teach Ahab that Jehovah was able to help whenever He chose to do so, even against immense odds.

Ahab was very pleased. He asked the prophet, "Who will do this? How do we proceed with the battle?"

The prophet answered, "The young officers of the commanders will lead you to victory."

Ahab said, "Who will attack first? Shall I wait for the Syrians to attack, or do I make the first move?"

The prophet answered, "You will."

At the prophet's instruction, Ahab assembled his army. He put 232 young officers first, with 7,000 soldiers behind them. They set out from the city about noon while Ben-hadad and his fellow kings were still drinking themselves drunk in their tent.

Ben-hadad's scouts told him, "There are men approaching from Samaria."

Ben-hadad said, "If they come in peace, take them alive. If they have come out for war, take them alive."

About that time, the Israelite army reached the first of the Syrian soldiers. Each one took the first soldier he came to and killed him. It threw the whole Syrian camp into panic. Soon the Syrians were fleeing toward the Jordan River with the Israelites in pursuit. Ben-hadad managed to escape on horseback with a few of his men. The Israelites continued to pursue them and inflicted heavy losses upon the Syrians.

The Syrians Come Again
(1 Kings 20:22-34)

The prophet warned Ahab to strengthen his position and do whatever was needed to be ready to fight again, because he said the Syrians would be back the next spring.

Meanwhile, the officials in Syria were trying to decide what had gone wrong. When Ben-hadad met with them, they thought they had figured out the problem. They said, "The god of the Israelites is a god of the hills" *[most Israelite towns were located in the hill country].* "That is where we made our mistake. We tried to attack them in their hills where their god protects them. If we will fight them on the plains, surely we will be stronger than they are."

They advised the king to prepare his army again. "Remove all the kings from their positions of command and replace them with officers. Then raise an army exactly like the one you had. Replace horse for horse, chariot for chariot, and man for man so that we can be ready to fight them on the plain. Then surely we will win." The plan seemed to be a good one, so Ben-hadad set out to do all they had suggested.

When spring came, Ben-hadad was ready. He took his army to Aphek (likely on a plain near the Sea of Galilee on the east side). The Israelites mustered their army also and went out to meet them. Their army was so much smaller they looked like two small flocks of goats in contrast to the Syrians spread out all over the countryside.

The prophet of God came back to Ahab and said, "This is what the Lord says: 'Because the Syrians think God is a god of the hills and not of the valleys, I will deliver this vast army into your hands and you will know that I am the Lord.'"

The first victory was to teach the Israelites God's power; this second victory was to teach the Syrians a lesson as well as the Israelites.

For seven days the two armies lay camped across from each other. On the seventh day, the battle was joined. Again, Israel won a decisive victory. As the Syrians were escaping, some went into the city of Aphek, and a portion of the wall collapsed and killed twenty-seven thousand of them.

Ben-hadad was fleeing for his life. He hid in an inner room in the city. After a time his officials came to him and said, "We have heard that the kings of Israel are merciful. Let us go to Ahab with sackcloth around our waist and ropes around our necks and plead for your life."

Ben-hadad was desperate to save his life, so he agreed to the plan. The men went to Ahab and said, "Your servant Ben-hadad says, 'Please let me live.'"

Ahab said, "Is he still alive? Why, he is my brother!"

Ben-hadad's men were quick to take this as a good sign. They said, "Yes, your brother Ben-hadad!"

Ahab said, "Go and get him." When Ben-hadad came out, Ahab invited him into his chariot as if they were the best of friends.

Ben-hadad began making all sorts of concessions to try to keep Ahab's favor. He said, "I will return the cities my father took from your father. I will let you set up your own market area in Damascus, just as my father did in Samaria."

Ahab answered, "On the basis of this treaty I will set you free." So Ahab and Ben-hadad made a treaty of peace and went their separate ways.

Label the probable location of Aphek on your map.

A Prophet Rebukes Ahab
(1 Kings 20:35-43)

God was not pleased with the treaty of peace Ahab had made with Ben-hadad. Therefore, God sent a prophet with a message to Ahab.

The prophet chosen to take the message was one of the "sons of the prophets." At God's word, he turned to one of the other prophets and said, "Wound me." But the second prophet refused.

The first prophet said, "Because you have not obeyed the word of the Lord, you will be killed by a lion as soon as you leave me." Sure enough, the second prophet turned away and a lion found him and killed him.

Meanwhile, the first prophet found another companion and made the same request. This man did as he was told and wounded the prophet. Then the prophet disguised himself to look like a wounded soldier returning from battle. He went out and stood by the way, waiting for Ahab to pass.

When the king came along, the prophet called out to him, saying, "While I was in the thick of battle, someone came along with a captive and told me to guard him. He told me that if I let the captive go missing, then I would have to give my life for his, or else pay a talent of silver. But I got busy here and there, and the man got away."

Obviously, the man wanted Ahab to pardon his offense, but Ahab said, "You already know your sentence. You have pronounced it yourself."

Then the prophet took off his disguise, and Ahab recognized him as one of the prophets. The prophet said, "This is the message from the Lord: 'You have set free a man that I had determined should die. Since you let Ben-hadad live, then you will give your life for his, your people for his.'"

Instead of accepting the rebuke humbly and praying for God's forgiveness, Ahab went to his palace in Samaria angry and sullen.

The "sons of the prophets" are mentioned in this story. In 1 Samuel 10:5-7, Saul was told he would meet a "company of prophets." Later when David fled from Saul's presence, he joined Samuel and a "company of prophets" (1 Sam. 19:18-24). Now, in this story, there are "sons of the prophets" together (1 Kings 20:35-43). The "sons of the prophets" are mentioned more than once in the stories about Elisha (see 2 Kings 2:3, 5, 7, 15; 4:1, 38; 6:1). It seems these must have been "schools" for the young prophets or groups of the prophets who lived together for their mutual benefit. Very little specific information is given about them. Obviously, in times when there were such men as Samuel and Elisha to work with the prophets, these would be good men. Without the influence of such good men, these companies of prophets could become centers of false prophets.

It was always very important that a prophet understand he was to obey an instruction from the Lord — even when it did not seem logical at the moment. That is why the first prophet who disobeyed was killed by the lion. all the "sons of the prophets" would learn the lesson of strict obedience. Their duty as God's spokesmen was a grave one — one to be handled with utmost care.

Naboth's Vineyard
(1 Kings 21:1-29)

Remember Jehoshaphat is still reigning in Judah while the divine record continues to tell of Ahab and his wickedness in Israel. Also remember that Ahab only reigned twenty-two years, so all of these stories are happening within that span of time.

Ahab's capital was in Samaria, just as his father's had been, but it seems that his personal home was in Jezreel. His home there is referred to as a "palace" also, but that does not mean Samaria had been abandoned. This story takes place in Jezreel. (Be sure Jezreel is labeled on your map.)

A man named Naboth owned a vineyard in Jezreel near the palace of Ahab. Ahab went to Naboth and asked to buy the vineyard. He offered to swap a better vineyard for it or to pay Naboth whatever price he set.

But Naboth refused, saying, "This property is my inheritance from my fathers. I do not want to let it go." The property was Naboth's and he had the right to refuse to sell.

Instead of accepting the refusal as a reasonable business experience, Ahab went home sullen and angry. He lay on his bed sulking and he refused to eat. Jezebel went in to see what was wrong. He told her, "I am upset because I asked to buy Naboth's vineyard, and he refused to let me have it."

Jezebel was amazed. She was used to kings who exercised absolute power and took whatever they wanted, with no thought for the welfare of others and no thought for the law of God. She said, "Is this how you act as king over Israel? Cheer up. I'll get the vineyard for you."

She wrote letters to the officials of the city and sealed them with Ahab's kingly seal. The letters said:

> Proclaim a special feast day and set Naboth in a place of prominence before all the people. Then seat some scoundrels opposite him and have them accuse Naboth of cursing God and the king. Then take him out and stone him to death.

The elders and nobles of the city did as they were told to do. They gave the feast, had men give false testimony about Naboth, stoned him to death, and sent word of their action to Jezebel. As soon as she heard the news, she went and told Ahab, "Get up and take possession of Naboth's vineyard because he is dead and cannot prevent it." Ahab was overjoyed and went to take possession of the vineyard.

Jezebel and Ahab thought the matter was settled, but God was very angry. God told Elijah, "Go down to meet Ahab king of Israel. He is in Naboth's vineyard where he has gone to take possession of it. Tell him what is going to happen to his household."

Elijah went to Ahab and said, "God says you have murdered a man and seized his property. As a result, the dogs will lick up your blood in the same place where they licked up Naboth's blood."

Ahab said, "So you have found me, my enemy!"

"I have found you," Elijah answered, "because you have sold yourself to do evil in the eyes of the Lord. God is going to bring disaster upon your whole house. Every male of your household will be killed whether he is slave or free. Your family will be destroyed as thoroughly as Jeroboam's family was, and as Baasha's family was, because you have provoked God to anger and have caused Israel to sin. Furthermore, dogs will eat the flesh of Jezebel by the wall of Jezreel. Dogs will eat those of your family who die in the city, and birds will eat those who die in the country."

Then the divine record describes Ahab: "But there was none like unto Ahab, which did sell himself to work wickedness in the sight of the Lord, whom Jezebel his wife stirred up. And he did very abominably in following idols, according to all things as did the Amorites, whom the Lord cast out before the children of Israel."

When Ahab heard the harsh message, he tore his clothes, put on sackcloth, and fasted. He went around meekly, grieving over the message.

God said, "Elijah, do you see how Ahab has humbled himself? Because he has humbled himself, I will not bring the predicted destruction in his day. I will wait and bring it upon his house in the days of his son."

Do you see God's mercy? Even with a man as wicked as Ahab, God allowed him the chance to change. God postponed the punishment of the whole family because Ahab humbled himself. Remember the prophecy. We will see its fulfillment soon — in the days of Ahab's son.

Micaiah Prophesies Against Ahab
(1 Kings 22:1-28; 2 Chron. 18:1-27)

After the treaty of peace Ahab made with Ben-hadad of Syria (or Aram), there were three years of peace between the kingdoms. But Syria held the city of Ramoth-Gilead that was supposed to belong to Israel. Ramoth-Gilead was in the territory of Gad on the east side of the Jordan River and was one of the cities designated as a city of refuge for the Israelites (see Deut. 4:41-43). Possibly of even more importance to Ahab, Ramoth-Gilead was located on the trade route known as the King's Highway. It was the first Israelite city caravans would pass through on their way south and the last city on their way north. Therefore, it was a very important city for collecting toll. It disturbed Ahab for such a city to be in the hands of an enemy. He discussed the matter with his officials, saying: "Don't you know that Ramoth-Gilead belongs to us and yet we are doing nothing to retake it from the king of Syria?"

Anytime you see the name "Gilead" attached to another name, you can know the city is located on the east side of the Jordan River. The name Gilead (or Galeed) was given to the east side when Jacob and Laban parted in peace when Jacob returned to Canaan with his wives and children (see Gen. 31:47). Sometimes the name is used in the Bible to refer to a small area between the Jabbok River and the Yarmuk River, but more often it is a general term for all the area belonging to the Israelites on the east side.

Label Ramoth-Gilead on your map. There will be repeated battles over this city in the chapters ahead.

About the time Ahab was considering what to do about fighting for Ramoth-Gilead, King Jehoshaphat from Judah came to visit him. Ahab told him what he was thinking about doing, and he asked, "Would you be willing to go with me to help me take Ramoth-Gilead?"

Jehoshaphat replied, "Yes. I am with you. My people and my horses are at your disposal." But Jehoshaphat insisted that they inquire of God before setting out on such a mission.

Ahab was willing to do so, and he called for his prophets — about 400 of them. There was only one problem, these were prophets of Baal rather than of Jehovah. The prophets came before the two kings, and Ahab asked them, "Shall I go to war against Ramoth-Gilead, or not?"

The prophets were quick to answer: "Go, for the Lord will deliver the city into your hands."

That sounded good, but Jehoshaphat knew they had not yet inquired of Jehovah, and the word of these false prophets meant nothing. So he said, "Is there not a prophet of Jehovah here whom we could ask?"

Ahab said, "Yes, there is one, but I hate him because he never says anything good about me. He is Micaiah the son of Imlah."

Jehoshaphat protested and insisted that he be brought. So Ahab sent for him. While they were waiting for Micaiah to come, the other prophets continued their gyrations. The kings were dressed in their royal robes and were holding court in the entrance of the gate of Samaria, with all the prophets out before them making their predictions. One prophet named Zedekiah had come prepared with a set of iron horns. He was saying, "God says you will gore the Syrians until they are destroyed." All the prophets were saying, "Attack Ramoth-Gilead and be victorious!"

Meanwhile, the messenger who had gone to get Micaiah was trying to give him some help so that

Micaiah could know how to please the king this time. The messenger said, "Look, all the other prophets are predicting victory for the king. Let your word agree with theirs this time."

Micaiah answered, "I can only tell him what the Lord tells me."

When Micaiah arrived, Ahab said, "Micaiah, shall I go to war against Ramoth-Gilead or not?"

Micaiah answered, "Go, attack, and be victorious for the Lord will give it into your hands." This was exactly the message the other prophets had been giving that Ahab had been enjoying, but Ahab knew it was too good to be true for a prophet of Jehovah to be giving him good news.

Ahab said, "Micaiah, how many times do I have to make you swear to tell me nothing but the truth? What has the Lord said?"

Micaiah answered, "I see Israel scattered upon the hills like sheep without a shepherd. The Lord says for them to go home in peace because they have no master."

Ahab turned to Jehoshaphat and said, "See. Didn't I tell you he never prophesies anything good about me?"

Then Micaiah continued:

I saw the Lord sitting on His throne with all the host of heaven gathered around Him. And the Lord said, "Who will go and lure Ahab into attacking Ramoth-Gilead so that he will die there?"

One suggested this, and another that, until one of the spirits said, "I will lure him. I will be a lying spirit in the mouth of his prophets."

The Lord said, "You will succeed. Go and do it."

So, the Lord has put a lying spirit in the mouths of all these prophets of yours. The Lord has decreed disaster for you.

The prophets of Ahab were filled with hate toward Micaiah. Zedekiah came forward and slapped Micaiah in the face. He asked, "Which way did that spirit from Jehovah go when he went from me to speak to you?"

Micaiah replied, "You will find out on the day when you go to hide in an inner room."

Ahab was angry, and he commanded, "Take Micaiah back to the ruler of the city and to Joash my son, and tell them to put this fellow in prison and feed him on bread and water until I return safely!"

Micaiah declared: "If you return at all, then Jehovah has not spoken through me. Mark my words, all you people."

Ahab is Killed
(1 Kings 22:29-40; 2 Chron. 18:28-34)

It is not surprising that Ahab went right ahead with his plans to fight against Ramoth-Gilead in spite of Micaiah's message, because he trusted in Baal rather than Jehovah to help him. But it is surprising that Jehoshaphat continued his plans to accompany Ahab, because Jehoshaphat was the one who had insisted upon hearing from Jehovah before going into battle. But both kings prepared their armies and started to battle.

Ahab was a little frightened by Micaiah's message, so he told Jehoshaphat, "I am going into battle wearing a disguise, but you go ahead and wear your royal robes." Ahab thought Jehoshaphat would be a decoy to draw attention away from himself. Ahab would be dressed as a common soldier so that the Syrians could not find him. Thus he and Jehoshaphat went into battle.

Meanwhile, Ben-hadad had ordered his thirty-two chariot commanders to find and kill Ahab: "Do not fight with anyone small or great except Ahab."

Therefore, when the commanders saw Jehoshaphat, they thought, "Surely this is Ahab." They pressed their way toward him, but he cried out and the Lord helped him. The Syrian soldiers saw that he was not Ahab and turned away.

Ahab was nowhere to be found. As the fighting continued, a Syrian archer looked around for a target and saw an Israelite soldier in a chariot. The archer drew back his arrow and shot the Israelite soldier through a joint in his armor. The soldier was Ahab. Ahab told his chariot driver, "Turn about and get me out of the fighting, for I have been wounded."

All day long the battle raged, and Ahab remained propped in his chariot. His blood ran down and pooled on the floor of the chariot. That evening he died. About sunset, the cry went out to stop the battle: "Every man go back to his own city and to his own land."

Ahab was brought to Samaria and buried. Ahab's chariot was washed by the pool of Samaria and the dogs licked up the bloody water. The fact that this was the pool where the prostitutes washed themselves is mentioned as a further sign of contempt piled upon Ahab in his death.

Additional information about Ahab was recorded in the historical records of the kings of Israel that were not preserved for us. A description of the palace he built using inlaid ivory was included in those records, as well as a list of the cities he fortified.

When Naboth was killed at Jezreel, Elijah prophesied: "In the place where dogs licked the blood of Naboth, they will lick your blood" (1 Kings 21:19). That place was Jezreel; yet the blood of Ahab was licked by dogs in Samaria. The fact that dogs licked his blood was a disgrace to Ahab, but do you remember that Ahab humbled himself when he heard Elijah's message? God sent Elijah back to tell Ahab that the disaster would not come until the days of Ahab's son (see 21:27-29). The prophecy will be fulfilled in its entirety in 2 Kings 9.

JUDAH

17th year of Jehoshaphat

The Prophet Jehu Rebukes Jehoshaphat (2 Chron. 19:1-3):

As one would expect, God was not pleased with Jehoshaphat's alliance with Ahab. He asked him, "Should you help the wicked and love those who hate the Lord? Because of this, the wrath of God is upon you. There is, however, some good in you for you have rid the land of the Asherah poles and have set your heart to seek Jehovah."

ISRAEL

Ahaziah — 2 years (evil)
(1 Kings 22:48-53; 2 Kings 1:1-18; 2 Chron. 20:35-37):

Chronological Note:
Most of the two years of Ahaziah's reign were at the close of Ahab's life. 1 Kings 22:51 says that Ahaziah began his reign in the 17th year of Jehoshaphat. But Jehoshaphat began his reign in the 4th year of Ahab's reign and reigned 25 years (1 Kings 22:41-42). But Ahab himself reigned 22 years (1 Kings 16:29). The 17th year of Jehoshaphat would still have been a year and a half or two years before the death of Ahab. Therefore, as was often done in that day, Aha-

Jehoshaphat's Further Reforms
(2 Chron. 19:4-11):

Jehoshaphat went out to all his people from Beersheba to the hill-country of Ephraim to bring them back to God. He set judges in all the major cities and told them, "Be careful how you behave because you are not judging for man but for the Lord who is with you when you render a verdict. Let the fear of God be upon you and judge righteously, for with Jehovah our God there is no injustice or partiality or bribery."

Jehoshaphat also encouraged the Levites and priests to do their work and to administer the law of the Lord and to settle disputes. They lived in Jerusalem. He admonished them to be faithful in their work.

To make the work of the Levites and the judges more efficient, Jehoshaphat set Amariah the chief priests over all the judges in all matters that pertained to God, and he set Zebadiah, the leader of the tribe of Judah, over the judges in all matters that pertained to the king.

Invasion of Moabites, Ammonites, and Men from Mt. Seir (2 Chron. 20:3-30):

After Moab rebelled against Israel following Ahab's death, they joined the Ammonites and some from Mt. Seir to fight against Judah.

Usually when the text mentions Mt. Seir, the people under consideration are the Edomites. Yet, the Hebrew word here is Meammonim, meaning those who lived by, or on the border of Ammon. Possibly it was a tribe called Maunites or Maonites, whose headquarters were in the city of Maon in the neighborhood of Petra, which was in the territory of the Edomites. If this is correct, then it may have been some Edomites and some of this non-Edomite tribe who joined the rebellion. The exact identity of these people is not vital to the lesson. Do not spend long in your class discussing the matter, but it is interest-

ziah must have been made co-regent with his father. Likely Ahaziah did not live long after his father died.

Ahaziah was very wicked. He walked in the ways of his father and mother and in the ways of Jeroboam the son of Nebat. That means he worshiped both Baal and the golden calves. Therefore, he greatly provoked the anger of Jehovah.

Rebellion of Moab (2 Kings 1:1; 3:4-5):

When Ahab was dead, Mesha, the king of Moab rebelled against Israel. The annual tribute of Mesha to the king of Israel was 100,000 lambs and 100,000 rams with their wool. The language used could refer to the wool of all the animals, or to the animals themselves. Either one would have been a large tribute.

ing to note the various people involved. Be sure Moab, Ammon, and Edom are labeled on your map.

As one would expect from their location, the invasion forces went around the southern end of the Dead Sea to attack Judah. Therefore, the report came to Jehoshaphat, "A vast army is coming against you from Edom. It is already at Hazazon-tamar" *(that is, En-gedi. Label En-gedi on your map.).*

Jehoshaphat himself had an army of over a million men, but it was not a mobilized, standing army. Caught by surprise, Jehoshaphat knew he had only one hope — Jehovah. He, therefore, ordered a fast throughout all Judah. The people came from every town in Judah to help Jehoshaphat seek help from God.

Jehoshaphat stood before the assembly in Jerusalem at the temple of the Lord, and he prayed:

Oh Jehovah God. Are you not the God who is in heaven? You rule over all the kingdoms of the world. Power and might are in your hand, and no one can withstand you. Did you not drive out the former inhabitants of this land and give it to the descendants of Abraham your friend? They have lived in it and have built a Sanctuary where you put your name, saying, "If calamity comes upon us, whether sword or famine, if we call upon you, you will hear us and save us."

Now the armies of Ammon, Moab, and Mt. Seir have come against us. You would not allow us to take their land when we came up from Egypt. See how they repay us for sparing them. They have come to drive us out of the possession you gave us. Will you not judge them, O God? For we do not have the power to face this vast army which is attacking us. We do not

know anything to do but call upon you.
We wait to see what you will do.

At that point, the word of God came upon
a Levite named Jahaziel who was in the assembly. He said:

> Listen, O King and all the people
> of Judah. This is what Jehovah says:
> "Do not be afraid or discouraged be-
> cause of this great army. The battle is
> not yours, but God's. Tomorrow,
> march down toward them. They will
> be climbing up the pass of Ziz, and
> you will find them at the end of the
> gorge in the desert of Jeruel. You will
> not have to fight. Just go and take up
> your positions and see the deliverance
> the Lord will bring to you."

Upon hearing this wonderful news, Jehoshaphat and all the people fell upon their faces
and worshiped God. The Levites led the
multitude in songs of praise to the Lord.

Early the next morning, the men of Judah
left for the wilderness of Tekoa. Jehoshaphat
encouraged them to have faith in God and in
His prophets. He appointed men to go before
the army, praising the beauty of God's holiness. They sang: "Give thanks to the Lord, for
His love endures forever."

The Bible says that while Jehoshaphat and
his army were approaching the enemy, God
set ambushes against the Moabites, Ammonites, and men from Mt. Seir. Who set the
ambushes? Since God had told the men of
Judah they would not have to fight, and since
the subsequent strife that erupted was against
the men of Mt. Seir, it was probably they
whom God used. Whoever it was, the three
groups involved in the invading army turned
upon one another. First the Moabites and
Ammonites destroyed the men of Mt. Seir and
then turned on each other. The slaughter was
so great that when the men of Judah arrived
and looked down upon the wilderness where

40

the great army had been, they saw only dead bodies all over the ground. No one had escaped.

Jehoshaphat and his men went down to collect the plunder and loot. There was so much, it took them three days to collect it all. They gathered in a valley to praise God for the victory. Therefore, the valley was called the Valley of Beracah (praise) from that day forward.

Then, led by Jehoshaphat, the men of Judah returned in triumph to Jerusalem. God continued to bless Jehoshaphat and Judah, and to deliver them from their enemies. Therefore, the kingdom had peace.

Jehoshaphat's Shipping Alliance with Ahaziah
(1 Kings 22:48-49; 2 Chron. 20:35-37)

Jehoshaphat did not heed the reprimands from Jehovah's prophets about his friendship with the family of Ahab. Jehoshaphat and Ahaziah agreed to work together to build a fleet of trading ships at Ezion-geber. The plan was for the ships to go to Ophir in the southern part of Arabia to bring back gold.

A prophet of the Lord named Eliezer came to Jehoshaphat and said, "Because you have made an alliance with Ahaziah, the Lord will destroy what you have made." Surely enough, the ships were wrecked and were not able to set sail to trade.

Ahaziah asked Jehoshaphat to try again, and let their men sail together, but Jehoshaphat refused.

The King James translation calls these "ships of Tarshish." That sounds as if these ships were designed to go across the Mediterranean Sea to the city of Tarshish (modern Spain), but it specifically says these ships were being built at Ezion-geber at the tip of the Gulf of Aqaba. Ships built there would sail down the Red Sea and out into the Indian Ocean. The term "Tarshish ships" or "Ships of Tarshish" had come to mean any long distance sailing vessels.

(Jehoshaphat continuing in Judah)

Ahaziah's Accident (2 Kings 1:2-18):
Ahaziah fell through a window in an upper story and was so severely injured there was a question of whether he would recover. He decided to send to inquire of the god of Ekron, Baal-zebub, whether he would get well. Ekron was in the territory of Philistia. Ahaziah showed his utter disregard for Jehovah by sending to inquire of an idol.

The angel of the Lord told Elijah: "Go

meet the messengers of Ahaziah and ask them
if there is no God in Israel. Is that why you
are going to consult Baal-zebub, the god of
Ekron? Go back and tell your master that he
will not leave his bed. He will surely die."

Elijah did as he was told, and the messengers returned to the king. When the messengers came back so quickly, Ahaziah knew they
had not had time to go to Ekron yet, so he
said, "Why have you come back?"

The messengers replied by telling him of
meeting a man who had rebuked them for
going to inquire of Baal-zebub and had said
Ahaziah would die.

Ahaziah inquired, "What was the man like
who met you?"

They said, "He wore a garment of hair
and a leather belt around his waist."

Ahaziah said, "That was Elijah the Tishbite." Then he commanded a captain of fifty
men to go and fetch Elijah.

The captain and his men came to Elijah
who was sitting on the top of a hill. The
captain spoke very abruptly to Elijah: "Man of
God, the king says for you to come down."

It was obvious that this captain did not
consider Elijah anything special. God wanted
to make a point about what it meant for God
to be with His prophet. So Elijah said, "If I be
a man of God, let fire come down out of
heaven and consume you and your men."
Immediately fire came down and burned up
the captain and his men.

When Ahaziah heard what had happened,
he sent another captain and his fifty. That
captain told Elijah, "Man of God, the king
says for you to come to him at once!"

Elijah replied to this captain also, "If I am
a man of God, let fire come down and devour
you and your fifty." Once again fire came
down from heaven and consumed the men.

Ahaziah was not getting burned, and he
had plenty of captains, so he sent another one
with his men. This captain had heard of the
fate of his predecessors. He gave a whole new
meaning to the term, "Man of God," when he

used it.

He came to Elijah and fell on his knees. He begged, "Man of God, please have respect for my life and the lives of these fifty men, your servants! Fire has already fallen from heaven and devoured the first two captains and their men. Please spare my life!"

The angel of the Lord told Elijah, "Go with him; don't be afraid." God's point had been made; the safety of His prophet was insured.

Elijah went with the captain to Ahaziah. When he got there he repeated the very message he had sent to Ahaziah through his messengers: "Because you sent to inquire of Baal-zebub, the god of Ekron, you will not leave your bed. You will surely die."

Ahaziah died as Elijah predicted. His brother Jehoram (or Joram) succeeded to the throne because Ahaziah had no son.

Baal-zebub means "Master of Flies" or "Fly-God." Some ancient peoples regarded the fly as having prophetic powers because they were governed in their going and coming by the weather. Evidence indicates that the people of Ekron may have represented this Baal as a fly, a fly-idol, and considered it had particular powers of prophecy.

As time passed, the Jews altered the name to Beelzeboul, lord of the heavenly dwelling, as a name given to the ruler of demons. Later Rabbins (teachers) altered it further to Beelzebel, lord of the dung-pile, to show their utter contempt for idolatry.

In Jesus' day, the term Beelzebub is found as a reference to Satan (Matt. 10:25; 12:24). In these references, the Greek word is Beelzebul to which we referred in the previous paragraph.

Elijah is Taken up into Heaven
(2 Kings 2:1-18)

When the Lord was about to take Elijah into heaven, He told Elijah what He would do and where Elijah was to go to meet Him. As Elijah and Elisha were about to leave Gilgal in the hill country of Ephraim, Elijah said to Elisha, "Stay here, because the Lord is sending me to Bethel."

Elisha replied, "As surely as Jehovah lives and you live, I am not leaving you." So they went to Bethel.

A company of prophets (sons of the prophets) came out to meet them at Bethel. They said to Elisha, "Do you know that the Lord is going to take your master from you today?"

Elisha said, "Yes, I know, but do not talk about it."

Then Elijah said to him, "Stay here, Elisha; the Lord has sent me to Jericho." Once again, Elisha swore that he would not leave Elijah's side.

When they reached Jericho, another group of prophets came out and asked Elisha, "Do you know that the Lord is going to take your master from you today?"

Elisha replied, "Yes, I know, but do not speak of it."

Then Elijah said, "Stay here, for the Lord has sent me on to the Jordan."

Elisha replied, "As the Lord lives and as you live, I will not leave you." So the two of them walked across the plain at Jericho to the Jordan River.

Fifty men from the company of prophets stood at a distance, facing the place where Elijah and Elisha had stopped at the river. Jericho was located a few miles from the river, on the slope leading into the hill country. Therefore, these prophets could see what happened at the river itself and then on the eastern slope beyond.

When the two men reached the river's edge, Elijah took his cloak, rolled it up, and smote the waters of the Jordan. The water divided to the left and right and the two men crossed over on dry ground.

When they had crossed over, Elijah asked Elisha, "What would you have me do for you before I am taken away?"

"Let me inherit a double portion of your Spirit," Elisha answered.

This request was not for twice as much of the Spirit as Elijah had, rather it was a request for the portion given to a firstborn child. As Elijah's successor, Elisha asked for the portion of Elijah's Spirit which would be proper for a firstborn son.

Elijah said, "You have asked a difficult thing. Nevertheless, if you see me when I am taken from you, your request will be granted, otherwise not."

As they were walking along and talking together, suddenly a chariot of fire and horses of fire appeared and separated them. Elijah was taken up into heaven in a whirlwind. What a truly awesome sight that must have been! Elisha cried out, "My father! My father! The chariots and horsemen of Israel!"

Elijah was gone, taken up into heaven in an extraordinary manner. He was one of only two men in all the history of the world to go to heaven without dying. The other was Enoch who lived before the flood (see Gen. 5:21-24; Heb. 11:5).

Though Elisha was grieved by the loss of his "master" and "father," he saw, now when all was quiet again, the cloak or mantle of Elijah lying on the ground. He picked it up and went back to the

Jordan. He struck the water with it and said, "Where now is Jehovah, the God of Elijah?" The water divided right and left, and Elisha crossed over.

The company of the prophets observed what happened, and they said among themselves, "Look, the Spirit of Elijah is resting upon Elisha." They went to meet Elisha and bowed to the ground before him, not in worship, but as a sign of deep respect for the prophet, and reverence for the Spirit of God which clearly was now upon Elisha.

Elijah had a reputation of appearing and disappearing. The sons of the prophets had seen him taken up into heaven in the whirlwind, but they thought he might have been put back down somewhere. They said, "We have fifty men available. Let them go look for your master. The Spirit of God may have put him down on some mountain or in some valley."

"No," Elisha replied, "do not send them." Elisha knew that Elijah was no longer on this earth.

The sons of the prophets insisted until Elisha was ashamed to refuse. So he said, "Send them." After three days, the fifty men returned to Elisha, who had remained at Jericho, and reported they could not find Elijah.

Elisha replied, "Didn't I tell you not to go?"

Now that Elijah's cloak has fallen upon Elisha, he will carry on the work of Jehovah in fine fashion. He is also a towering character, as was Elijah, but their stories are somewhat different. Elijah had to stay in hiding because his life was in danger. Times change a little, and Elisha's relationship with the kings was less stormy. Only five of Elijah's miracles are recorded, but at least twelve of Elisha's are related in the next few chapters of 2 Kings. Elisha lived to be an old man, and his work spanned the reigns of four kings of Israel. It is impossible, however, to establish an exact chronology for the miracles told, so we will deal with them in the order in which we come to them in the Bible text.

Elisha Purifies a Spring of Water
(2 Kings 2:19-22)

While Elisha was still at Jericho, the men of the city came to him and said, "Look, our lord, this town is well situated, as you can see, but the water is bad, and the land unproductive."

Elisha said, "Bring me a new bowl and put salt in it." The bowl was brought as he asked.

The prophet went out to the spring and threw the salt into it, saying, "This is what the Lord says: 'I have healed this water. Never again will it cause death or make the land unproductive.'" The water remained good ever after.

Some Youths Jeer at Elisha
(2 Kings 2:23-25)

Elisha left Jericho to go to Bethel in the hill country. As he was walking along the road, some youths came out of the town of Bethel and mocked Elisha. These were boys old enough to know better. In them was reflected the spirit of the idolatrous city of Bethel. They cried out, "Go on up, you baldhead. Go on up, you baldhead."

Elisha looked around and called down a curse on them in the name of the Lord. Elisha was conscious, not of his personal honor, but of his role as God's prophet in troubled times. It was important that the people of Jehovah be taught to respect those who spoke for the Lord. Even the law had stated that stubborn and rebellious sons should be put to death (Deut. 21:18-21).

Jehovah caused two female bears to come out of the woods. The bears mauled forty-two of the youths. Elisha went on his way to Mount Carmel and from there returned to Samaria.

JUDAH

18th year of Jehoshaphat
2nd year of Jehoram, son of Jehoshaphat

Chronological Note:

When we compare 2 Kings 1:17 and 3:1, there is a distinct problem in chronology. It seems that Jehoshaphat appointed his son Jehoram co-regent with him about the time he was preparing to go with Ahab to fight against Ramoth-Gilead. Therefore, in the second year of Jehoram's co-regency which was Jehoshaphat's eighteenth year, Jehoram of Israel began his rule.

After this early co-regency, there is a gap of two or three years and once again Jehoshaphat makes Jehoram co-regent. This second co-regency began in the fifth year of Jehoram of Israel (see 2 Kings 8:16). This would have been about the 22nd year of Jehoshaphat.

The Jehoram in Judah is the son of Jehoshaphat, of the lineage of David. He is married to Athaliah, the daughter of Ahab and Jezebel. Therefore, the Jehoram of Judah is the brother-in-law of the Jehoram of Israel. See the family tree below.

Do not let the repetition in the names confuse you. The reigning families in the two kingdoms are related by marriage, and names are repeated in the family, just as names are repeated in families today. The information about the kings will be shown in the correct columns to help you keep them straight.

Remember, also, that these kings are called by more than one name. For example, both Jehorams are also called Joram. Do not let it confuse you.

ISRAEL

Jehoram (or Joram) — 12 years (evil) (2 Kings 3:1-9:28):

Jehoram was evil in God's sight, but not like his father and mother. For example, he repudiated the sacred stone (or obelisk) of Baal which Ahab had made. He did, however, encourage the worship of the golden calves.

Jehoram's Family:

The account becomes somewhat confusing in these chapters because there are kings in both kingdoms with names alike. Before we go further, let us take time to look at the relationships. Ahab and Jezebel were the parents of King Ahaziah who fell through the upper window and died. Ahaziah did not have a son, so he was succeeded by Jehoram (or Joram) who was also a son of Ahab and Jezebel.

In addition to these men, Ahab and Jezebel were the parents of a daughter named Athaliah. She married Jehoram (or Joram), the son of Jehoshaphat, as a seal to the treaty of peace between their fathers. That means that wicked Athaliah now lives in Judah while two of her brothers reign in Israel, and while her own husband Jehoram is first co-regent with his father Jehoshaphat, and then king on his own. Jehoram and Athaliah have a son named Ahaziah who will succeed his father to the throne. Learn the chart below.

Memorize this Family Tree

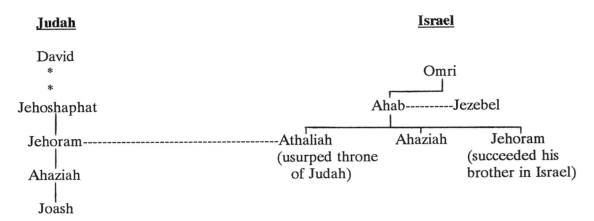

Judah   **Israel**

David
*
*
Jehoshaphat
|
Jehoram--Athaliah   Ahaziah   Jehoram
| (usurped throne   (succeeded his
Ahaziah   of Judah)   brother in Israel)
|
Joash

Jehoshaphat and Jehoram Fight Moab
(2 Kings 3:6-27)

We have already noted that Moab rebelled against Israel when Ahab died. King Mesha of Moab refused to pay his tribute any longer. Then, we noted that Moab joined Ammon and men from Mt. Seir to fight against Judah. Now, in this story, Jehoram of Israel decides to try to re-take Moab, and he calls upon Jehoshaphat to help him. It was not hard to persuade Jehoshaphat to join the effort, possibly because of the invasion Moab had made against Judah only a short time earlier.

When Jehoram of Israel sent messengers to Jehoshaphat asking him to help him fight against Moab, Jehoshaphat responded, "I will go with you, and I am as you are, my people as your people, my horses as your horses." Jehoshaphat suggested they take their combined armies around the southern end of the Dead Sea to reach Moab.

Notice on your map that to get from Judah to Moab, one had to go either around the northern end of the Dead Sea and then south to Moab, or around the southern end of the Sea and then north to Moab. By going around the southern end of the Sea, Jehoram would move south from Samaria with his men, join Jehoshaphat in Judah, and continue south into Edom's territory where they were joined by the king of Edom and his army. Edom was under Jehoshaphat's control at this time, so Edom's soldiers could be counted on to help Judah in time of need.

The territory south of the Dead Sea is very dry, so after a seven days' journey, the armies were out of water. By now they were on the southern edge of Moab's territory. Jehoram cried out, "Has the Lord called us three kings together only to hand us over to Moab?"

Jehoshaphat asked, "Is there no prophet of the Lord here that we may inquire of God through him?"

An officer of Jehoram answered, "Elisha the son of Shaphat is here. He used to be Elijah's servant."

Jehoshaphat had confidence in Elisha, so all three kings went to the prophet. When Elisha saw Jehoram king of Israel, he said, "What do we have to do with one another? Go to the prophets of your father and of your mother."

Jehoram said, "No, because it was Jehovah who called us three kings together to hand us over to Moab."

Elisha replied, "As surely as the Lord Almighty lives, whom I serve, if it were not for the presence of Jehoshaphat king of Judah, I would not waste any time with you. But now bring me a harpist."

While the harpist played for Elisha, the Spirit spoke to the prophet and said, "This is what the Lord says: 'Make this valley full of ditches. There will be neither wind nor rain, yet this valley will be filled with water, and you, your cattle, and your other animals will drink.' This is an easy thing for God; He will also hand Moab over to you. You will overthrow every fortified city and every major town. You will cut down every good tree, stop up all the springs, and ruin the good fields with stones."

They did as they were told, and the next morning at the time for morning sacrifices, there it was — water flowing from the direction of Edom! And the land was filled with water as Jehovah had said.

This blessing turned out to be a twofold blessing. The Moabites had mobilized every man, young and old, to fight, and they were stationed on the border of Moab. Early that morning, the sun was shining on the water in the distance, and it looked red like blood. The Moabites shouted, "That's blood!" They thought Israel, Judah, and Edom had fallen out with one another and had slaughtered one another with a great slaughter just as they themselves had done in a battle recently (see 2 Chron. 20). They said, "These kings must have slaughtered one another. To the plunder, Moab!"

But when the Moabites rushed into the Israelite camp, they found the soldiers alive and well. The Israelites rose up and fought the Moabites until they fled. Then they invaded the land of Moab and destroyed the cities and ruined the fields by covering them with stones. Only the capital city of Kir-hareseth was left with its stones in place.

When the king of Moab saw that he was being defeated, he took a special force of seven hundred swordsmen to break through to the king of Edom, but he failed. Then, in desperation, he took his firstborn son, and offered him as a sacrifice on the city wall.

The Bible says, "And there was great indignation against Israel," and they stopped fighting and went home. The Bible does not explain why wrath came upon Israel at this point. Usually such an expression is describing wrath from God. In the absence of more details, it is better to leave it just as the text has it. The battle ended, with Moab defeated, and wrath against Israel.

Judah	Israel

Judah

Death of Jehoshaphat (1 Kings 22:45, 50; 2 Chron. 20:33-34; 21:1):

After a reign of twenty-five years, Jehoshaphat died and was buried in the City of David. He had been a righteous king, who had made numerous efforts through the years to bring his subjects to faithful service to God. He had succeeded in destroying the outward signs of idolatry in the land, but the high places were not destroyed, and the hearts of the people were not wholly set on serving Jehovah.

Jehoram (or Joram) — 8 years (evil) (2 Kings 8:16-24; 2 Chron. 21:1-20):

Remember that this Jehoram of Judah is a brother-in-law to the Jehoram reigning in Israel at the same time, because this Jehoram is married to Athaliah the daughter of Ahab and Jezebel and, therefore, a sister to Jehoram of Israel.

Jehoram reigned alone after his father died. He was very wicked because he walked in the ways of Ahab. Nevertheless, because of His promise to David, God was not willing to destroy Jehoram and his house.

Look back to 2 Samuel 7:13-14. In that passage, God said that if a descendant of David sinned, God would punish him, but He would not destroy his lineage on the throne the way He had destroyed Saul's house. That is exactly what we will observe happening with Jehoram.

Jehoram Kills his Brothers (2 Chron. 21:2-4):

Jehoshaphat had six sons besides Jehoram. He had given them many gifts of gold, silver, and other articles of value and had put them in charge of fortified cities of Judah. But he had reserved the position of king for Jehoram because he was his firstborn son.

As soon as Jehoshaphat was dead and Jehoram in control, Jehoram murdered all his brothers, plus some of the princes of Judah.

Israel

Jehoram, the son of Ahab, still ruling in Israel.

Jehoram of Judah began ruling as co-regent with his father in the fifth year of Jehoram of Israel (2 Kings 8:16). Jehoshaphat died about two or three years later, leaving Jehoram ruling alone in about the seventh or eighth year of Jehoram of Israel.

That left him as the only legal heir to the throne.

In this awful deed, Jehoram was conducting himself much more like a pagan king than a king of God's holy people. The corrupt influence of Jezebel had certainly been transplanted to Judah through the evil influence of Athaliah.

Edom Revolts (2 Kings 8:20-22a; 2 Chron. 21:8-10a):

Edom had been under the control of Israel since the days of David, and had continued to be held by Judah until now. After the death of Jehoshaphat, everything fell apart for Judah because of the terrible wickedness of Jehoram.

Edom revolted. Jehoram took his army and tried to bring them back under his control, but he failed. The Edomites surrounded him and his chariot commanders. Jehoram and his men broke through the lines by night and fled back home.

Libnah Revolts (2 Kings 8:22b; 2 Chron. 21:10b):

Libnah rebelled about the same time Edom rebelled. Libnah was a city on the southwest edge of Judah, a little northwest of the city of Gath, on the old border between Israel and the Philistines.

Again, the Bible points out that the reason for the revolt was that Jehoram had forsaken the Lord, the God of his fathers.

Jehoram Receives a Letter from Elijah (2 Chron. 21:11-15):

Notice verse 11. In contrast to his father Jehoshaphat and grandfather Asa, who destroyed idols on the high places, and tried to turn the people back to Jehovah, Jehoram *built* high places and encouraged his people to worship the idols. He "caused" the people to commit fornication and led Judah astray.

A letter arrived from Elijah the prophet. According to the chronology that we have followed, Elijah had already gone to heaven before this event. There is no information given to let us know how this letter reached Jehoram. In absence of detailed information, it is useless to speculate. The letter said:

> Thus saith the Lord, the God of David: "You have not walked in the ways of your father Jehoshaphat and of Asa. Instead you have walked in the ways of the kings of Israel and have led Judah to prostitute themselves just as the house of Ahab did to Israel. You murdered your own brothers, better men than you. Therefore, now the Lord is about to strike your people, your sons, your wives, and everything you have with a heavy blow. You yourself will become very ill with a lingering disease of the bowels until your bowels will come out."

Invasion of the Philistines and Arabians (2 Chron. 21:16, 17):

The Lord stirred up the wrath of the Philistines, and they joined with Arabians from deep in the Arabian Desert to attack Judah. They invaded the land and carried away the wealth found in the king's palace. They also took the king's sons and his wives. He was left with only one son, Jehoahaz (also known as Ahaziah). He was left with only his wife Athaliah. It would have been better for Judah if she had been carried away.

One son was left. There was still an heir to David's throne. Do you see God's promise to David is holding true even though Jehoram is being severely punished for his wickedness? Contrast Jehoram's punishment with the punishment against such men as Jeroboam whose whole family was wiped out. God's providence works!

The Prophet Obadiah
(The Book of Obadiah)

Most students of the Bible believe that Obadiah wrote his prophecy against Edom about this time (ca. 845 B.C.), although some believe he came much later. We choose to look at his little book at this point because the circumstances fit better here than anywhere else. Edom was first conquered by David (2 Sam. 8:12-14), and it had remained under the control of Judah after the kingdom divided. But now, Jehoram of Judah is very, very wicked. He is having trouble on every hand. Edom rebels — and then rejoices over the trouble Judah is having. God is allowing Jehoram to be chastised by the trouble coming upon Judah, but He is not pleased over Edom's attitude, and He sends the prophet Obadiah to cry out against her sins. Edom, too, will someday face her judgment.

In order to fully understand the little book of Obadiah, you must remember that the Edomites were descendants of Esau, the twin brother of Jacob — the sons of Isaac. Edom is another name for Esau, just as Israel is another name for Jacob. The message of the book is:

Jehovah's Message: Call the nations to war against Edom (verse 1):
The message from Jehovah through Obadiah concerns Edom. News has come from Jehovah, and the nations are being called to come in battle against Edom.

Edom is deceived by her pride (verses 2-4):
Edom has completely lost sight of how insignificant she is. Her pride has led her to believe she is invincible. Like the eagle who builds his nest upon the cliffs, Edom cries, "Who thinks he can bring me to the ground?"

The answer is God! He says to Edom, "Though you build your nest even among the stars, I will bring you down."

Edom is to be completely destroyed (verses 5-9):
Edom's destruction will be complete. If thieves came to steal, they would not take everything. And when the grape-gatherers harvest the grapes, they do not pick every grape. But every thing Edom has, even the things hidden away, will be taken. The "friends" she relies on will not be her friends at all. Esau [Edom] could not see this. God would utterly discredit the wisdom of which Edom was so proud. Her mighty men would be slaughtered.

The reason for Edom's destruction (verses 10-14):
Because of the violence done to Edom's brother Jacob, she will be cut off forever. In the day that strangers came and raided Jacob and plundered his possessions, Edom was as one of them. It was not right for Edom to rejoice in her brother's destruction. God says, "You should not have entered their gates to take your share of the plunder. You should not have blocked the escape of those who fled, and you should not have turned them over to their captors."

The Day of the Lord, a Day of Judgment for Edom (verses 15-16):
As Edom has done, it shall be done unto her. As she has drunk and swallowed Judah, so the nations will drink of Edom — on and on until she is completely gone.

Triumph of Mount Zion over Edom (verses 17-21):

In this section, the deliverance of God's people is contrasted with Edom's downfall. In fact, Israel would be a flame to burn the house of Esau for stubble. The symbol of the victory depicts a spiritual over-coming of Edom, the symbol of unregenerate, profane men.

In the prophetic writings, Edom came to be used in a figurative sense to refer to unregenerate mankind, in contrast with Israel or Judah (Amos 9:12; Acts 15:17; Ezek. 35, and others). Verses 17-21 of Obadiah seem to be Messianic, and in such a context, Edom would definitely be used in a symbolic sense of unregenerate mankind — that is, the lost, those in open rebellion against God.

If, as we have shown, Obadiah wrote his book at this time, he was the first of the writing prophets. There had been many prophets through the years — such as Moses, Samuel, Elijah, Elisha, as well as many others who are mentioned only a few times or whose names are not told. Moses wrote the first five books found in our Bibles and Samuel may have written at least portions of I Samuel. But this is the first prophet to record his prophetic message rather than history.

Think about it: Why did prophets begin writing their messages? Up until this point, God would send a prophet to deliver a specific message. Even if the king were as evil as Ahab, someone recorded the message for later generations to see — such as in the case of Elijah. But the kingdoms grew more and more wicked. There were messages God wanted recorded as a witness that God warned before He punished. Therefore, God's Spirit guided these men in writing their message as proof that God had spoken. (See Isaiah 30:8, and a host of similar passages throughout the writings of the prophets.)

Prophetic Themes

In teaching the prophets, one must remember that, unfortunately, they are among the least known books of the Bible. Teachers must resolve to give the prophets special attention in both studying them and teaching them.

To help teachers with the prophets, we are including summaries of the prophetic books as we come to their place in the history of the kingdoms of Israel and Judah. These summaries are designed to simplify and emphasize each prophet's message. We have tried to reduce each prophetic book to a manageable lesson. In addition, we have tried to emphasize particular points here and there to help the teacher know what special lessons should be brought out about a given prophet.

To help teachers and students further, we want to devote just a little space to prophetic themes in general. If the teacher will firmly fix these themes in mind, it will soon be second nature to see these points as each prophet is studied. Therefore we present here a list of the most prominent prophetic themes, with a brief discussion of each one:

1. *Repent — The prophets were sent forth in crucial times in the history of Israel and Judah. It was always the unfaithfulness of the people that brought calamity upon them. Even as God prepared to chastise His people, He would extend His mercy in the call to repent.*

2. *The Day of Jehovah — The "day of Jehovah" is the day of reckoning that comes in the lives of nations and individuals. It is a day of judgment upon the evil and of deliverance for the righteous.*

There have been many "days of Jehovah" throughout the course of history, as God has determined the time has arrived for various nations or individuals to receive the judgment necessary as a result of their behavior.

3. *God's concern for the nations — The more one studies and thinks about this idea, the more one can see the emphasis upon this theme. First, God will not demand that His people be righteous, and then allow the world to behave anyway it wants without rebuke. Therefore, He calls upon the nations to measure up to His requirements, and chastises them if they do not. Secondly, He promises redemption for the nations, as well as for the Jews.*

4. *The Messiah — The Messiah is coming. This message is the shining message of the prophets. He is coming to do the Lord's will. He will save, and He will destroy, among the nations as well as among Israel.*

5. *A new spiritual order — Parallel with the concept of the Messiah, God's Priest-King, is the idea of the new spiritual order which the Messiah will inaugurate. Whether characterized as the "mountain of the Lord's house," or as a kingdom, or a grand temple, the reference is to the church.*

Essentially, the prophets preached God's message to a faithless nation. Some of the finest preaching in the Bible is found in the prophets. The beauty of the language, the vivid, graphic imagery, the different personalities of the writers, the great ideas discussed, the poignant emotions revealed, all make the prophets worthy of careful study. It is our hope that the brief studies of the prophets in this book will lay a good foundation for more in-depth studies of these great books.

JUDAH

Jehoram Falls Ill (2 Chron. 21:18-20):

After the invasion and devastation caused by the Philistines and Arabians, God smote Jehoram with an incurable disease of the bowels. *(From the description, it is likely he had amoebic dysentery.)* He was sick and in agony with the disease for two years before he finally died.

His people made no fire in his honor as they had with the previous kings. He was buried in the City of David, but *not* in the tombs of the kings.

One of the saddest epitaphs possible is given about Jehoram. He "departed without being desired," or as more modern translations express it, he passed away "to no one's regret." There were still enough good people left in Judah to grieve over the wickedness that had filled the land and, therefore, to feel

ISRAEL

Jehoram, the son of Ahab, still reigns in Israel.

relieved when such a wicked king died.

Jehoram was succeeded by his son Ahaziah (or Jehoahaz), but before we continue with his history, let us finish the stories told about Elisha at this point in the Bible text. Remember, in order to tell the stories of Elisha in the kingdom of Israel, we leave the history of Judah in the background, but the kingdom still exists — we only pause to continue observing the mighty effort God was making at this time to try to bring His people back to Him before it was too late.

More Stories About Elisha

If the chronology we have used is correct, Elisha became Elijah's attendant before Ahab died. Then Elijah was carried to heaven in the whirlwind about the time Ahaziah died and Jehoram became king in Israel. Elisha's work continued through the reigns of Jehoram, Jehu, Jehoahaz, and into the reign of Joash. There is no way to know for sure exactly when the events of his life happened. Whoever recorded the history of Elisha's work by the inspiration of God (the writer's name is unknown), was much more concerned with the miracles and teaching of Elisha than in the chronology. Therefore, the stories are told together in a group. There are various hints about the chronology, but we will continue to tell them as they appear in the text. Do not be surprised to see these stories rearranged in some work that has tried to follow the chronology precisely.

Elisha Increases a Widow's Oil
(2 Kings 4:1-7)

The wife of one of the sons of the prophets came to Elisha and said, "My husband is dead, and you know how he feared the Lord. But now his creditors have come and are demanding my two sons as slaves."

Elisha asked her, "How can I help you? What do you have in your house?"

She said, "I have nothing but a little oil."

Elisha told her, "Go to all your neighbors and borrow every vessel you can get. Then go into your house and shut the door behind you and your sons. Pour oil into the vessels, and as each one is filled, put it to one side."

The widow did as Elisha said. Her sons would bring her a jar and she would fill it. They would set it aside and bring another. When all the vessels were filled, she said, "Bring me another one."

One of her sons replied, "There is not another," and the oil stopped flowing.

The woman went and told Elisha what had happened, and he told her to sell the oil and pay her debts. He told her she and her sons could live on the rest of the proceeds.

A Shunammite Woman
(2 Kings 4:8-37)

One day Elisha passed through the city of Shunem which was located at the southwestern foot of the Hill of Moreh in the valley of Jezreel. A well-to-do woman lived there, and she invited Elisha to come in and eat at her house. After that, whenever Elisha passed that way, he stopped to eat.

Remember, there were no McDonalds or Quincys in that day. Eating and lodging while traveling were more difficult then.

After a time, the woman spoke to her husband, saying, "I know that this man who comes by often is a holy man of God. Let us make a small room on the roof and furnish it with a bed, a table, a chair, and a lamp. Then he can stay there when he comes by." Her husband agreed to this very considerate idea and it was done.

One day, Elisha had come by and had gone to his room and had lain down. He called his servant Gehazi to him and said, "Call the Shunammite."

Gehazi brought her and Elisha said, "You have gone to all this trouble for us. What can we do for you? Would you like for us to speak on your behalf to the king, or to the commander of the army?"

The woman declined any favors by saying, "I have a home among my own people."

Privately, Elisha asked Gehazi, "What can be done for her?"

Gehazi said, "Well, she has no son, and her husband is old."

Elisha said, "Call her." Once again, she came and stood in the doorway. Elisha said, "About this time next year, you will hold a son in your arms."

The woman was astonished. She said, "Don't deceive me, O man of God!"

But she did become pregnant, and about that time the next year, she gave birth to a son just as Elisha had predicted.

Some years passed, and likely some of the stories told later happened during these years. But, we will continue the story about this woman and her son at this point just as the Bible text has it. It will be less confusing than rearranging the text to fit the chronology.

Some years passed, and the son of the Shunammite woman grew. One day he went out in the field with his father and the reapers. After a while, he said, "My head! My head!"

The boy's father told a servant to take the child to his mother, but it seems he did not realize how seriously sick the boy was. The child sat on his mother's lap until noon — and then tragedy struck. The boy died in his mother's arms.

The mother carried his body up to Elisha's room and tenderly laid it on the bed. Then she called to her husband, and asked him to send a servant and a donkey so that she could go to the man of God quickly and return.

Her husband did not know why she wanted to go, so he said, "Why go to him today? It is not the New Moon or the Sabbath."

She said, "It is all right."

She saddled the donkey and told the servant, "Lead on, and do not slow down for anything unless I tell you." They struck out across the Jezreel Valley, heading for Mt. Carmel where Elisha lived.

When Elisha saw her coming he sent Gehazi to meet her. "Look," he said. "There is the Shunammite. Run to meet her and see if everything is all right with her and her husband and son."

Elisha knew something must be wrong for her to come at that time, and he knew it must be something about her family.

When Gehazi got to her and asked her, she would not stop to talk to him. She just said, "Everything is all right."

When she got to Elisha, however, she grasped his feet in supplication. She could say nothing at first because of her distress. Gehazi came over to push her away, but Elisha said, "Leave her alone! She is in deep distress, but the Lord has hidden it from me and has not told me why."

Finally she cried out, "Did I ask you for a son, my lord? Didn't I tell you not to raise my hopes?"

Elisha was very concerned, and he made immediate efforts to try to help her. He turned to Gehazi and said, "Gird yourself up, take my staff and run. If you meet anyone, don't even take time to say hello. Lay my staff on the boy's face."

The boy's mother said, "I will not leave you." So Elisha got up and went with her.

Gehazi went on ahead and laid the staff upon the boy's face, but nothing happened. Gehazi returned to meet Elisha, who was now on his way, and he said, "The boy has not awakened."

When Elisha arrived in his room, the boy was lying dead on his bed. Elisha went in, shut the door, and prayed to the Lord. Then he stretched himself out over the body of the boy. As he lay upon the body, the boy's flesh began to grow warm again. Elisha got up, walked about, and once more stretched himself out upon him. The boy began to sneeze. He sneezed seven times and opened his eyes.

Elisha called Gehazi and said, "Call the Shunammite." When she came, Elisha said, "Take your son."

She came in, fell at Elisha's feet, and bowed to the ground in profound gratitude. Then she took her son and went out.

Elisha Purifies Stew
(2 Kings 4:38-41)

Elisha went to Gilgal in the hill country of Ephraim at a time when there was a famine in the region. While the sons of the prophets were meeting with him, he told his servant, "Put on a large pot and cook some stew for these men."

One of the men went into the field to gather herbs and found a wild gourd vine. He gathered some of its gourds and filled the lap of his robe full. When he came back, he shredded them into the stew. He did not know they were poisonous and very bitter.

The stew was dipped out, but when they began to eat, they cried out, "O man of God, there is death in the pot." It was the bitterness of the wild gourd that let them know something was wrong.

Elisha said, "Bring me some meal." When it was brought, Elisha cast it into the pot and said, "Now, pour some out to each one so that everyone may eat."

There was nothing harmful in the pot after that.

Elisha Feeds 100 Men with 20 Loaves
(2 Kings 4:42-44)

Elisha continued with the sons of the prophets for a time. One of the problems they faced regularly was that of finding enough food. One day a man came from Baal-shalishah (located west of Gilgal) bringing twenty loaves of barley bread.

Elisha said, "Give it to the people to eat."

"How can I set this before a hundred men?" asked his servant.

Elisha replied, "Set it before them because the Lord says they will all eat and have food left over." The servant set it before the people, they ate, and had food left — just as the Lord had said.

Elisha Heals Naaman of his Leprosy
(2 Kings 5:1-27)

The Syrian (Aramean) king had a general in his army by the name of Naaman. He was very much esteemed in the eyes of his master, but he was a leper.

The term leprosy in the Bible covered a range of skin conditions, and even mildew in the case of objects. Some forms of these diseases were much more serious than others. Obviously, Naaman's leprosy was not yet debilitating, so either it was not as serious a form as some, or it was not yet advanced to that point. Either way, it was a grievous nuisance.

On one of their raids into Israel, the Syrians had captured a little maid, and she had become a servant to Naaman's wife. One day the girl told her mistress, "If only my master could see the prophet who is in Samaria! He would cure him of his leprosy."

This word was passed along to Naaman, and he told the king. The king of Syria was eager for his servant to be healed, so he said, "By all means, go. I will send a letter to the king of Israel."

The name of the Syrian king is not given, nor is the name of the Israelite king given. Therefore, there is no way to place the time of this event.

Naaman left Syria, taking with him ten talents (750 pounds) of silver, six thousand shekels (150 pounds) of gold, and ten changes of clothes. He took along a letter to the king of Israel from the king of Syria which said, "With this letter I am sending my servant Naaman to you so that you may cure him of his leprosy." Somewhere in the transmission of the information from the little Israelite girl to the Syrian king, sight had been lost of the prophet in Israel who was to do the healing.

The king of Israel was frantic when he got the letter. He tore his clothes and ranted, "Am I God? Can I kill and raise people from the dead? Why does this fellow send someone to me to be cured of his leprosy? See how he is picking a fight with me?"

When Elisha heard of the king's reaction he sent word: "Why have you torn your robes? Send the man to me, and he will know there is a prophet in Israel."

So Naaman and his company left the king and went to Elisha's house. He stopped at the door with all his chariots, his horses, his servants, and all his gifts. Elisha did not even come out of his house to see the splendor of the company. Instead he sent a messenger out to say, "Go and wash yourself seven times in the river Jordan, and your flesh will be restored and you will be cleansed."

Naaman was highly insulted! He turned to go back home, saying, "I thought that he would surely come out and stand and call on the name of his God, wave his hand over the spot and cure me of my leprosy. If all I have to do is take a bath, then the Abana and the Pharpar, rivers of Damascus, are certainly better than all the creeks in Israel! Couldn't I wash in them and be clean?" So he went away in a rage. He also was still a leper.

Then one of his servants approached him and pled with him gently: "Father, if the prophet had told you to do some great thing, would you not have done it? How much more, then, when he says, 'Wash and be cleansed'?"

Naaman listened to the words of his servant and went down to the Jordan to dip the required seven times. His flesh became as clear as that of a little child's.

Now Naaman's heart was filled with gratitude for his cleansing. He went back to Elisha's house with all his servants and stood before the prophet. Naaman said, "Now I know that there is no God in all the earth but in Israel. Please accept a gift from me."

Elisha replied, "As surely as Jehovah lives, I will take nothing." Even though Naaman insisted, Elisha refused to take anything.

Then Naaman said, "If you are not going to let me give you anything, then let me have as much soil as two mules can carry. I will build an altar with this earth, and I will never again make burnt offerings and sacrifices to any God but Jehovah. But I hope I may be forgiven for one thing: when my master enters the temple of his god Rimmon to bow down, and he is leaning on my arm, and I bow down there also, may Jehovah forgive me for this."

Elisha said, "Go in peace," or as we might express the thought, "All is well; it is as you will."

Elisha's servant Gehazi had observed all these happenings and had seen the obvious wealth of Naaman. After Naaman left, Gehazi said to himself, "My master has been too light on Naaman the Syrian and has not taken any of the things Naaman brought for him. As the Lord lives, I will go after him and accept some of those gifts."

Gehazi ran after Naaman. When the Syrian general saw someone running after him, he stopped his chariot and met Gehazi, saying, "Is everything all right?"

"Yes," Gehazi said, "but my master sent me to say: 'Just now two young men of the sons of the prophets came to me from the hill country of Ephraim. Give them, if you please, a talent (75 pounds) of silver and two outfits of clothes.'"

Naaman was happy to comply with the request, so he said, "By all means take two talents (150 pounds) of silver." Urging Gehazi to accept the silver, he put it into two bags, and got two changes of clothes ready for him to take. Naaman also sent two servants back with Gehazi to carry the heavy load.

When they got back close to the house of Elisha, Gehazi sent the servants back to Naaman while he hid the silver in the house. Then he went in and stood before Elisha as if nothing had happened.

Elisha said, "Where have you been, Gehazi?"

"I have not been anywhere," Gehazi said.

But Elisha said, "Was not my spirit with you when the man got down out of his chariot to meet you? Is this the time to be taking money, or accepting clothes, olive yards, vineyards, flocks, herds, or other gifts? Naaman's leprosy will be upon you and upon your descendants forever."

Gehazi went out from Elisha's presence a leper. His skin was as white as snow — and his would never be healed as Naaman's had been.

Elisha Makes an Ax-head to Float
(2 Kings 6:1-7)

The company of the prophets needed new quarters in which to live, because they had outgrown the place they had. They said to Elisha, "Look, the place where we meet with you is too small for us. Let's go to the Jordan, and each man get a pole, and let's build a new place to live."

Elisha said, "Go."

One of them asked, "Won't you please go with us?"

"I will," Elisha said, and he went with them.

After they arrived at the Jordan, they began cutting poles. As one of the men was chopping a tree, his ax-head slipped off the handle and fell into the river. The man was very upset. He cried out, "Oh, it was borrowed!"

Elisha asked, "Where did it fall?"

The man showed him and Elisha cut a stick, threw it in the place where the ax-head fell, and made the iron float to the top. "Lift it out," he said. So the man reached out and got the ax-head back.

Elisha Traps Some Blinded Syrians
(2 Kings 6:8-23)

The Syrians (or Arameans) were the most constant enemy of the kingdom of Israel at this point in history. The battles Ahab fought were only the early part of a long series of conflicts between the two little kingdoms. There were Syrian raids into Israel even when there were not open battles. Remember, the little girl who first told Naaman's wife of a prophet in Israel was a captive that had been taken during one of the raids. In the story about to be told, there were frequent raids.

This is another story that is impossible to date. Neither the king of Syria nor the king of Israel is named, and since the conflicts spanned several kings, there is no way to guess. Therefore, we will spend no time speculating.

The king of Syria was at war with the king of Israel. The Syrian king would consult with his officers and say, "We will set up camp in such and such a place," planning thus to catch the Israelite forces by surprise.

But Elisha, the man of God, would send word to the king of Israel, saying, "Be careful and do not go to such and such a place because the Syrians will be there." The king of Israel would send scouts to see if the warning was well-founded, and he learned that Elisha was always right, and he was saved from defeat time and again.

The Syrian king was extremely upset. He called his servants together and said, "Won't you please tell me who is on the side of the king of Israel?" He thought one of his servants must be passing along information about his plans to the king of Israel.

One of his servants, however, said, "That is not the problem, O my lord. But Elisha, the prophet in Israel, is telling the king of Israel what you are saying even in your bedroom."

The king of Syria said, "Find where he is, and tell me so that I can send and bring him here."

Word came soon: "He is in Dothan." Dothan was a city just south of the Jezreel valley in Israel. The Syrian king sent horses and chariots and a great army to surround the city by night.

When morning came, the young assistant of Elisha went out early and saw the army. He exclaimed, "Oh no! My master, what shall we do?"

Elisha said, "Don't be afraid. We have more on our side than they." Then Elisha prayed, saying, "Lord, please open his eyes so that he may see." God opened the young man's eyes, and what a spectacular sight! The mountains were full of horses and chariots of fire round about Elisha.

As the enemy approached them, Elisha prayed, "Please make these soldiers blind." And God smote the Syrian army with blindness.

Elisha told the Syrians, "This is not the way, nor the city you want. Follow me, and I will take you to the man you are after." So Elisha led them from Dothan to Samaria, the very capital of Israel.

When they reached Samaria, Elisha prayed again: "Oh Lord, open the eyes of these men that they may see." God opened their eyes and they saw they were in the very middle of Samaria, and completely at the mercy of the Israelites.

The king of Israel was excited. He asked Elisha, "My father, shall I smite them? Shall I smite them?" He was thrilled to have this many enemy soldiers at his mercy.

Elisha answered, "No, you will not smite them. Would you kill those whom you take captive with your sword and bow? Feed them bread and give them water to drink, and let them return to their master."

After the soldiers had eaten, they were sent back to Syria. For a time the Syrians gave up on their raids, and they stayed out of Israel. God was teaching the Syrians about His great power. Jehovah is God over all the earth.

God struck these soldiers blind, yet one man, Elisha, could lead the whole group from the city of Dothan to Samaria, a distance of a little more than ten miles. Perhaps, they were not totally blind in the sense of not being able to see anything before them, but rather blind in the sense that they were unable to recognize anything before them. Therefore, they could not recognize Elisha whom they had come to capture, nor could they recognize the landmarks of the area around them. The point was that God could protect His servant from harm. The soldiers must have gone home with a profound respect for this prophet.

The Siege of Samaria
(2 Kings 6:24-7:20)

Ben-hadad, the Syrian king, gathered a great army together again and went up to besiege Samaria. A siege meant that no one went in or out of the city. Famine was always a problem at such times, so there was a famine in Samaria. Food was so scarce that a donkey's head sold for eighty shekels (about 40 ounces) and a fourth of a cab (1/2 pint) of dove's dung sold for five shekels (about two ounces).

The expression "dove's dung" may be literal, because there have been cases where dung was collected for eating in times of severe famine. It may also be used figuratively of a very miserable kind of food which the Arabs call sparrow's dung. It is seed pods.

The king of Israel was passing by on the wall when a woman cried out, "Help me, O king."

61

He said, "If the Lord will not help you, what can I do? Can I give you anything from the threshing floor or the winepress? What is your problem?"

The woman answered, "This woman and I made a deal. She said, 'Let us eat your son today, and tomorrow we will eat my son.' So we cooked my son and ate him. The next day I said, 'Give up your son so we can eat him,' but she has hidden him and will not give him up."

Cannibalism was fairly common in long sieges. Moreover, this very kind of situation was prophesied by Moses as something that would happen if Israel became unfaithful (Deut. 28:52-57).

The king was terribly upset over this dreadful situation. He tore his robes, and the people saw that he wore sackcloth beneath his other garments. Of course, no wicked king of Israel ever thought of blaming Israel's calamities upon his own sin and unfaithfulness — he blamed it all upon God. He swore that the head of Elisha would not remain on his shoulders that day.

Apparently Elisha was living in Samaria during the siege because he was with the elders of the city. The king sent a messenger ahead of him, but before the messenger arrived, Elisha told the elders, "Do you see how this murderer is sending someone to cut off my head? When the messenger arrives, shut the door and hold it shut. His master will not be far behind."

The messenger came, followed soon by the king. The king said to Elisha, "This disaster is from the Lord. Why should I wait on Him any longer?" Obviously, Elisha had been telling the king and the elders to wait for God's deliverance. And, just as obviously, the king had no faith in God's word.

Elisha said, "Hear what Jehovah says, 'This time tomorrow, seven quarts of flour will sell for a shekel and three gallons of barley will sell for a shekel at the gate of Samaria.'"

The officer who assisted the king said, "Why, even if the Lord opened the windows of heaven, could such a thing happen?"

Elisha replied, "You will see it with your eyes, but you will not eat of the food."

Meanwhile, there were four Israelite men with leprosy who sat just outside the city gate. They were experiencing great difficulty finding anything to eat. They discussed the matter among themselves this way: "Why should we just sit here until we die? If we say let us go into the city, there is a famine there and we will die. And if we stay here, we will die. Let us, therefore, go and throw ourselves upon the mercy of the Syrians. If they spare us, we will live; if not, we would die anyway."

The lepers arose and went to the Syrian camp in the late evening. When they came to the outermost fringes of the camp, they were amazed to find no one there — no guards, no one! The lepers did not know what to think as they crept forward step by step.

The Bible interrupts their story to tell what had happened to the Syrians: Jehovah had caused the Syrians to hear the noise of chariots, and the sound of horses, as if a great army were coming upon them. When they heard the sound, the Syrians said, "The king of Israel has hired the kings of the Hittites and the kings of the Egyptians to come upon us!" In panic they jumped up and fled. They did not take time to saddle their horses or donkeys. They fled on foot and left everything behind just as it was.

The lepers cautiously went into a tent, ate and drank, and carried out the silver, gold, and raiment. Then they went into the next tent and took all the valuables from it and hid them. Abruptly they stopped and said to one another: "We are not doing right. This is a day of good news and we are not telling anyone. If we wait until morning to tell this, we might suffer punishment. Let's go and tell the king."

They went back to Samaria and told the gatekeepers, "We went into the Syrian camp and nobody was there. Their donkeys and horses were tied, and the camp is standing just as they left it."

The gatekeepers shouted the good news, and soon word came to the king in the palace. By now it was night, but the king of Israel arose. He said, "I'll tell you what this is. The king of Syria knows we are starving, so they have left their camp; but they are not gone, only hiding. They are saying, 'When they come out, we will take them alive and go into the city.'"

One of the king's officers said, "Let some men take five of the horses that are left in the city, and let them go and see what has happened."

It was a good plan, so the king sent out two chariots to see what the situation was. The men followed the trail of the Syrians from their camp all the way to the Jordan River. The whole road was strewn with clothing and equipment discarded by the Syrians as they fled. The scouts came back and reported their findings. With joy, the people rushed out and plundered the camp of the Syrians. Soon seven quarts of flour could be bought for a shekel and three gallons of barley for the same price, as God had predicted through Elisha.

The king had put a certain officer in charge of the gate, and the people were in such a rush to find food, they trampled the man to death. This officer was the one who had said, "Even if the Lord should open the windows of heaven, could this happen?" when Elisha prophesied that food would be abundant and cheap. Elisha had told him, "You will see it with your own eyes, but you will not eat it." That is exactly what happened!

The story told above of the siege of Samaria is one of the hints we have about the chronology of the period. The name of the Syrian king is given as Ben-hadad, but the name of the Israelite king is not given. The Syrian king who fought Ahab was named Ben-hadad, and this story is recorded before we are told of the death of that Ben-hadad, so it is likely the same one. If so, the king of Israel would have been Jehoram the son of Ahab. The story fits easily into the time frame of Jehoram's reign because Ben-hadad was killed and succeeded by Hazael toward the close of Jehoram's reign. Jehoram's last battle was against the Syrians led by Hazael (see 2 Kings 8:28).

There is one additional point, however, that makes it impossible to be dogmatic about the time even though the above explanation seems logical. The name "Ben-hadad" was more than a personal name among the Syrian kings. The prefix "Ben" meant "son of," and Hadad was the name of their god. Therefore, the kings called themselves "Son of Hadad." The Syrian king Asa hired to attack Baasha called himself Ben-hadad (see 1 Kings 15:18). The Syrian king who fought Ahab was Ben-hadad (see 1 Kings 20:1). That particular Ben-hadad was killed by a man named Hazael who ruled for a time (see 2 Kings 8:14-15), and then was succeeded by his son who was also called Ben-hadad (see 2 Kings 13:3). Since Syria was such a bitter enemy of Israel at this point, each of these kings fought Israel more than once. The kings of Israel were all wicked, so there were numerous times when God allowed them to be brought low. Elisha's work overlapped with the Ben-hadad of Ahab's day, through Hazael's reign, and into his son Ben-hadad's reign. It could, therefore, have been either of these Ben-hadads.

Remember, the chronology is not as important at this time as the effort God was making to try to awaken His people to their need to rely upon Him. We give these notes to help you understand the period. Do not become alarmed if you see different reference books arranging the stories in different orders. No one knows for sure how they fit with the kings at this time.

Land is restored to the Shunammite Woman
(2 Kings 8:1-6)

At some point, Elisha warned the Shunammite woman, in whose house he had stayed, that a famine was coming in Israel. He told her, "Go away with your household and stay somewhere else, because Jehovah has appointed a famine in the land which will last seven years."

Remember, this is the woman whose son was raised from the dead. It seems she was a widow by the time this story occurred, but her husband was described as old when we first met her (see 2 Kings 4:14).

She followed Elisha's advice and went to the southern coastal plain and stayed in the territory of the Philistines seven years. At the end of that time, she returned to Israel and went to the king to ask him to restore the property that had been hers.

Just as she was reaching the palace to speak to the king, Gehazi the servant of Elisha was inside talking to the king. The king had said, "Tell me about all the great things Elisha has done."

Gehazi had reached the point of telling how Elisha had raised the dead to life again, when word came to the king that the Shunammite woman wanted to see him. Gehazi said, "This is the woman, my lord the king, and this is her son whom Elisha restored to life."

The king asked the woman about it, and she told the story. Then the king assigned an official to take care of her needs. He said, "Give back everything that belonged to her, including all the income from her land from the day she left the country until now."

God's providence was at work again. She "happened" to approach the king at the same time Gehazi was telling her story — and therefore, the king was eager to help her.

Do you remember the last time we met Gehazi in the story? Do you remember he was stricken with leprosy, white as snow? Lepers were banned from society, so it is unusual to find a leper talking to a king. That is why some scholars place this story before the story of Naaman told in chapter 5. That placement may be true, or it may be that Gehazi was telling his own tragic story as part of the story of Elisha.

Back to our Two-Column Style

There are a few more stories about Elisha, but the rest of them can be placed into the history of the kings of Israel and Judah. By these miracles, God continued to substantiate the reputation of Elisha as His servant and spokesman.

JUDAH

Ahaziah (Jehoahaz, Azariah) — 1 year (evil) (2 Kings 8:25-9:28; 2 Chron. 22:1-9):

After the very wicked Jehoram, the son of Jehoshaphat, died, he was succeeded by his son Ahaziah. This Ahaziah did not rule as long as some of the other wicked kings, so he did not have time to do as much harm in the land, but he was a very wicked man.

Ahaziah was the youngest son of Jehoram

ISRAEL

12th year of Jehoram, the son of Ahab and Jezebel

This Jehoram worshiped the golden calves that Jeroboam had made, and he was a wicked king, but he was not as bad as his father and mother. He reigned only twelve years. This Jehoram was already reigning when we started the stories about Elisha. Some of the and Athaliah. He was the one available to rule because the Philistines and Arabians had slain all the older sons. He was only twenty-two years old when he came to the throne, and he reigned only one year.

Remember, his mother was Athaliah who was a daughter of Ahab and Jezebel. That means the Jehoram who was reigning in Israel was Ahaziah's uncle. Look back to the family tree of Ahab's family and Jehoshaphat's family. Ahaziah walked in the ways of the house of Ahab, with his mother encouraging him in every wrong doing.

Chronological Note:
2 Kings 8:26 says that Ahaziah was 22 years old when he began to reign; 2 Chronicles 22:2 says that he was 42 years old. But since his father Jehoram was only forty when he died (2 Chron. 21:20), then certainly 22 is the correct reading.

stories about Elisha took place within the twelve years of Jehoram's reign, but not all of them.

Elisha Meets with Hazael (2 Kings 8:7-15):

At Mt. Horeb (Sinai), God had told Elijah that among the changes in personnel that would be made in the area, Hazael would replace Ben-hadad as the king of Syria (1 Kings 19:15). The time has come.

Elisha went to visit Damascus, the capital of Syria. Ben-hadad the king was ill. He was told, "The man of God has come here." So Ben-hadad sent Hazael, saying, "Take a gift with you, and go meet with the man of God, and inquire of Jehovah whether I will get well from my illness."

Hazael went to Elisha, carrying with him forty camel-loads of the finest things of Damascus. He came in and stood before Elisha and said, "Your son Ben-hadad, king of Syria, has sent me to ask you if he will get well from his illness."

Elisha replied, "Go and tell him, 'You will surely recover.'" But then Elisha confided to Hazael, "Nevertheless the Lord has shown me he will surely die."

There was silence then as Hazael perhaps pondered the meaning of this strange revelation. Elisha began gazing very intently at Hazael, until Hazael felt embarrassed. Then the man of God began to weep! Hazael was puzzled, and said, "Why are you crying?"

Elisha answered, "Because I know all the harm you will do to the children of Israel, burning their forts, killing their young men with the sword, bashing their little ones to pieces, and ripping open their pregnant women."

Hazael took a different view of his ability to do such things to the Israelites. He said, "How could I, but a dog, do such great things?"

Elisha replied, "The Lord has shown me that you will be king over Syria."

Hazael returned to his master, who said, "What did Elisha tell you?"

Hazael answered, "He told me that you will surely recover."

But the next day Hazael took a thick cloth, dipped it in water, and smothered Ben-hadad to death.

Thus the strange words of Elisha were made clear. If nature followed its course, Ben-hadad would get well. But his illness was not the only factor. Hazael's own ambition led him to destroy his master and reign in his stead.

Ahaziah and Jehoram Fight for Ramoth-Gilead
(2 Kings 8:28-29; 9:14b, 15a; 2 Chron. 22:5-6)

Ahaziah, the king of Judah, joined forces with his uncle Jehoram, king of Israel, to fight against Hazael, king of Syria, for the city of Ramoth-gilead. This is the same city that Ahab and Jehoshaphat fought the Syrians for when Ahab died. Ahab did not succeed in taking the city at that time, and it was still in the hands of the Syrians more than twelve years after Ahab died.

In the course of the battle, Jehoram was wounded, and he went home to Jezreel to recover. After a time, Ahaziah (here called Azariah in 2 Chronicles) left the armies still besieging Ramoth-gilead while he himself went to Jezreel to visit Jehoram. Be sure you know where both cities are on your map.

Therefore, as we begin the next portion of the story, both kings are in Jezreel and the army is in Ramoth-gilead. Jehoram is wounded, but well on the way to recovery.

Ahaziah, the grandson of righteous Jehoshaphat and of wicked Ahab, is continuing to reign in Judah.

Jehu Anointed to be King (2 Kings 9:1-13):

In this story Elisha carries out the last change that God had designated to be done when He spoke to Elijah at Mount Horeb (1 Kings 19:16).

Elisha called one of the sons of the prophets to him and said, "Take this bottle of oil and go to Ramoth-gilead. Find Jehu the son of Jehoshaphat, the son of Nimshi. Pour the bottle of oil on his head and say, 'This is what the Lord says: I am anointing you to be king over

Israel.' Then leave at once."

The young man went to Ramoth-gilead and found the captains of the army, and he said, "I have a message for you, O captain."

It was Jehu who said, "For which one of us?"

"To you, O captain," the young man replied.

Jehu and the young man went into the house and the prophet poured the oil upon Jehu's head. He said, "This is what the Lord says, 'I have anointed you king over the people of the Lord, even over Israel. You are to destroy the house of Ahab your master in order that I may avenge the blood of my servants the prophets at the hand of Jezebel. I will make Ahab's house like that of Jeroboam the son of Nebat, and like the house of Baasha. Dogs will eat Jezebel in Jezreel and there will be none to bury her.'" Then the messenger opened the door and fled.

Jehu came out of the house, just a little stunned perhaps, and one of his fellow officers said, "Is everything all right? What did that crazy fellow want?"

Jehu replied, "You know the man, and what he wanted."

They said, "That is not true. Tell us what he said."

Jehu answered, "He told me the Lord has anointed me king over Israel."

This announcement was received with instant enthusiasm by Jehu's fellow officers. Each man took his cloak and spread it before Jehu on the steps and blew the trumpet, saying, "Jehu is king."

Jehu Proceeds to Jezreel and Kills Jehoram (2 Kings 9:14-26):

Jehu told his fellow captains, "If you are with me in this thing, then see to it that no one escapes from here to go warn Jehoram in Jezreel." Then Jehu rode his chariot toward Jezreel to find Jehoram.

Meanwhile, in Jezreel, a watchman was on the tower of the wall. He saw Jehu's troops approaching, and he called out, "I see a band of men coming this way."

Jehoram said, "Send a horseman out to meet them and see if anything is wrong."

The horseman rode out and said to Jehu, "The king says, 'Do you come in peace?'"

Jehu answered, "What do you have to do with peace? Fall in behind me."

The watchman reported that the messenger had come to the troop, but that he was not returning. So Jehoram sent another messenger. He did not come back either.

Again the watchman reported, "He has met them, but he is not coming back." Then he added, "The driving is like that of Jehu the son of Nimshi, because he drives like a madman."

Commanding that chariots be brought, Jehoram and Ahaziah drove out to meet Jehu, each in his own chariot. They met in the field that had belonged to Naboth. Jehoram said, "Is it peace, Jehu?"

Jehu answered, "How can there be peace as long as the idolatry and witchcraft of your mother Jezebel is in the land?"

Jehoram turned to flee, and he cried out to Ahaziah, "There is treachery!" But Jehu drew his bow all the way back and shot Jehoram through the heart, and he fell down in his chariot.

Jehu told Bidkar his captain, "Pick him up and throw him into the field of Naboth, because you remember when you and I rode with Ahab and heard the prophecy God made about him saying, 'Surely I have seen the blood of Naboth and of his sons, and I will require your blood in this place.' So cast him into the field as Jehovah said."

Jehu Kills Ahaziah king of Judah
(2 Kings 9:27-28; 2 Chron. 22:7-9):

God had ordained that Ahaziah be destroyed also in this purge of the house of Ahab. When Ahaziah saw that Jehoram was slain he fled for his life. Jehu told his men, "Kill him too!" so they set out in pursuit.

The accounts in both Kings and Chronicles are very brief. There is not enough data given to determine exactly where Jehu's men caught up with Ahaziah, or exactly how he was killed. He was fleeing toward Samaria to try to find a hiding place. Possibly the men caught him

Jezebel is Slain (2 Kings 9:30-37):

When Jezebel heard that Jehu had come to Jezreel, she painted her eyes and arranged her hair and kept watch for him from her on the way and killed him, or he made it to Samaria, was captured, and brought back to the ascent of Gur near Ibleam to be killed.

Ahaziah's body was taken back to Jerusalem and was buried in the City of David with his fathers, because he was the grandson of Jehoshaphat who had followed the Lord with all his heart.

window. As Jehu came in at the gate, she said, "Have you come in peace, you Zimri, murderer of your master?"

Jehu looked up and said, "Who is on my side? Who?"

Two or three eunuchs looked out the window, and Jehu called to them, "Throw her down."

The eunuchs seized Jezebel and threw her out the window. She struck the ground, and some of her blood splattered upon the wall and on the horses. Jehu and his men calmly drove forward and trampled her body under their horses and chariots.

Jehu went inside and ate and drank. After a time he said, "See about that cursed woman, because she was a king's daughter." But when they went out to bury her, they found the dogs had been busy before them. The dogs had devoured her body, leaving only her hands, feet, and skull.

The servants went back and told Jehu the gruesome news. He said, "The word of the Lord has come true. He told Elijah the Tishbite, 'In the portion of Jezreel, the dogs will eat the flesh of Jezebel, and the carcass of Jezebel will be as dung upon the face of the ground so that no one will be able to say: Here lies Jezebel.'"

Jehu Destroys the Sons of Ahab
(2 Kings 10:1-10):

So far Jehu had not moved at all to secure the capital of the kingdom. At this point he could have been considered a rebel. So he prepared to deal with Samaria. Remember that Israel's army was at Ramoth-gilead and that all the captains there were on Jehu's side. Jehu himself is still in the city of Jezreel, where he has killed Jehoram and Jezebel.

Jehu was shrewd. He wrote letters to the rulers of Samaria, to the elders, and to those who oversaw the rearing of seventy sons of Ahab. He told them, "You have the sons of

Ahab with you; you have chariots and horses, a fortified city and weapons. Therefore, as soon as you get this letter, choose the best of your master's sons, and set him upon his father's throne, and fight for your master's house."

The elders and those in charge of Ahab's descendants were terrified. They said, "If two kings could not stand before him, how could we stand?" So they wrote back to Jehu, saying, "We are your servants. We will do as you say. We will not make any man king."

Jehu replied, "If you are really on my side, then bring the heads of your master's sons to Jezreel by this time tomorrow."

The leaders of Samaria did as Jehu commanded: they beheaded the seventy sons of Ahab and brought the heads to Jezreel. Jehu said, "Pile them in two heaps at the entrance of the city gate until the morning."

The next morning Jehu went out to the gate. Jehu called out to the people gathered there, "You people are righteous. I, on the other hand, have killed my master! But I ask you: Who killed these?" This was Jehu's way of involving the people in his rebellion.

Jehu continued, "Be assured that not one word will fail of all that God said would happen to the house of Ahab. The Lord has done exactly what He said He would do!"

Jehu Kills the Leaders of Jezreel
(2 Kings 9:11);

Jehu went throughout the city of Jezreel and killed all the remaining relatives of Ahab. To make the purge complete in Jezreel, he also killed all of Ahab's chief men, his close friends, and his priests. There were no survivors of Ahab left in the city — whether friend or relative.

Then Jehu headed toward the city of Samaria to finish the purge there.

Jehu Kills the Princes of Judah
(2 Kings 10:12-14; 2 Chron. 22:8):

As Jehu was on his way to Samaria, he met forty-two men at a meeting house of the shepherds. He said, "Who are you?"

They replied, "We are relatives of Ahaziah, and we have come down to greet the families of the king and queen."

Jehu said, "Take them alive." He commanded that they be taken to the cistern of the meeting house, and slain.

Jehu Meets Jehonadab (2 Kings 10:15-16):

After Jehu left the shepherd's gathering place where he had killed Ahaziah's relatives, he continued on his way to Samaria. He met a man named Jehonadab, the son of Rechab. Jehu greeted him, saying, "Are you in accord with me, as I am with you?"

"I am," Jehonadab answered.

"If so, give me your hand," Jehu said. He helped Jehonadab into the chariot with him, and said, "Come with me and see my zeal for Jehovah."

This Jehonadab was an interesting man. This is all we are told about him at this point, but he established a tradition in his family. His descendants would drink no wine, nor build houses, nor sow seed, nor plant vineyards, but would live in tents and be nomads. Jehonadab lived about 842 B.C. Two hundred and fifty years later, just before the destruction of Jerusalem, his descendants were still faithfully keeping that tradition (see Jer. 35:1-19).

****

****

Athaliah — 6 years (evil)
(2 Kings 11:1, 3; 2 Chron. 22:9-12):

When Athaliah learned that her son Ahaziah was dead, she moved swiftly to place herself in power. She killed all of her son's children, her own grandchildren, and proclaimed herself ruler of Judah.

Joash, the Son of Ahaziah, Spared
(2 Kings 11:2-3; 2 Chron. 22:11-12):

When Athaliah tried to kill all the seed royal, she missed one. Ahaziah's sister was Jehosheba. She was the wife of Jehoiada the high priest. Jehosheba stole the infant Joash and his nurse away from the other sons of the

Jehu — 28 years (evil)
(2 Kings 9:1-10:36; 12:1; 2 Chron. 22:7-9):

When Jehu reached Samaria, he finished destroying the house of Ahab and became the official king as God had anointed him to be.

Jehu Destroys the Baal Worshipers
(2 Kings 10:18-28):

Jehu gathered the people together and said, "Ahab served Baal a little, but Jehu will serve Baal much! Now gather all the prophets, priests, and ministers of Baal together because I am going to hold a great sacrifice for Baal. Anyone who fails to come will die!" But Jehu was speaking deceitfully because he was planning to kill the ministers of Baal.

king. Joash was hidden in the temple of God for six years.

Once again, God's promise to David, that his seed would rule upon his throne forever, hung by one tiny thread, the life of a helpless baby. This was the third generation with only one rightful heir to the throne: Jehoram was the only one because he killed all his brothers. Ahaziah was the only one because an enemy had killed all the other sons. And now, Athaliah has killed all the children of the king that she could find. Yet one is left. Do you see God's providence? His promise would be kept.

Word was sent throughout the whole kingdom of Israel for all Baal worshipers to assemble. People came from all over the land and filled the temple of Baal from one end to the other. Jehu told the keepers of the wardrobe, "Bring out robes for all the worshipers of Baal."

Jehu and Jehonadab went into the temple of Baal, and Jehu gave the order: "Look around you, and be sure there are no servants of Jehovah in here. This is for servants of Baal only."

Jehu had posted eighty soldiers outside, and had warned them, "If any of you lets any of the men I am placing in your hands escape, it will be your lives for their lives."

As soon as Jehu had finished offering the sacrifice, he commanded his men, "Go in and kill them; let no one escape."

The soldiers rushed in and killed the Baal worshipers from one end of the temple to the other. Then they went in to the inner shrine of Baal and brought out the pillars of Baal. Most of the pillars were of wood, and they were burned. One was of stone, so it was crushed. They also broke down the house of Baal and made it into a public latrine, or restroom.

So Jehu destroyed Baal worship in Israel. The wicked family of Ahab was destroyed and the immoral worship of Baal was defeated. What a great day in Israel!

Jehovah's Promise to Jehu (2 Kings 10:30):

Jehovah said to Jehu: "Because you have done well in doing what is right in my sight, and you have done to the house of Ahab all that I had in mind, your descendants will rule after you for four generations upon the throne of Israel."

This is one more prophecy we will watch to see fulfilled.

Victory is Short-Lived (2 Kings 10:29-33):

Though Jehu had destroyed Ahab's family, and had devastated Baal worship, and had told Jehonadab to watch his zeal for the Lord, he did not bother to worship Jehovah correctly. He went back to the worship of the golden calves which Jeroboam had set up at Dan and Bethel. He paid no attention to God's law. How sad! He had the opportunity to turn his entire kingdom back to Jehovah, and he failed. That means the mighty effort God had put forth, and was continuing to put forth through the work of Elisha, was not having the effect God wanted.

Therefore, judgment was inevitable!

Only a few years after Jehu killed Ahab's family, God spoke through the prophet Hosea and said, "Yet a little while, and I will avenge the blood of Jezreel upon the house of Jehu" (Hos. 1:4). Why would God avenge the blood of Ahab's house upon Jehu, when Jehu did what God wanted when he slew Ahab's family? The answer is that Jehu's subsequent behavior demonstrated that he did not carry out God's command to kill Ahab's family out of a love for God, but rather God's instructions exactly coincided with Jehu's own ambitious desires. Jehu obeyed God only until his own personal goals were met, and then ignored God the rest of his life.

The Assyrian Empire

The Bible story was easy so long as it was about one family, growing into a nation, and then of that one nation as it served God or failed to do so. Then the kingdom divided, and the story became more complicated. But now it becomes even more involved, because other nations are touching Israel and Judah so often.

Before we go further in our history of the kingdoms of Israel and Judah, we need to look at an empire that has arisen northeast of Israel. All of the kingdoms we have met so far in our study were small. Israel, Judah, Syria, Moab, Edom, Ammon, Philistia, and Phoenicia were all tiny kingdoms located within about 12,000 to 15,000 square miles (much less than the size of the state of Alabama). Egypt was the strongest people we have encountered. At various periods of history, Egypt controlled land far beyond its natural borders. At this time, though Egypt was still relatively strong, it did not reach very far beyond the Nile River Valley.

Judah	**Israel**

Many nations rose and fell during the Biblical era that do not play any part in the Bible story. The Bible mentions only those nations which directly touched God's chosen people in some way. The early history of Assyria is an example of one of the nations that had been growing for many years, but they are just now touching the Israelites in our history. Their capital was at Nineveh on the Tigris River, many miles away from Israel. The Assyrians were the first people to build an army capable of conquering an extensive empire. Assyria was already in existence as a nation by the time the Israelites conquered the land of Canaan. They grew rather strong then, but did not touch the Israelites. Their power waned for a number of years, and then began to rise again about the time Solomon's kingdom divided into Israel and Judah. Their power continued to rise and wane, depending upon the forcefulness of each king.

The Assyrian kings kept very detailed records of their exploits, and vast libraries of their records have been found in their ruins. From their records, the name Assyria has come to be almost synonymous with cruelty and ruthlessness. Their kings would record: "I conquered the cities…I caused much slaughter, I destroyed, I devastated, I burned. I took their fighting men prisoners and impaled them on sharpened stakes in full view of their cities" (Story of the Bible World, by Nelson Beecher Keyes, p. 76).

In 859 B.C. a powerful ruler came to the throne in Assyria. Shalmaneser III ruled from 859 B.C. until 824 B.C. In 853 B.C., a few years before Ahab died in Israel, Shalmaneser III attempted to invade the area of Canaan. For the battle, Ahab king of Israel and Ben-hadad king of Syria laid aside their differences and joined a coalition led by Irhuleni king of Hamath against the Assyrians. Although Shalmaneser defeated the coalition, it was not a decisive enough victory for him to move ahead with his conquests. There were several more attempts by Shalmaneser III to invade, which were resisted with some degree of success by Ben-hadad and Irhuleni. The Bible does not tell of this first contact with the Assyrians. (See the inscription of Shalmaneser III on the Kurkh Stele, now in the British Museum. Documents From Old Testament Times, Edited by D. Winton Thomas, pp. 47-48.)

Take a map of the Bible lands. Label Nineveh on the Tigris River. Also label the little kingdoms of Hamath, Syria, Israel, and Judah. Note how far they were from Nineveh, but also note that these little kingdoms were directly in Assyria's path to Egypt, which was Assyria's primary goal in that direction. Assyria will be a major enemy to Israel and Judah very soon in our story.

JUDAH	**ISRAEL**

Athaliah, the usurper, continues to reign in Judah.

Historical Note — The Assyrians Force Jehu to Pay Tribute:

Hazael came to power in Syria just a short time before Jehu came to power in Israel (about 842 B.C.). At the same time, Shalmaneser III was continuing his efforts to conquer the countries all along the Mediterranean Coast.

Shalmaneser attacked Damascus in 841 B.C. Hazael stood alone against him. Irhuleni of Hamath was dead; Jehu would not help. The Assyrian forces defeated the Syrian army and reached the walls of Damascus, but could not take the heavily fortified city.

At some place (the location of which is uncertain), Jehu went and submitted himself to the Assyrian king. Shalmaneser erected a monument which has been called the Black Obelisk. On this stone pillar there are a number of relief panels showing various kings coming to submit to Shalmaneser. One of them is Jehu. With the picture is an inscription which reads: "The tribute of Jehu, son of Omri."

The Bible does not mention this encounter with the Assyrians.

It is ironic that Jehu was called the son of the man whose dynasty he had destroyed in order to be king. The fact that Jehu was referred to as the son of Omri is evidence of the power and reputation which Omri established in his comparatively short reign.

Hazael Begins to "Cut Israel Short" (2 Kings 10:32-33):

The threat of Assyrian invasion was removed after Shalmaneser's last effort to subdue Syria in 837 B.C. Neither Shalmaneser nor his son was able to threaten Syria again for about 25 years. This left Hazael free to turn his attention to Israel.

After saying Jehu was not faithful to God, the very next verse says, "In those days the Lord began to cut Israel short." King Hazael came against Israel in raid after raid and succeeded in taking all the land east of the Jordan River.

Take a new map of the land of Israel. Label all the territory on the east, north of the Arnon River, as belonging to Syria. Compare it to the map you already have of Israel's territory in the days of Jeroboam. Moab has been out of Israel's control since the death of Ahab (label Moab). Now, for the first time since they conquered the land in Moses and Joshua's day, Israel controls no territory on the east side of the river. We will watch how Israel's territory continues to shrink

Jehu and Israel are reaping the consequences of their continuation of the idolatry introduced by Jeroboam the son of Nebat.

****

7th year of Jehu

Joash (Jehoash) — 40 years (evil)
(2 Kings 11:1-12:21; 2 Chron. 22:10-24:27)

Jehoiada Elevates Joash to the Throne in Judah (2 Kings 11:4-12; 2 Chron. 23:1-11):

Jehoiada the high priest carefully laid his plans to restore the house of David to the throne. From the story, we do not see any popular support for Athaliah. The people of the land must have been grieving, thinking the royal line of David had been broken.

First, Jehoiada called to him the captains of hundreds of the royal bodyguard. The Carites and the guard likely corresponded to the groups called the Cherethites and Pelethites in David's day. Jehoiada did not take the corps of the bodyguard into his confidence, only the captains. Five of them are named in 2 Chronicles 23:1.

Jehoiada swore the men to secrecy and then showed them the young king who was now seven years old. The captains went out through Judah gathering Levites, plus the heads of the major families, out of all the kingdom, and brought them to Jerusalem. Jehoiada made an agreement with them all. He said, "Behold, the king's son will reign as the Lord said concerning the sons of David."

Then he told them his plan. Usually the shift of guards changed on the Sabbath. One shift left; another shift went on duty. Jehoiada divided the incoming priests and Levites into three groups, because this time there would be many more than usual. The outgoing shift he divided into two groups, and, instead of going home, they remained at the temple.

Jehoiada stationed one group to keep watch on the king's house. In other words, they were stationed at the temple to watch for any force that might come from Athaliah. Another group guarded the doors of the temple. Another guarded one of the main gates to the outside.

When the men came, they did not bring their weapons lest they arouse suspicion. Jehoiada gave them shields, bucklers, and swords from the temple armory. The five captains were likely in charge of the corresponding five groups of priests and Levites.

Jehoiada's plans were carried out to perfection and with complete secrecy. The Levites surrounded the child-king when he was brought forth. They put the crown upon Joash's head, gave him a copy of the law of God which he was to keep as king (see Deut. 17:18-20), and Jehoiada and his sons anointed him. Then the people applauded and shouted, "God save the king."

Athaliah is Executed (2 Kings 11:13-16, 20; 2 Chron. 23:12-15, 21):

Athaliah heard the noise of the people shouting and came to the temple to see what was happening. She saw the young king standing by a pillar of the temple. She saw the captains, the Levites, and the people who were gathering. Trumpets were sounding, the Levites were singing, and the people of the land were rejoicing. She tore her clothes and cried, "Treason! Treason!"

Jehoiada calmly ordered the captains to take her, and if anyone seemed inclined to go to her rescue, take him too. He said, "Bring her forth between the ranks, and anyone who follows her, kill him with the sword." He had also ordered, "Let her not be slain in the Lord's house," so they seized her at the gate where horses entered the palace grounds and executed her there.

"...And all the people of the land rejoiced. And the city was quiet, because Athaliah had been slain with the sword at the palace."

Jehoiada Renews the Covenant (2 Kings 11:17-20a; 2 Chron. 23:16-21):

Joash was only seven years old when he became king, so Jehoiada was the true leader of the people during the early years of his reign. It was Jehoiada, therefore, on this day of celebration when the new king was anointed, who called upon the assembled people to renew their covenant with God. This was the same covenant that God had first made with the people at Mt. Sinai soon after they came out of Egyptian bondage. As God stated it then, "If you will obey me fully, and keep my covenant, then I will be your God and ye shall be my chosen people out of all the earth" (Exod. 19:3-6). Now, after years of unfaithfulness, Jehoiada led the people in renewing their promise to obey God and to conduct themselves as God's chosen people. Only then would they have the right to expect God's blessings.

On this occasion, the people joined into the covenant readily. Then, having made that agreement, they went to the temple that had been built to Baal in Jerusalem and destroyed it. They crushed the altars and idols, and killed Mattan the priest of Baal.

Then Jehoiada, the guards, the Levites, and the people escorted Joash to the palace where he took his place upon the throne. Thus the rightful king, David's descendant, once more ruled in Judah. As long as Jehoiada lived, Joash was faithful to God and the majority of the people were faithful also.

The contrast between the two kingdoms continues. When Jehu killed the Baal worshipers in Israel, he did not lead the people in renewing their covenant to serve Jehovah. He turned instead to the false worship of the golden calves. He and his people gave up the chance they had to renew their right to God's blessings. In contrast, when Jehoiada led the people of Judah in destroying the worship of Baal, he also led them in renewing their service to Jehovah, thus renewing their right to His blessings.

One additional thing to note: Every individual in the kingdoms did not follow the example of the king — whether for good or evil. For example, Jehu was very wicked, but righteous Elisha and his followers were alive at the same time. In the same way, Jehoiada was righteous and was trying to lead the people to be righteous, but there were individuals across the land who were quietly worshiping Baal on the hillsides. That is why the welfare of the kingdoms could change so quickly. Both elements — righteousness and wickedness — existed all the time. It depended upon the leaders of the people as to which side was in prominence at any particular moment.

Joel the Prophet
(The Book of Joel)

Joel is another prophet whose work is somewhat difficult to date. He most likely prophesied in the early years of Joash, perhaps around 830 B.C. He did his work in the kingdom of Judah.

Judah had been badly corrupted by the wickedness brought in by Athaliah the daughter of Ahab and Jezebel. She had worked hard to destroy belief in Jehovah and to build up Baal worship. During the twelve years of Jehoram's reign, the one year of Ahaziah's reign, and the six years of Athaliah's own reign, Judah had fallen badly.

Even though Jehoiada had renewed the covenant between Judah and God, the people still sacrificed and burnt incense on the high places. Joel's prophecy was not in conflict with Jehoiada's work, but rather in support of his efforts to win the people back to God.

The message of Joel is built around a severe locust invasion that had come to the land of Judah. Joel's message was: If you do not take warning from this locust invasion and truly repent, then there will be a much worse invasion, one of armies which will ravage the land. His entire book is written in beautiful Hebrew poetry. Let us look briefly at his message:

The Devastation of the Locusts (Joel 1:2-12):

This locust swarm was surely one of the worst the land had ever suffered. Joel challenged them to inquire whether there had ever been a locust swarm this bad. The various stages of the locust had eaten everything green and had even eaten the bark from the trees, leaving their branches white. All of society had suffered — drunkards, priests, farmers, and vine growers.

Call to Repentance (Joel 1:13-20):

Joel calls upon the priests to repent. He tells them to call a sacred assembly to fast and mourn. He warns that the day of the Lord is nigh. Call on the elders and all the people to cry unto the Lord. Do you not see the devastation all around us? Our food has been cut off; our storehouses are in ruins; our cattle and sheep are suffering; even the wild animals pant for help because the waters are dried up. It is time to call upon the Lord.

The Day of the Lord (Joel 2:1-11):

"The day of Jehovah" is an expression often used in the Bible for any day of judgment or day of wrath from God against a people. In this case, Joel uses vivid imagery of a battle: the chariots, the horses, and the ranks of the army are pressing forward. The destruction and burning is everywhere, and there is no stopping the force. The description cleverly mixes the figure of the locust swarm with the prophecy of a far worse invasion of an army. As in so many of the descriptions of judgment, there is mention made of the sun and moon being darkened and of earthquakes. These were expressions describing total upheaval in the kingdom being judged.

Judah	**Israel**

A Second Call to Repentance (Joel 2:12-17):

The remedy is true, heartfelt repentance. "Rend your hearts and not your garments" (2:13). Return to the Lord and perhaps He will leave a blessing instead of a curse. Call for a solemn assembly to weep and pray before the Lord. No one is exempt — bring the nursing infant and the bridegroom from his chamber. Pray for God's mercy.

Promise of Blessings (Joel 2:18-27):

If Israel will repent, Jehovah will restore prosperity and will more than make up for that which was lost through chastisement. He will drive the army far away. The land will be green again. The trees, the pastures, the fig trees, and vines will be rich again because there is abundant rain in the land. Rejoice, O people, in the Lord your God. You are repaid for all the locust destroyed. God has shown His mercy. "Then you will know that I am in Israel, that I am the Lord your God, and that there is no other..." (2:27).

Outpouring of God's Spirit (Joel 2:28-32):

After these days Jehovah will pour His Holy Spirit upon all people, young and old, male and female. Then, once again, signs of judgment will appear before the great and terrible day of the Lord.

This is the passage quoted by Peter on the day of Pentecost to explain what was happening on that day when the Spirit of God came upon the apostles (Acts 2:16-21). The prophecy was fulfilled in its entirety in that first century A.D. when God poured out His Spirit upon the apostles and prophets through whom God was revealing His new law for all generations to follow.

Victory Promised to God's People (Joel 3:1-21):

God promises, through Joel, that all enemies of His people will be defeated. The nations are challenged to gather their armies and bring them to the valley of Jehoshaphat (Judgment of Jehovah) where God will judge them. He says that He will make Zion a stronghold for His people, one which foreigners will never again invade. Jehovah promises wonderful blessings upon Judah. These blessings will flow freely, but the countries of those who stand against God's people will be desolate.

These promises of great blessing for God's people could never be brought to fruition in the physical kingdoms of Israel and Judah because the people never turned to God with their full hearts. Their history gives only a glimpse of what God would have been willing to do for them if they had been faithful. Since they were not, God fulfilled His promises for blessings in the spiritual blessings offered in the New Testament. Now all who want to be can be a part of God's chosen people, as individuals all over the world voluntarily submit themselves to the rule of God. As God's chosen people, His kingdom, we will never be invaded or harmed. God will judge all others who reject His will.

JUDAH	**ISRAEL**

Joash Takes Two Wives (2 Chron. 24:3):

Still under the leadership of Jehoiada, Joash took two wives chosen for him by the high priest. He begat sons and daughters.

Jehu is continuing to reign in Israel.

Judah

Joash Commands that the Temple be Repaired (2 Kings 12:4-5; 2 Chron. 24:4-5, 7):

Joash decided to have the temple of Jehovah repaired. Athaliah had not destroyed the temple, but she and her cohorts had severely abused it. They had broken into the temple and had taken sacred objects to use for their Baal worship.

Joash gave orders to the priests to collect all money brought for offerings at the temple. This would include the half shekel each Israelite male paid each year, money brought in connection with personal vows, and money given as a free will offering.

The king also told the priests and Levites: "Go to the towns of Judah and collect the money due annually from the people to repair the temple of your God. Do it now."

But the Levites delayed and did not gather the money.

23rd year of Joash (2 Kings 13:1)

Repairing of the Temple (2 Kings 12:6-16; 2 Chron. 24:6-14):

About the time Jehoahaz came to the throne in Israel, Joash (or Jehoash) moved forward with his plans to repair the temple.

Joash saw that the priests had made no move to repair the temple so he called Jehoiada and the other priests to him and said, "Why have the breaches in the temple not been repaired? Do not take any more money from your acquaintances." The priests agreed not to take any more money, nor to be in charge of the repair work.

Some have charged that the priests had been guilty of embezzling funds, but the charge is uncharitable and fails to take into account the realities of the situation. According to the law of Moses, at least a portion of the money collected

Israel

Death of Jehu (2 Kings 10:34-36):

Jehu's zeal for ruling was not nearly as strong as his zeal for destroying Ahab's house. Therefore, his reign of 28 years was not illustrious. He died and was buried in Samaria. His son Jehoahaz received a much weakened kingdom.

Jehoahaz — 17 years (evil) (2 Kings 13:1-8):

Jehoahaz is the first of four generations of Jehu's descendants that will sit upon his throne.

Character of Jehoahaz (2 Kings 13:2-3):

Jehoahaz was wicked and continued in the sin of Jeroboam the son of Nebat. Therefore the Lord gave Israel into the hands of Hazael and of his son Ben-hadad continually.

by the priests was for their own maintenance and to provide for the expense of worship. It is very hard to take money which is already being spent for regular purposes and decide to do something special with it in addition to what is already being done.

Joash commanded that a chest be made with a hole bored in the lid and that it be set near the entrance to the temple. The money which the people gave was deposited in the chest. The people gave their money gladly. The priests who guarded the entrance watched the box regularly, and when they saw the box was full, the royal secretary and high priest emptied the money into bags, and the chest was returned to its place. Much money was collected this way.

The money was paid to the carpenters, builders, masons, and stone-cutters who were doing the repair work. Timbers, hewn stones, and other necessities were purchased with the money. The silver and gold brought were not used to make any vessels until the repair work was done. Then the extra was used to make vessels to use in the temple worship. The work of restoration was done according to the original plan of the temple.

The workmen were not required to keep specific account of the way the money was being spent because they were acting with complete honesty in their work.

It had been about 150 years since the temple had been built by Solomon, so age itself would have made repairs necessary.

Death of Jehoiada (2 Chron. 24:14b-16):

During the life of Jehoiada the worship of the temple was faithfully carried on. Jehoiada was the human instrument which God used to preserve the house of David from destruction.

By now Jehoiada was very old. He died at the age of 130 years. As a tribute to him for

Jehoahaz and Israel are Brought Low (2 Kings 13:7):

Since Jehoahaz was very wicked, Israel was brought very low under him. At one point Jehoahaz was left with fifty horsemen, ten chariots, and ten thousand footmen. Hazael and the Syrian army had nearly destroyed his forces.

Take the map that you have already started showing Israel's decreased territory. Indicate on your map that Jehoahaz was left with only a token army in the territory immediately surrounding the city of Samaria. God nearly allowed the kingdom of Israel to be destroyed by Syria, a kingdom that had been smaller than Israel in their early days.

Jehovah Takes Pity Upon Israel (2 Kings 13:4-6):

Finally, in desperation, Jehoahaz sought Jehovah's help, and the Lord listened because He saw how Hazael was oppressing Israel. The Lord provided a deliverer (a savior) for Israel. With God's help, Israel began to make a startling recovery which continued through the days of Jehoahaz's son Joash and into the days of Jeroboam II after him.

Even when Jehoahaz sought God's help and He came to their rescue, the people still did not turn away from their idolatry. They continued to worship the golden calves, and the Asherah pole (or groves) remained in Samaria.

his service to the house of David, and to the house of God, he was buried in the City of David with the kings.

37th year of Joash (Jehoash) king of Judah (2 Kings 13:10)

Sins of Joash (2 Chron. 24:17-19):

After Jehoiada's death the princes of Judah came to Joash and bowed before him. He listened to their requests (which must have been to allow idolatry), and he and his people forsook the temple worship and served the Asherah poles and the idols. Therefore the wrath of God came against Judah and Jerusalem. God continued to send prophets to warn, but the people would not hear.

Stoning of Zechariah (2 Chron. 24:20-22):

As the idolatry in Judah resumed, Jehovah spoke by the mouth of Zechariah the son of Jehoiada. He said, "This is what God says: 'Why do you transgress the Lord's commandment? You will not prosper. Because you have forsaken Jehovah, He has forsaken you.'"

The people, at the command of Joash, stoned Zechariah to death. Thus Joash repaid his benefactor Jehoiada for his kindness by murdering his son!

As Zechariah died he said, "May the Lord see this and call you to account."

Hazael Devastates the Kingdom of Judah (2 Kings 12:17-18; 2 Chron. 24:23-24):

Having rendered Israel impotent, Hazael turned his attention to Judah and to Philistia. First he attacked and captured the Philistine city of Gath and then turned toward Jerusalem. Even though he had brought a small army with him, he was able to intimidate Joash into surrendering. Some of the officials of Judah were killed. Thus the Lord delivered Judah and Joash into Hazael's hands as a

Joash (Jehoash) — 16 years (evil) (2 Kings 13:9-14:16; 2 Chron. 25:17-25):

Joash (or Jehoash) of Israel is the second of four generations of Jehu's descendants that would sit upon the throne of Israel according to the word of the Lord (2 Kings 10:30).

Chronological Note:

If Jehoahaz began his reign in the 23rd year of Joash of Judah and reigned 17 years, then he would have died in Joash's 40th year. Since Joash of Israel began in the 37th year of Joash of Judah instead of his 40th year, then he must have begun to reign as co-regent with his father at that time. Jehoahaz must have died just a short time before Joash of Judah died. The two Joash's (or Jehoash's) overlapped reigns by two or three years.

judgment against them because of their idolatry. In fact, 2 Chronicles shows that this invasion was in direct judgment of Joash's killing of Zechariah, as well as the idolatry of Judah. Joash took all the valuable objects from the temple that his fathers had dedicated, the gifts he himself had dedicated to the temple, the gold in the treasury of the temple, plus additional gold from his own house, and paid Hazael to leave Jerusalem alone.

Death of Joash (2 Kings 12:19-21; 2 Chron. 24:25-27):

When Hazael withdrew from Jerusalem, he left Joash severely wounded. Two of Joash's own officials conspired against him to kill him because of the blood of Zechariah the son of Jehoiada. They killed him in his bed and buried him in the City of David, but not in the sepulchers of the kings.

Note that this is the second of the wicked kings of Judah who were not buried with the other kings. Wicked Jehoram was not (2 Chron. 21:20); and now Joash is not even though his benefactor Jehoida was buried with the kings even though he did not rule upon the throne (2 Chron. 24:16).

Amaziah — 29 years (evil) (2 Kings 14:1-20; 2 Chron. 25:1-28):

Chronological Note:

The only way to get the chronology to work out is to assume a co-regency of Amaziah and his father Joash. Amaziah began his reign in the second year of Joash of Israel. Joash of Israel, however, began his rule in the 37th year of Joash of Judah. Joash of Judah ruled a total of 40 years. The second year of Joash of Israel would have been the 38th or 39th year of Joash of Judah. Therefore, Amaziah must have reigned with Joash his father for a year or so, as was often done.

Jehoahaz Dies (2 Kings 13:8-9):

Jehoahaz died only three years before Joash of Judah died. That left Joash of Israel reigning alone, after a co-regency with his father.

Hazael of Syria Dies (2 Kings 13:22-25):

Hazael oppressed Israel all the days of Jehoahaz. God did not let him completely destroy Israel, however, because of God's promise to Abraham, Isaac, and Jacob. God was still trying to hold to Israel as His chosen people, and to bring them back into a covenant relationship with Himself.

Hazael died after a very long rule and was succeeded by his son Ben-hadad. It was from Ben-hadad that Joash of Israel was able to recover part of the territory Hazael had taken.

2nd year of Joash

Elisha's Deathbed Prophecy (2 Kings 13:14-19):

Even though Joash (Jehoash) was sinful and continued in the ways of Jeroboam the son of Nebat, the relationship between him and Elisha was much more cordial than that of Ahab and Elijah.

By now, Elisha was a very old man. His active work had covered fifty or more years. Elisha fell ill with his last sickness, and Joash went to visit him. Joash wept and said, "My

Amaziah's Character (2 Kings 14:1-4; 2 Chron. 25:1-2):

We are told Amaziah "did that which was right in the sight of the Lord, yet not like David his father." In other words, Amaziah served God in his early years as king, but not as zealously as David had. The high places remained in the land and the people continued to offer sacrifices and to burn incense there.

Unfortunately, Amaziah became more and more wicked as the years passed.

Amaziah Avenges his Father's Death (2 Kings 14:5-6; 2 Chron. 25:3-4):

As soon as Amaziah's kingdom was secure, he executed the officials who had murdered his father. He did not punish their sons, however, because of the ordinance in the law which stated: "The fathers shall not be put to death for their children, nor the children be put to death for their fathers; each one shall die for his own sins" (Deut. 24:16).

In Israel, if a man killed the king, he killed the rest of the king's family also, and then made himself king. Now, in Judah, a king has been murdered, but the murderers are executed as criminals rather than becoming king.

father! My father! The chariots and horsemen of Israel."

These were the same words Elisha himself had used when Elijah was taken to heaven (2 Kings 2:12). The words meant: "The power and defense of Israel." Joash recognized his need for the help of Jehovah to overcome the Syrian threat. He dreaded the thought of not having Elisha around to help.

Elisha said to him, "Take up your bow and arrows."

When Joash was ready, Elisha said, "Draw the bow." Then the old prophet laid his hands over the king's hands and said, "Open the east window and shoot." Then as Joash shot the arrow, Elisha said, "The Lord's arrow of victory over Syria! You will smite the Syrians at Aphek until you consume them."

The prophecy of Elisha was not yet complete. He commanded Joash to take up his arrows and smite the ground with them.

According to Keil and Delitzsch, the word smite, when used of an arrow, means to shoot the arrow into the target, in this case, into the ground. Such an action would parallel what Elisha had already instructed Joash to do.

The prophet had already shown the king what the shooting of the arrows would mean. Each one would be a victory for Israel over the Syrians. When Joash fired only three arrows into the ground, it indicated a lack of zeal in obtaining God's promised blessing.

Elisha was angry at Joash and said, "You should have smitten the ground five or six times. Then you would have completely destroyed the Syrians. Now you will defeat them three times."

After this, Elisha died and was buried.

A Dead Man Comes to Life (2 Kings 13:20-21):

Every spring Moabite raiders would enter the country. One time some Israelites were burying a man, when they saw a band of raiders approaching. They hastily laid the body in the nearest tomb, intending to flee from the raiders. The tomb happened to be the one in which Elisha's remains lay. When the dead body touched Elisha's corpse, the man came to life and stood up. Once more God had underscored His support of His prophets and His own great power.

Amaziah Plans an Expedition Against Edom (2 Chron. 25:5):

Remember that Edom had rebelled against Judah in the days of Jehoram (2 Kings 8:20). Amaziah wanted to regain control over them, hence this invasion.

Amaziah called all the people of Judah together and assigned them to commanders of hundreds and thousands. Then he counted all his available soldiers and found he had 300,000 chosen men able to go to war.

Joash Defeats the Syrians Three Times (2 Kings 13:23-25):

By now Hazael of Syria was dead and Ben-hadad was reigning in his stead. (*Possibly Ben-hadad served as co-regent with his father for a time. See 2 Kings 13:3*). Joash defeated Ben-hadad three times just as Elisha had prophesied, and he recovered the Israelite towns that Hazael and Ben-hadad had taken earlier.

Amaziah Hires Mercenaries from Israel
(2 Chron. 25:6-10)

Amaziah feared that his 300,000 men would not be strong enough to defeat the Edomites so he hired an additional 100,000 soldiers from the Israelites for a hundred talents of silver (about 3 3/4 tons). But a man of God came to him and said, "O King, these troops from Israel must not go with you because Jehovah is not with Israel. Even if you and your men fight courageously in battle, God will overthrow you before your enemy. Jehovah has the power to help you or to defeat you."

Amaziah said, "What about the hundred talents I paid for these men?"

The man of God replied, "The Lord can give you much more than that."

So Amaziah sent the mercenaries home. The Israelite soldiers were enraged at being dismissed.

Amaziah's Success in Edom (2 Kings 14:7; 2 Chron. 25:11-12):

Amaziah led his forces to the Valley of Salt and slew 10,000 men of Seir. His army also captured 10,000 more men, took them to

Soldiers of Israel Wreak Havoc in Judah (2 Chron. 25:13):

To vent their anger, and possibly to take spoils that could replace the spoils they had

Judah	Israel
the top of a cliff, and threw them down so that they were all dashed to pieces.	hoped to take in battle, the mercenary Israelite soldiers raided the towns of Judah and Benjamin in the north along the border between Israel and Judah. They killed 3,000 people and carried off a great deal of plunder.

<table>
<tr><td>

Amaziah Turns to Idols (2 Chron. 25:14-16):

When Amaziah returned from slaughtering the Edomites, he brought their gods back with him. He set them up and began worshiping them as his own. The Lord was very angry and He sent a message to Amaziah through a prophet: "Why are you seeking the gods of this people? They were not able to deliver their own people out of your hands."

Amaziah was tired of listening to God's prophets. He said, "Have you been appointed one of the king's advisers? Stop. Do you want to be killed?"

The prophet said, "I know that God has determined to destroy you because you have done this, and have not listened to my advice."

</td><td>

This story explains why Amaziah soon sought a battle with Israel.

</td></tr>
</table>

War Between Amaziah and Joash
(2 Kings 14:8-14; 2 Chron. 25:17-24)

Amaziah sent messengers to Joash (Jehoash) challenging him: "Come face me."

Joash sent back a scornful reply, saying, "A thistle in Lebanon sent word to a cedar of Lebanon saying, 'Give your daughter to my son in marriage.' About that time a wild beast stepped on the thistle and crushed it underfoot. You have defeated Edom and now you are arrogant and proud. You had better stay at home. Why cause your own downfall and that of Judah?"

Amaziah continued to insist on battle because God intended to deliver him and Judah over to Joash because they had sought the gods of Edom. The two kings met in battle at Beth-Shemesh in northwestern Judah. Joash completely defeated Amaziah's army, captured Amaziah, and brought him to Jerusalem. There, Joash tore down about six hundred feet of the walls of the city. He took the gold, silver, and other valuables from the temple treasures. He also took Amaziah's own fortune and some hostages and returned to Samaria.

Judah	Israel
15th year of Amaziah Amaziah ruled fifteen years after the death of Joash (Jehoash) of Israel (2 Kings 14:17).	## Jeroboam — 41 years (wicked) ### (2 Kings 14:23-29) Jehoash (Joash) died and was succeeded by his son Jeroboam. This Jeroboam is referred to as Jeroboam II to distinguish him from Jeroboam, the son of Nebat, who was

the first king of divided Israel.

Jeroboam II was wicked and did not turn back from the idolatry introduced by Jeroboam the son of Nebat.

Jeroboam II was the third descendant of Jehu's to reign upon the throne.

The Bible does not tell much about Jeroboam's deeds. During his rule God continued to "save" Israel from her enemies (2 Kings 14:26-27). God sought to show Israel His mercy in order to bring them back to Himself. He explained His purpose, He warned, and He exhorted the people through the prophets which He sent to Israel at this time. We have already seen Obadiah and Joel come along. They were the earliest of the writing prophets. Now we will see a second group come along beginning with Jonah and including Amos, Hosea, Isaiah, and Micah.

Jeroboam ruled about twenty-six years before Uzziah began to rule in Judah. Then their rules overlapped about fifteen years. Under their rules, the territories of Israel and Judah, if combined, would have almost equalled the extent of Solomon's empire.

One of the factors that made this expansion possible was that Assyria was in a period of decline between the reign of Shalmaneser III (859-824 B.C.) and that of Tiglath-pileser (745-727 B.C.). With Assyria weakened, there was no enemy to oppose the expansion of Israel and Judah. God's mercy was with the little countries and He helped them in an effort to bring them back to Him.

Israel prospered — but the prosperity was illusory. As soon as Jeroboam died, Israel collapsed like a house of cards. The end of Israel is nigh, and it is chilling to realize how quickly the nation went from the prosperity of Jeroboam's day to utter destruction only twenty-five years later.

Jonah the Prophet
(The Book of Jonah)

Jeroboam II began his rule in about 786 B.C. Jonah prophesied during the days of Jeroboam. The record says of Jeroboam: "He restored the border of Israel from the entrance of Hamath unto the sea of the Arabah, according to the word of Jehovah, the God of Israel, which He spake by His servant Jonah the son of Amittai, the prophet, who was of Gath-hepher" (2 Kings 14:25). Apparently Jonah foretold the restoration of Israel. Thus most students date Jonah about 790 B.C. The exact date is uncertain.

Other than the brief note in 2 Kings, the only other information found about Jonah is in the book that bears his name. Let us now briefly survey the book of Jonah.

We have already noted that Assyria was in a period of decline in Jonah's day. This situation pleased all patriotic Jews. It was, therefore, extremely distasteful to Jonah to be commanded to go warn the people of Nineveh to repent or be destroyed. When God told Jonah to go preach to the people of Nineveh, he refused and went to Joppa where he found a ship going to Tarshish (southern Spain), about as far from Nineveh as he could go. Look on your map of Bible lands and find Nineveh; then see how completely Jonah had turned his back on God's call by starting off across the Mediterranean Sea toward Tarshish.

Jonah runs away from God (chapter 1):

The Lord spoke to Jonah saying, "Go preach to the city of Nineveh, for I have seen its great wickedness." But Jonah did not want to preach to the people of Nineveh, for fear they would repent and be spared (Jonah 3:10-4:2). So he paid the fare and got on a ship going to Tarshish.

When the ship set sail, the Lord sent a fierce storm after the boat. The sailors called upon their gods; they threw the cargo out to lighten the boat — but nothing worked. The captain went below deck and found Jonah fast asleep. The captain urged him, "How can you sleep? Get up and call on your god. Maybe he will notice us and will help us."

The sailors cast lots to find out whose fault it was that the storm had come upon them, and the lot fell on Jonah. He told them, "I am a Hebrew, and I worship Jehovah the God of heaven, the One who made the sea and the land." This terrified the sailors because Jonah had already told them he was running away from the Lord.

The storm grew worse, and the sailors asked, "What should we do to make the sea calm down for us?"

Jonah replied, "Throw me into the sea, and the storm will cease, because I know this is my fault."

The sailors did not want to throw Jonah overboard, so they tried their hardest to row back to land, but the storm only grew worse. Reluctantly they threw Jonah into the sea. They cried to Jehovah: "Do not hold us accountable for this man's life, O Lord, because you have done as you pleased."

As soon as Jonah was cast overboard, he was swallowed by a great fish. Then there was a great calm. The sailors were deeply impressed. They sacrificed to Jehovah and made vows to Him.

Both the Hebrew and the Greek words mean a great sea creature of some kind, not necessarily a whale or a fish. Jesus used the Greek word for great sea creature when He referred to Jonah's story in Matthew 12:40. Most English translators have chosen to use the word whale to convey the meaning in the word — and, indeed, the whale is a great sea creature. Do not spend time debating over the shape of this sea creature. Stopping to debate a minor detail would destroy the point of the prophet's message.

Jonah runs toward God (chapter 2):

Jonah was in the belly of the fish three days and three nights, but he was alive and fully aware of his plight. Jonah prayed earnestly to the Lord from the stomach of the creature, while that creature swam about in the depths of the sea. Was anyone ever more hidden away than Jonah? Yet the prayer of Jonah came before God, and God heard!

Jonah learned that there is no escape from God, nor is there any release from man's responsibility in this life to serve Jehovah. Jonah said, "What I have vowed I will do. Salvation is from the Lord." Then the Lord caused the fish to vomit Jonah forth upon dry land.

Jonah runs with God (chapter 3):

This time when God commanded Jonah to go preach to the people of Nineveh, he went and preached, "Forty more days, and Nineveh will be overthrown."

No indication is given about where Jonah was when the fish spit him out, nor how long it was before the second call came for him to go to Nineveh. Such facts are irrelevant to the story.

The preaching of Jonah deeply impressed the Ninevites, and they declared a fast. All of them, small and great, put on sackcloth. Even the king took off his royal robes and dressed in sackcloth. He issued a proclamation that neither man nor beast was to eat or drink while everyone sought Jehovah's favor. The king even sat in the dust.

When Jehovah saw the reaction of the city to His warnings, He had compassion upon them and determined not to destroy the city.

Jonah runs ahead of God (chapter 4):

God's refusal made Jonah very angry. He said, "This is exactly what I told you would happen. This is why I tried to run away to Tarshish. I knew you are a gracious and compassionate God who turns away from His fierce anger."

Jehovah asked Jonah, "Do you do well to be angry?" But Jonah did not answer.

Jonah went out to the east of the city and made himself a shelter and sat in its shade to see what would happen to the city. God caused a vine to grow up over the shelter to provide shade. Jonah was very happy to have the vine. Then God caused a worm to gnaw the vine and it died. Now Jonah was exceedingly angry.

God said, "Do you have a right to be angry about the vine?"

Jonah said, "I am so angry I could die."

God made His point: "Jonah, you are concerned about your gourd vine though you did nothing to cause it to be here. It sprang up overnight and died overnight. Should I not be concerned about this great city?"

Do not think that God was joking about Assyria being destroyed. If they had not repented on this occasion, Nineveh and the entire empire would have fallen. Throughout her history, there were enemies who arose on all sides, and even from within the borders of her conquered territories. If God had chosen to bring about her downfall, He could have helped any one of these enemies, and Assyria would have been helpless. The day will come in our study that Assyria does fall, and God's message is that they are receiving exactly the judgment they deserve (the book of Nahum). But this time, they listen to the message of the prophet, and their judgment is postponed. God's mercy was extended — even to a wicked nation like Assyria.

In the book of Jonah, we see, as we did in the book of Obadiah, Jehovah is not just the God of Israel. He is God of all the earth. This theme is vastly enlarged in the other prophets. As Israel falls into conflict with other nations, God brings all the nations into the scope of His great plan, first, as He pronounces judgment upon the nations that have long forsaken Him and turned to gods of sticks and stones. But then, in the prophets, God also reveals His plan to bring all nations into His family and into His covenant. Thus the prophets truly serve as a transition from the old order, which crumbles even as they speak, to the new which they announce and foretell in the most glorious of words.

We are also impressed that Israel's failure is not God's failure. Even while Israel falls, God reveals His plans for a kingdom that shall never be destroyed. The prophets' messages constitute a vital part of the unity of the Bible and of the unity, excellence, and fairness of God's plan. It will be interesting to observe how God uses the fall of Israel as the occasion to declare Himself unto all the nations in preparation for the gospel of the Messiah to be preached "among all the nations" (Luke 24:47).

JUDAH

ISRAEL

Death of Amaziah (2 Kings 14:18-20; 2 Chron. 25:26-28):

After Amaziah turned away from God, his servants conspired against him in Jerusalem. He fled to Lachish, but his servants sent after him and slew him there. He was buried at Jerusalem in the City of David.

It seems there was an interval of eleven years before Uzziah took over as king in Judah (compare 2 Kings 14:1, 17, 23 with 2 Kings 15:1).

Uzziah (Azariah) — 52 years (good) (2 Kings 14:21-22; 15:1-7; 2 Chron. 26:1-23):

After Amaziah was killed, the people of Judah took Azariah (Uzziah) and made him king in his father's stead. He was only sixteen years old when he became king. He ruled for fifty-two years.

Character of Uzziah (2 Kings 15:3-4; 2 Chron. 26:4-5):

Uzziah was a good king for most of his life. He was aided by a prophet named Zechariah, and as long as Uzziah sought the Lord,

Jeroboam II is continuing to reign in Israel.

27th year of Jeroboam II

he prospered. The high places were not removed, however, and the people continued to
worship at such places. Idolatry had taken root
by now in the heart of the common man.

Uzziah's Successes in War (2 Kings 14:22; 2 Chron. 26:2, 6-8):

Uzziah went forth and fought the Philistines and tore down the walls of Gath, Jabneh,
and Ashdod. He built his own fortresses in the
area of Ashdod and in other places among the
Philistines. God gave Uzziah victory against his
various enemies — the Arabians and the Meu-
nim. Even the Ammonites sent him gifts
(tribute).

Uzziah also succeeded in restoring Elath
(Eloth) to Judah's control. Elath was a port at
the head of the Gulf of Aqaba. Copper was
mined in the vicinity, and Elath was the door
of commerce to and from the Red Sea.

Uzziah's Building and Agricultural Projects (2 Chron. 26:9-10):

Uzziah strengthened the walls of Jerusalem, part of which had been torn down by
Jehoash of Israel (2 Chron. 25:23). He also
built towers in the wilderness and cisterns for
water. Uzziah loved farming and had many
cattle and vineyards.

Uzziah's Army (2 Chron. 26:11-15):

Uzziah possessed a trained army of
307,500. It was a highly trained fighting force.
Uzziah provided his soldiers with the best
weapons and armor available. He also made
engines of warfare for the defense of Jerusalem.

The fame of Uzziah spread far and wide
because God highly blessed him (2 Chron.
26:8b, 15b).

*Since the text makes a special point that
Uzziah provided the weapons for warfare, it
seems that the soldiers had been bringing their
own weapons to battle under the previous kings.*

92

Judah	Israel

Take a new map of Canaan. Show how Jeroboam II was able to extend his kingdom of Israel "from the entering of Hamath unto the sea of the plain" (that is, the Dead Sea) (2 Kings 14:25). Also show how Uzziah extended his borders to include most of old Philistia, down through Edom to Elath on the tip of the Gulf of Aqaba. Note that even the Ammonites and Arabians on the edge of the desert were defeated or paid tribute to him.

Note that the two kingdoms together nearly equal the total land controlled by David and Solomon. This is the largest the kingdoms have been since they divided in the days of Rehoboam and Jeroboam I.

But look at the contrast in the kingdoms. God was blessing Uzziah and helping him extend his borders because Uzziah was righteous. In contrast, Jeroboam II was wicked, but God was allowing Israel one more chance to see that God could help when He chose to do so. It is at this point in history, when things look more prosperous in Israel than they had in years, that a new prophet steps out on the stage of history. Amos comes to say the prosperity has not brought about the desired gratitude on the part of the people. They are just as deeply involved in idolatry as before. They have not turned to Jehovah — therefore <u>judgment is inevitable!</u> Amos is the first to say the end was definitely coming. It was too late to avoid it. More prophets follow Amos in Israel, but their message was to pronounce doom. God always warned before He brought destruction.

Notice, however, that Amos is saying that judgment is inevitable to <u>Israel</u>, not to Judah. Though Judah is warned in Amos' book, her judgment was not yet assured. There was still some good in Judah — but Israel's sin was full.

Amos the Prophet
(The Book of Amos)

Amos was a stern man of the wilderness, and his background is evident all through his writings. He was a native of Tekoa which was about five miles south of Bethlehem and ten miles from Jerusalem. The city was built on a hill overlooking the wilderness of Judah, one of the most desolate areas in Canaan. He was from a lowly background — a herdsman of sheep and a gatherer of sycamore fruit (1:1; 7:14). Nevertheless, Amos shows an amazing understanding of the history and attitudes of the nations around him, as well as of Israel and Judah. Perhaps he had visited some of the cities and areas mentioned as he traveled to market with his sheep. God called Amos from following his flocks and sent him to preach to the kingdom of Israel.

In taking time to note Amos' background and to marvel at his understanding of world affairs, we are in no way minimizing the inspiration of God. Though God's Spirit not only could, but did, increase a prophet's understanding of conditions around him, yet He also used the man's own circumstances and personality in conveying the message. For example, the tone of Amos' writing is very different to Hosea's writing, even though both prophets were giving the message of doom to the little kingdom of Israel.

Amos lived during the days when the reign of Jeroboam II in the north overlapped with the reign of Uzziah in the south. He adds the further note that his work in Israel was "two years before the earthquake," but this does not help pinpoint the date because nothing else is known about this earthquake. Most scholars date his work about 760 to 755 B.C. Let us look briefly at his message:

93

God's Judgments on all the Nations (chapters 1-2):

The theme of the book is emphatically one of judgment and doom. First the Lord announces judgment against the various nations around Israel: against Damascus (Syria), Gaza (Philistia), Tyre (Phoenicia), Edom, Ammon, and Moab. Then He turns closer home and cries out in condemnation of Judah, "because they have rejected the law of the Lord, and their lies have caused them to stray as their fathers did. Therefore I will send a fire upon Judah, and it will consume the palaces of Jerusalem."

He comes even closer home to Israel herself and gives a matching summary of her sins, though the rest of the book will continue the description of the judgment coming upon Israel. The sins of Israel named here are: social injustice; forsaking Jehovah and her covenant with Him; idolatry with its sacred fornication; and ritualistic, formalistic worship. Listen to God's cry of denunciation: "I will not turn away their punishment because they have sold the righteous for silver, and the needy for a pair of shoes. They even pant after the dust on the head of the poor. A man and his son will use the same religious prostitute."

God had done so much for Israel: He destroyed the Amorites before them; He brought them out of Egyptian bondage; led them through the wilderness; raised up prophets and Nazarites from among their own children. Yet they had despised the Lord; they had forbidden the prophets to prophesy, and had given the Nazarites wine to drink. Therefore, God warns that the impending judgment could not be avoided. Israel had sinned to the fullest, and God would wait no longer. No matter how fast or how strong their army was, it would flee away naked in the day of judgment. "Look, I am going to press you down as a cart loaded with sheaves. You will not be able to escape, no matter how fast or strong you are."

Basis for God's Judgment (chapters 3-6):
Chapter 3:

God had blessed both Israel and Judah far above any of the other nations, but that only gave them more responsibility to obey Him. Since they had not fulfilled their responsibility, God would punish them for their iniquities. "Listen to me, O Israel. You are the only ones I have known from all the families of the earth; therefore I will visit upon you all your iniquities."

Amos asked a series of rhetorical questions: "Shall two walk together unless they have agreed? Will a lion roar before he sights his prey? Will a young lion growl from his den, if he has taken nothing? Can a bird be caught in a snare where no net has been set for him?..." He ends with a question just as evident as the others: "Shall there be evil (judgment) in a city, and the Lord hath not done it?" or to express it in more modern speech: "When disaster comes to a city, has not the Lord caused it?" Amos says, "The Lord has revealed His plans for destruction to His prophets. Who can refrain from telling it?"

God had urged His people to return to Him, and they had ignored His pleas. Now God is warning of destruction, and they continue to ignore the message. Therefore:

> Call the people of Ashdod and of Egypt to witness that Israel is no better than the heathen. They do not even know how to do right anymore. Therefore, O Israel, I am sending an adversary who will pull down your fort, and your palaces will be plundered. The only rescue Israel can expect is as when a shepherd rescues two legs of his sheep, or an ear, from the mouth of the lion.
>
> When I bring upon Jacob the consequences of his evil, I will cut off the horns of the altar of Bethel, and I will destroy the winter-house along with the summer-house, and the houses

richly decorated with ivory will perish.

Chapter 4:

God had sent chastisements upon them to try to awaken them to repentance but nothing had helped. "Yet have ye not returned to me, saith the Lord" follows the description of each calamity. Since they had not repented, the warning is given to "prepare to meet thy God, O Israel." Judgment was coming and could not be avoided. The Creator, the All-knowing, the Lord, the God of hosts will come against them.

Hear this message, you cows of Bashan [*the wicked wives*] who live in the mountain of Samaria, who crush the poor and say to your husbands, "Bring us another drink." The Lord has testified that the days are coming when you will be taken away with hooks.

Continue your self-serving worship, because it pleases you. I have caused you to suffer famine, yet you have not turned to me. I gave you drought, and you have not returned to me. I struck you with blight and locusts; I sent you diseases such as there were in Egypt; I caused your young men to be slain with the sword; I have overthrown certain of your cities as I overthrew Sodom and Gomorrah — yet you have not repented.

Therefore, I plan to deal with you, O Israel. Prepare to meet your God!

Chapters 5-6:

The cry from Jehovah continues through the prophet:

Hear the message of lamentation, O house of Israel. The virgin of Israel is fallen; there is none to raise her up.

Seek Jehovah and you will live. Do not seek the idols of Bethel, Gilgal, and Beersheba. Seek Jehovah and you will live — otherwise He will break out like fire in the house of Joseph.

These people hate the one who reproves them in the gates; they cannot stand the one who speaks truthfully. You have trampled the poor and have extorted his wheat from him. You will not live in the fine houses you have built, nor will you drink wine from the nice vineyards you have planted. I know every one of your transgressions — you who afflict the just, and take bribes. The one who is prudent knows to stay quiet in such an evil time.

Seek good and not evil. Hate the evil and love the good. Establish justice in your courts. If you do, there is a chance the Lord will show kindness unto you.

Woes are placed against all classes of society — the wealthy ruling class, the women of Samaria. Woe to those who want the day of the Lord to arrive, thinking it would be a day of judgment only to their enemies and a day of glory for them. Instead: "That day will be one of darkness and not light; there is no refuge from this judgment. It is as a man who flees in panic from a lion, only to run into a bear; or as one who goes into his home and leans on his hand against the wall and is bitten by a snake."

Woe to the extravagant and vain worship of the day. The empty rituals of Israel's worship were despised by God:

I hate, I abhor your feasts. Your worship services mean nothing to me. Even if you offer me your sacrifices, I will not accept them. Take away the noise of your songs. Instead, let justice roll down like a great waterfall, and righteousness as a mighty river.

From the days of wandering in the wilderness, you have not worshiped me. You have served your images which you made yourself. Therefore you will go into captivity beyond Damascus.

Woe to those who are at ease, to the complacent, in Zion; to those who think they have it made in the mountain of Samaria:

Go look at Calneh, then at Hamath. Look at Gath of the Philistines. Are your borders any more secure than theirs — you who put off the day of reckoning, who loll upon your beds of ivory; the ones of you who eat the lambs out of your flocks and the stalled calves, who have your parties, drink your wine, and anoint yourselves — but who are not grieved over the problems of Joseph. Therefore you will go into captivity! I will raise up a nation, O house of Israel, that will afflict you all the way from Lebo-hamath to the brook of the Arabah.

The Lord knew of their wickedness. They oppressed the poor and were unjust in all their dealings. Although they had built houses of hewn stone and had planted vineyards, judgment would come, and they would not enjoy their luxuries. Amos gives a clearer insight into the extravagance of the day than any other writer. He describes their winter houses and summer houses. The people lay upon their beds of ivory and engaged in revelry and banqueting with no thought for the evil day coming. But they did not grieve over the idolatry in the land.

Therefore Judgment is Inevitable (chapters 7-9):
Chapter 7:

God allowed Amos to see visions of the destructions pending. The first was of a locust swarm that would destroy the crops. Amos prayed: "Forgive, I beg of you, because the land cannot stand it." God listened and refrained.

Then Amos saw a fire that would destroy the whole land. Again Amos prayed: "O Lord, please stop. How can Jacob stand such a thing?" And again, God refrained from sending the fire.

But then God showed Amos a wall that was leaning and told him to measure it with a plumb-line. God was letting Amos see how far Israel had drifted from God's original plan for them. "Therefore," God said, "I will not pass by them again. The high places and sanctuaries will be left desolate, and I will rise against the house of Jeroboam with the sword." Amos did not plead for Israel again. He could see why God was saying their judgment was inevitable. They had gone too far.

There is an interlude in the message as Amaziah, a priest of the golden calves at Bethel, tries to stop Amos. He told Jeroboam that Amos was causing trouble in the land and then told Amos, "Go, run back to Judah, and prophesy and earn your salary there, but don't prophesy at Bethel any more, because it is the king's sanctuary."

Rather than leaving as he had been commanded, Amos defended his right to speak: "I am not a prophet, nor am I one of the fraternity of the prophets. Rather, I was a herdsman and a keeper of sycamore trees, and Jehovah told me, 'Go prophesy to my people Israel.' So you listen to the word of Jehovah! You tell me, 'Don't prophesy against Israel, and don't drop your word against the house of Isaac.' Therefore, this is what Jehovah says to you: 'Your wife will be a harlot in the city, and your sons and your daughters will fall by the sword, and you yourself will die in an alien land, and Israel will surely be led captive from his own land.'"

Chapter 8:

The Lord showed Amos a basket of ripe summer fruit, and said, "The time is ripe for my people Israel; I will spare them no longer. The songs of the palace will be wailing; there will be many dead bodies, and they will cast them out in silence." What a chilling thought! The nation is ripe for plucking!

> Listen to this, you who swallow up the needy and cause the poor of the land to fail. You say, "When will the new moon and the sabbath be over so that we can cheat people out of their money, and you buy the poor for silver and the needy for a pair of shoes."
> Jehovah has sworn by the excellency of Jacob [*that is, by Himself*], saying, "I will never forget any of their works. I will cause the sun to go down at noon, and I will darken the earth on a clear day. I will turn your feasts into mourning and all your songs into crying. I will cause everyone to wear sackcloth and to shave their heads.

Then the Lord made a very unusual prophecy. His people had rejected His word from the time He first began speaking to them, so now He predicts a day when He would cease to speak to them: "Behold, the days come when I will send a famine in the land, not a famine of bread, nor a thirst for water, but of hearing the words of Jehovah. People will wander from sea to sea, from north to east seeking the word of Jehovah and shall not find it." [*As we proceed with the history, this is one more prophecy we will see fulfilled.*]

Chapter 9:

Amos said, "I saw the Lord standing beside the altar, and He said, 'Strike the pillars of the temple and break them in pieces upon the head of all of them. The rest I will slay with the sword. If they dig down to Sheol [*the realm of the dead*], I will take hold of them there; if they climb up to heaven, I will bring them down. No matter where they go, I will command the sword, and it will slay them.

"Are you not as the Ethiopians to me, O children of Israel? Behold, the eyes of the Lord are upon the sinful kingdom to destroy it from the face of the earth. But I will not completely destroy the house of Jacob. I will sift Israel among all the nations like grain is sifted in a sieve, yet not one grain will fall on the earth. All the sinners of my people will die by the sword, those who say, 'Nothing bad will happen to us.'"

As in the other prophesies of the day, God included a hope of future glory for His people. After the destruction to come, there would be a day of renewal. It is very important to note that it was the wicked kingdom and wicked individuals that were to be destroyed. God said He would sift the house of Israel among the nations as in a sieve, and the chaff, or the sinners, would die by the sword. However, not one kernel, or righteous one, would fall. God has always been able to see each righteous individual and preserve him even in the midst of severe punishment of the wicked.

The book closes with a bright ray of hope. A remnant will be returned, and in that day the tabernacle of David will be rebuilt. In Amos' day, David's seed no longer reigned in the northern kingdom of Israel. Even Judah would soon crumble in judgment, leaving David's tent torn and tattered in the wind. But through the Spirit, Amos was allowed to see a day when that tattered and torn tent would be revived and enlarged so that the remnant of all men and all nations that bear the name of Jehovah would become a part of that house. In Acts 15:16-17, James quotes this passage to show that the Gentiles were included in the blessings given in the New Testament. This was not a material prosperity that was being predicted, but a spiritual remnant with spiritual blessings in Christ.

The Prophecy of Hosea
(The Book of Hosea)

The prophet Hosea stands in sharp contrast to Amos. Amos told the people that judgment was coming and that they deserved every heartache approaching because of their wickedness. The justice of God is vividly portrayed in the book of Amos as we see God determined to punish the wicked. If that were the only picture we had of Jehovah, however, it would be an incomplete one. Hosea comes on the scene and shows that judgment is indeed inevitable, but that God's heart was broken because His people had made it necessary. The wrath of God was aroused against Israel by her constant idolatry and by her gross immorality, but wrath was not the only emotion He felt as He observed Israel's unfaithfulness. He also felt the pain of unrequited love. God's chosen people did not return His love.

Throughout the book God rebukes Israel for her wickedness and idolatry, but He does so, not only from the standpoint of righteous indignation that a husband would feel who finds his wife unfaithful, but also through the heartbreak of unrequited love.

Since Hosea prophesied in the days of Jeroboam king of Israel, as well as in the days of Uzziah, Jotham, Ahaz, and Hezekiah in Judah, he most likely began prophesying late in Jeroboam's reign. His work is usually dated about 750 to 725 B.C., barely later than Amos. He spoke to the northern kingdom of Israel, and the judgment he predicts is to Israel, not Judah, though Judah is warned to take heed lest she have the same fate come upon her.

Israel's Adultery (chapters 1-3):
Chapter 1:
The story of Hosea and Gomer is the key to understanding the whole book. In 1:2 Hosea was told to go take a "wife of whoredom," that is, a woman who was reared under the influence of idolatry and in whom the seeds of unfaithfulness were already sown. Through Hosea's experiences with Gomer as she turned from him to take lovers, God revealed His own grief at Israel's rejection of Him.

Hosea took the wife as he was told and she bore him three children. Each child was given a prophetic name. The first son was named Jezreel — "Jehovah scatters" — foretelling that God would scatter His people for their sins. "I will soon punish the house of Jehu for the massacre at Jezreel. I will put an end to the kingdom of Israel."

The second child was named Lo-ruhamah — "without mercy." God said, "I will not longer show mercy to the house of Israel, though I will still show it to the house of Judah." God's judgment this time would be without mercy. It seems there was some question about whether this child was Hosea's.

The third child was named Lo-Ammi — "not my people" — signifying God's rejection of Israel. This child definitely was not Hosea's, just as Israel was no longer God's people. His covenant with them was broken; it no longer existed. (*The covenant had stated "I will be your God and ye shall be my people." Now God says "...for you are not my people, and I am not your God.")*

Yet even here, as God declares that Israel no longer deserves the title of God's people, He looks to the future and sees a day when a purified, spiritual Israel would be His people — "like the sand on the seashore which cannot be counted or measured." In that day, "those who had been called 'not my people' will be called 'sons of God.' There will be a new leader, and the people will be united under Him." [*This passage is fulfilled in the New Testament as Jews and Gentiles are united under the Messiah, and those who had not been God's people could become His sons. What a blessing!*]

Chapter 2:

In chapter 2 God makes the comparison between the story of Gomer and Israel. God is pictured as the husband; the nation as the unfaithful wife; and the individuals within the nation as the children. God speaks to the nation throughout the chapter. He calls upon the children to plead with their mother to put away her whoredoms lest He strip her of her blessings. God turns away from her in disgust. "She is not my wife, neither am I her husband." She might still claim to be His wife, but she had turned away from Him as a harlot. Let her remove every trace of her adultery and return to her husband in loving service or she would be put away forever.

God would have no more mercy upon her children of whoredom than He had upon the wicked wife: "I will not show my love to her children, because they are children of adultery. Their mother has conceived them in disgrace."

"Israel (the wicked wife) has gone to seek new lovers in the Baalim. She thinks they give her blessings." But God says, "I will hedge her way with thorns so that she can not find her lovers." God's hope was that, if her blessings were removed, Israel would come back to her first husband (God) seeking a reconciliation.

God had given Israel many blessings, but she had used them in her sacrifices to Baal. She had not acknowledged that God was the one who gave her everything she had. Therefore He was going to remove all her blessings and leave her stripped naked before her lovers — "and no one will take her out of my hands." None of her lovers would be willing to help the filthy harlot that was uncovered.

God had given her various feasts and special days, but she had corrupted them until they were no longer His days but "hers." She had regarded the various gifts and blessings as rewards from the Baalim for her faithful service to them. Therefore God would show her foolishness by turning the land into a jungle where wild beasts would live.

But God is gracious. The Baalim had lured Israel away from God, but now He seeks to lure her back. An enemy will carry her away into the wilderness, but that enemy is only a tool in the hand of God as He carries out His plan for regaining His wife's love. "I will lead her into the desert and speak tenderly to her." The place of punishment would become a place to purge the nation. Israel's blessings would begin again as soon as the wickedness was judged and put away. The new relationship would be very close. "In that day," declares the Lord, "you will call me 'my husband,' not 'my master.'" Her love for God would so completely fill her mind that even the memory of the Baalim would pass away.

Chapter 3:

To help the prophet understand God's position, Hosea was commanded to go to his estranged wife Gomer, show his love to her, and bring her back to him again. Hosea did this and showed how God would speak kindly to Israel to bring her back to Himself. But like God's love, Hosea's love would not overlook her wickedness: Gomer would be required to prove herself to Hosea. She would have to prove her changed attitude by refraining from sin for "many days." Thus Israel would be punished, her government and religion would be destroyed, and she would be exiled in a foreign land. Yet even that punishment would be for her eventual welfare. A spiritual remnant is promised — an Israel who would return and seek the Lord their God and David their king.

The millenialists believe that God will yet bring Israel back to Jerusalem and will renew His covenant with her and give her the blessings promised in the prophets. But if so, the Gentiles have no right to a covenant relationship with God. The physical kingdoms of Israel and Judah were soon carried into captivity as such prophets as Hosea predicted. A purified remnant returned to the land, determined to renounce idolatry and to serve God devotedly. Unfortunately, most who returned were not truly faithful. Therefore God was not able to bless them as He would have, just as He had not been able to bless them through the preceding years. The small spiritual remnant who truly kept their covenant relationship with God was enlarged in the New Testament to include Gentiles also — those who had not been God's people but could now be His. Passages such as Hosea 1:10 and 2:21-23 are quoted in the New Testament (Rom. 9:25-26; 1 Pet. 2:10) to show that the Gentiles have been accepted.

Prophetic Discourses: The Ungodliness of Israel and its Inevitable Punishment (chapters 4-13):
These discourses are, of course, really God's discourses presented almost as if there were a trial in which the Lord presents the evidence which will justify the actions He is about to take against Israel.

Chapters 4-6:
Jehovah has a suit against Israel because there is no truth, no goodness in the land, and no knowledge of the Lord. There is nothing but swearing and the breaking of oaths, and killing, and stealing. Therefore the land is devastated.

Hosea said, "My people perish for lack of knowledge" (4:6), and God blames the priests. They led the people into error. God will punish them for their deeds. [*According to the law of Moses, the priests and Levites were to teach the people, to keep the knowledge of God's law alive in the land. See Deuteronomy 17:10-11; 33:8-11.*]

Their whoredom and drinking have taken away the people's common sense. They ask advice from a stump, and their walking sticks talk to them. The people are completely given over to idolatry and fornication.

Judah is warned to leave Ephraim alone because he is joined to his idols. Nevertheless Judah will also stumble and will share in the chastisement God has in store for Israel. [*Ephraim was the largest, most prominent tribe in the northern kingdom of Israel. Therefore, throughout the prophets, the name Ephraim is used interchangeably with the name Israel. And, since Ephraim was the son of Joseph, the expression "house of Joseph" is often used in the same way.*]

In chapter 6 Hosea exhorts the people to repent and return to the Lord. Jehovah Himself laments over the unfaithfulness of Israel and Judah. They have transgressed their agreement with God and have completely turned away from Him.

Israel's Corrupt Political Condition and the Consequences (Chapters 7-8):
The king and the princes delight in wickedness. They are all adulterers. They prepare their hearts like an oven to do evil. They devour their judges, and their kings have fallen.

Ephraim consistently turns to the wrong sources for help. He is like a silly dove with no understanding. They turn to Egypt and to Assyria. They do everything but turn to God.

Israel has transgressed God's covenant and broken His law. Their kings are set up without His approval; they have set up their idols. They have sowed the wind; they shall reap the whirlwind. As Israel has increased the number of his idols, he has simply multiplied his sins. God wrote for Israel the ten thousand things of His law, but they are strange things to Ephraim, things he obviously knows nothing about. Therefore Jehovah does not accept their sacrifices. He will remember their iniquity and will punish their sins. They will return to Egypt. [*Several times in Hosea and in other prophetic writings, Egypt is used as a symbol of bondage. Their literal captivity, however, would be at the hands of Assyria (5:13; 7:11; 9:3; 10:6; 11:5).*]

Israel's Religious and Moral Apostasy — Its Punishment: Exile and Destruction (chapters 9-11):

Ephraim has played the harlot, therefore they will not dwell in Jehovah's land. They shall return to Egypt [*captivity*] and will eat unclean food in Assyria. The time has come for their sins to be visited upon them.

God says, "I regarded Israel like grapes one might find in a wilderness, or like the first ripe figs, but they chose to reject me and to worship idols. I will leave Ephraim bereaved of children" (9:10-12).

Hosea says, "My God will cast them away because they did not listen to Him, and they shall be wanderers among the nations" (9:17).

As Israel has been blessed, he has increased his idolatrous altars. Because of the calves of Bethaven [*Bethel*], the people of Samaria will be in terror. Their idols shall be carried away to the king of Assyria. [*There is a play on words in this passage. The name Bethel meant "house of God," but by placing their golden calves there, they had turned it into the "house of vanity, the house of emptiness" — Beth-aven instead.*]

Israel has sinned more than in the days of Gibeah (Judges 19:10-30). [*On that occasion, almost the whole tribe of Benjamin was wiped out.*] He needs to seek the Lord, but because he is filled with evil-doing, destruction of the fortresses and of the cities awaits.

When Israel was a child God loved him and called His son out of Egypt (see Matt. 2:15). Nevertheless, the more God reached out to them, the more they sacrificed to the Baalim. They will not return to Egypt, but the Assyrian will be their king.

The anguish of God over losing the people He loved is expressed when He says, "How shall I give thee up, Ephraim? How shall I cast you away, Israel?" (11:8). The compassions of Jehovah were kindled within Him. He would not utterly cast them away. "They will come trembling like a bird out of Egypt [*their captivity*], and as a dove out of the land of Assyria, and I will make them to dwell in their houses," says the Lord (11:11).

Israel's Apostasy and God's Fidelity (Chapters 12-13):

Ephraim feeds on the wind [*emptiness*]. Jehovah not only has a controversy with him but with Judah also. Jehovah will punish Jacob according to his deeds. In the womb he took his brother by the heel. In his manhood, he had power over the angel, and prevailed (Gen. 32:24-28). He met God at Bethel, and God spoke to him, even Jehovah, the covenant God of Israel.

Ephraim is a Canaanite. He says I have become rich. He says, "In all my labors they shall find no iniquity that were sin" (12:8). Ephraim, God says, has been completely faithless while God has blessed and sought to do only good for His people.

When Ephraim spoke, he made people tremble, but when he offended in Baal, he died. The people of Ephraim made for themselves silver images of their calves and said, "Let the men that sacrifice kill the calves" (13:2). Therefore they will pass away as the morning fog, as the early morning dew, as chaff blown from the threshing floor, as smoke from the chimney.

Judah	**Israel**

God says, "I am Jehovah your God from the day when you were in the land of Egypt. Thou shalt have no god but me. I knew you in the wilderness, in the land of great drought" (13:4-5).

Nevertheless, Israel turned away from God. The Lord now stalks them as a lion or a leopard. As a bear that has lost her cubs, He will meet them and will tear their hearts. He will devour them as a lioness.

It will be Israel's destruction that he is against the Lord. Who will save him? His sin is laid up in store. It is time for his punishment.

Though he is fruitful among his brethren, the Lord will cause the east wind to blow, and his spring will dry up. Samaria will bear her guilt; she has rebelled against her God. They will fall by the sword.

Israel's Conversion and Pardon (chapter 14):

Jehovah calls to Israel, "Return, O Israel, to your God. Come and ask Him to remove your iniquities" (14:1).

Israel needs to say, "Assyria will not save us, and we will not say anymore to the works of our hands, 'You are our gods'" (14:3).

The Lord will heal Israel. He will be like the dew to refresh them. The Lord will be like the olive-tree, and His people will come again to His shade. He will bless Israel and will restore their blessings.

Though both Hosea and Amos are declaring the time has come for judgment, the nation is ripe for picking — yet the cry goes out from Jehovah, "Return, O Israel, to your God. Ask Him to remove your iniquities." Even this late in their history, and in the increase of their wickedness, God would have been glad to accept them back if they had only repented. The story of the divided kingdom is a very sad story, but the sad part is not because they were punished, but because they refused to listen to the warnings and return to God. God's mercy is as evident as His justice in the prophets. God's justice could not ignore their wickedness, but His mercy made Him long that conditions could be different.

JUDAH	**ISRAEL**
15th year of Uzziah	**Death of Jeroboam II (2 Kings 14:28-29):** Jeroboam died in the fifteenth year of Uzziah king of Judah. Remember that Jeroboam was the third descendant of Jehu to rule in fulfillment of the promise God made to him (2 Kings 10:30).
	Look back at your map of the land in the days of Uzziah and Jeroboam II. Remember the land looked more prosperous than it had in a long time. That is why the message of Amos and Hosea stands out in such sharp relief. Why predict destruction now? Things look great — but that prosperity is about to end!

Judah	Israel

Judah

Israel

Chronological Note:
A comparison of 2 Kings 14:23 and 15:1, 2, 8 shows that apparently there was a twenty-two year gap between the reign of Jeroboam and the reign of his son Zechariah.

38th year of Uzziah

Zechariah — 6 months (wicked)
(2 Kings 14:29b; 15:8-12):
Zechariah was the fourth and last descendant of Jehu to sit upon the throne of Israel. God's promise was now fulfilled to Jehu. Jehu and his sons had been wicked and had continued in the way of Jeroboam the son of Nebat. Therefore as soon as His promise was fulfilled, God put an end to the dynasty.

Six months after he began his rule Zechariah was dead, slain by a man named Shallum. The Bible says Shallum slew him "before the people" and reigned in his stead.

****

39th year of Uzziah

Shallum — 1 month (wicked)
(2 Kings 15:13-15):
Shallum only ruled one month in Samaria before he was slain by Menahem.

****

39th year of Uzziah

Menahem — 10 years (wicked)
(2 Kings 15:16-18):
Menahem continued in the ways of all the kings of Israel. He was a ruthless man. When he made himself king, there were certain cities that would not open to him [*that is, accept his rule*]. He destroyed the city of Tiphsah and slashed even pregnant women, killing them and their unborn babies.

Uzziah's Sin and Punishment (2 Kings 15:5; 2 Chron. 26:16-21):
Uzziah had been a righteous king and a very successful one. But, unfortunately, success went to Uzziah's head. He determined to offer incense in the temple, an act only the priests could do. Azariah the high priest, with 80 other valiant priests, went into the temple after him.

Azariah said, "It is not right for you to

Historical Note: Tiglath-Pileser III
In 745 B.C., about the time that Jeroboam died in Israel, and the next two kings were

Judah	Israel

Judah (left column)

offer incense to the Lord. That is for the priests, the descendants of Aaron, to do. Leave the sanctuary, because you have been unfaithful, and you will not be honored by the Lord for what you have done."

Uzziah, who already had a censer in his hand ready to burn incense, was very angry at the priests. While he was enraged, leprosy broke out in his forehead. The priests examined the place, and saw that indeed he had leprosy. They hurried Uzziah out of the temple, but the king needed no special urging because he knew the Lord had smitten him.

Uzziah had leprosy from this time until he died. He had to live in a separate house, while Jotham his son was in charge of the palace and exercised actual rule of the people. This is another example of a co-regency.

There is not enough data given for us to know precisely when this event occurred.

50th year of Uzziah

52nd year of Uzziah

Israel (right column)

murdered, a very powerful king arose in Assyria. His name was Pul, but he took the title of Tiglath-pileser III (also spelled Tiglath-pilneser in the scripture). He proved to be the most forceful king Assyria had seen. Having pulled the warring factions together in his empire, he set out on a determined campaign of conquests. He ruled until 727, only six years before the fall of Samaria.

Invasion of Tiglath-Pileser III (Pul) Into Israel (2 Kings 15:19-20; 1 Chron. 5:26):

It was not long before the Assyrian king turned his attention to the west. No army or coalition of armies could stand against him. He marched to the sea and forced Syria, Phoenicia, Israel, and Arabia to pay tribute. Israel's share was 1,000 talents of silver (about 37 tons) — a staggering amount for a country so small. Menahem raised the money by taxing every wealthy man one and one-fourth pounds of silver each. By the way, that would work out to 59,200 wealthy men in Israel at that time.

Pekahiah — 2 years (wicked) (2 Kings 15:22-25):

When Menahem died, he was followed by his son Pekahiah. Pekahiah was evil and soon followed his father in death. One of his captains, Pekah, conspired against Pekahiah and killed him in the palace in Samaria.

****

Pekah — 20 years (wicked) (2 Kings 15:25-31; 16:1-5; 2 Chron. 28:5-15):

Pekah was one of the captains of Pekahiah's army. He conspired against Pekahiah. Taking fifty men of Gilead with him, Pekah went to the palace in Samaria and killed the king and two officials. Then Pekah proclaimed

Uzziah Dies (2 Kings 15:6-7; 2 Chron. 26:22-23):

Remember that for some time before Uzziah died, his son Jotham had ruled as Regent. When Uzziah died, he was buried in a field for burial that belonged to the kings. That is, he was buried close to the normal burying place, but not in the sepulchers with the other kings because he was a leper.

This is the third king of Judah who was not buried in the tombs of the kings. Jehoram and Joash were not because of their wickedness. Uzziah was a good king, except for his effort to offer incense, but he was a leper, and was therefore unclean. He was buried near the kings, but not with them.

Isaiah Receives his Commission to Prophesy (Isa. 6:1-13):

In the year king Uzziah died, Isaiah saw the Lord sitting upon a throne, high and lifted up, and his train [*the skirt of His robe*] filled the temple. Above Him stood the seraphim. Each seraph had six wings. With two he covered his face, with two his feet, and with two he flew. One cried to another, "Holy, holy, holy is Jehovah of hosts: the whole earth is full of His glory."

At this, the foundations shook, and the house was filled with smoke. Isaiah was afraid and said, "Woe is me! It is all over for me, because I am a man of unclean lips, living in the midst of a people of unclean lips, and I have looked upon the King, Jehovah of hosts."

One of the seraphim took a hot coal from the altar before the Lord and brought it and touched Isaiah's lips with it. He said, "See? This has touched your lips, and your iniquity has been taken away, and your sins forgiven."

Then Isaiah heard the voice of the Lord, saying, "Whom shall I send, and who will go for us?"

It is interesting that Isaiah was bold enough to say, "Here I am. Send me."

himself king.

Pekah was very wicked and continued in the idolatrous ways of all the kings of Israel before him.

One wonders if there was a little time that Isaiah waited to see if some celestial messenger would be chosen. In some way, he felt that this was something _he_ was expected to do.

Immediately, the Lord accepted Isaiah's offer. He told the prophet what the mission was: "Go, and tell this people, 'Hear, but understand not. See, but do not perceive.' Make their hearts fat, make their ears heavy, and shut their eyes, lest they see with their eyes, and hear with their ears, and understand with their heart, and turn again, and be healed."

God's command was to preach to a stubborn and rebellious people what they did not want to hear. To hear further teaching from God would only make them more stubborn.

But God said, "Preach my will to them until they stop their ears, and close their eyes."

To explain the principle, we use this old illustration: when someone is determined to nail himself into a coffin, God will hand him the nails. From another viewpoint, God is making sure that none can say he had no chance to know better. God always warned His people before He punished them, hoping they would repent, but knowing that by now they had become so wicked they would only refuse to listen.

Isaiah asked, "Lord, how long am I to do this?"

The Lord replied, "Until the cities lie in ruins with no inhabitants, and the land is utterly destroyed."

What chilling news! The certain result of Israel's rebellion and disobedience would be national destruction.

Warning: Keep your Perspective in the Study:

This book is a study of the divided kingdom, with an *introduction* to the prophets as you come to them in their proper place in history. Up until this point, the prophets that have been introduced have been short ones that could be looked at relatively quickly and easily. But now we come to the longest book in the Bible, next to Psalms. Do not forget what you are studying. It is beyond the scope of this material to make a detailed study of Isaiah, or of any other prophet, but we hope to give enough of a synopsis here to give an insight into his message. It is a beautiful book, worthy of a much more detailed study.

If you interrupted your study of the history, and turned to the prophet for a detailed study, you would defeat what you are trying to do on this time through the period. You would lose the thread of the history, and you would fail to see what is happening to the two little kingdoms. Use this study to form the foundation for a later, detailed study of the prophets.

The Prophet Isaiah
(The Book of Isaiah)

Isaiah was a prophet in Jerusalem and Judah, though he cries out against both Israel and Judah. Both are wicked by now. He has been called the prince of the prophets. There are several reasons for this. The beauty of his language, the soaring heights of his imagery, the richness of his visions, all contribute to Isaiah's reputation. But, in our thinking, more than anything else, it is Isaiah's emphasis upon all the great prophetic themes, and especially his many passages on the nature and work of the Messiah and of His kingdom that make him the greatest of the prophets.

His career began in the last year of Uzziah (Isa. 6:1), and lasted well into Hezekiah's reign after the fall of Samaria. In fact, Jewish tradition says he was one of the many innocents slain during the reign of Manasseh.

It is readily obvious that the book falls into two portions: Chapters 1-39 and Chapters 40-66. In the first 39 chapters there is a good deal of material that can be arranged chronologically with the history of the kings. Therefore we will include those portions at their proper places, but at this point, we want to discuss briefly the overall structure and teaching of the book.

Visions and Discourses Relating to Israel and Judah, and to the Nations (chapters 1-39):

God's Messages to Israel and Judah (chapters 1-12):

Through the prophet, Jehovah preaches to His people, telling them of the wickedness He has found among them. The sins of Israel and Judah are graphically set forth, but there are brilliant flashes of light from a better day in the future.

Israel's sins are her idolatry (2:5-8; 8:19), her immorality (1:15; 3:9-11; 5:8, 11, 18-23; 10:1-2), her ritualism (1:11-15), and the vanity of the lifestyle of her people (3:16-24; 5:11-12). Jehovah must punish such wickedness to uphold His great name. They have become as Sodom and Gomorrah (1:10; 3:9); very well, they must be treated as Sodom.

But the mountain of the Lord's house will be exalted above the nations, and the word of the Lord will go forth from Jerusalem (2:1-4). The virgin shall conceive and shall bring forth the One who shall be called Immanuel (7:14). In the devastated lands of Zebulun and Naphtali, Isaiah sees a great light shining (9:1-2), the light of a Son that is born, who shall be called Wonderful Counsellor,

Mighty God, Everlasting Father, Prince of Peace (9:6-7). A shoot will put forth from the stump of Jesse. The Spirit of Jehovah will be upon Him, and He will delight in obeying Jehovah. The wolf will dwell with the lamb, and a child shall play at the den of the asp (11:1-8). No one will hurt or destroy in God's holy mountain because the earth will be full of the knowledge of Jehovah as the water covers the sea (11:9).

God's Messages for the Nations (chapters 13-23):

In the prophets God shows clearly that He is the God of all the world. He will not reprove sin among His people and let it go unchallenged among the nations. All men are accountable before God. Babylon, Philistia, Moab, Syria, Ethiopia, Egypt, Edom, Arabia, and Tyre are all dealt with. Their sins and their punishment are all set forth in detail.

Contrast Between Israel, God's People, and the Nations (chapters 24-27):

God's judgments will be against the whole earth, not just individual nations. They have transgressed the laws, violated the statutes, and broken the everlasting covenant (24:5). With sound and fury, Isaiah sets forth the punishment upon the nations in strong contrast with the glory and blessings of God's people. The prophet says, "Come, my people, enter into your chambers, and shut your doors about you. Hide yourself for a little moment, until the indignation be passed. For, behold, Jehovah comes forth out of His place to punish the inhabitants of the earth for their iniquity. The earth will disclose her blood, and shall no more cover her slain" (26:20-21).

A Series of Rebukes and Promises Regarding Israel's Future (chapters 28-35):

"Woe to the crown of pride of the drunkards of Ephraim" (28:1). That crown will be trodden under foot in the day when he is judged. Jehovah will become a crown of glory unto His people.

His people refuse to be taught. They complain, "It is precept upon precept, line upon line." Therefore they will be taught their lesson by men of a foreign language.

Jehovah will destroy the lies and falsehoods upon which His people have come to depend, and He will lay in Zion a corner stone of a dependable foundation (28:16).

Jehovah will show Judah how foolish her "wise" men are and how blind are her seers. He says, "Since this people come to me with their mouth, and their lips honor me, but their heart is far away, and what they fear is the commandment of men, I am going to do an amazing thing among this people, and the wisdom of their wise men will perish" (29:13-14).

In chapters 30-31 the Lord asks why Israel relies upon Egypt. "Woe to the rebellious children that ask advice, but not from me. They make alliances, but not with my Spirit" (30:1). Therefore they will all be ashamed because of a people who cannot help them (30:5).

The Lord says to His people, "You have no way of escaping your doom, no way at all, unless you turn to me. I can defeat the Assyrians. At Topheth I have prepared the funeral pyre for Assyria. The breath of Jehovah, like a stream of brimstone will kindle it" (30:27-33).

In chapter 32 the Lord tells of a righteous king who will rule, and the fool shall no more be called noble. Paragraphs similar to 32:1-8 are often found in the prophets. The point is impressed how distorted men's thoughts become when God is forsaken, and how foolish their ideas.

As in 3:16-24, the women of Jerusalem are warned in 32:9-15. They are reproved for their carelessness. Their land will be smitten and deserted until the Spirit of the Lord is poured out upon it again.

Jehovah will be the helper in trouble: "O Jehovah, be gracious unto us; we have waited for thee: be thou our arm every morning, our salvation in the time of trouble" (33:2). The land is devastated, but the Lord says, "Now I will arise; now will I lift up myself; now will I be exalted."

In chapter 34 God tells of the vengeance which He will take against Edom. It will be utterly abandoned, a place where the jackal and ostriches roam. [*Remember that Edom is widely used in the prophets to contrast the future of the nations of unregenerate men and the future of God's people.*]

Therefore in chapter 35, God tells of the blessings to come in Zion. "The desert shall rejoice, and blossom as the rose" (35:1). The eyes of the blind will be opened, and the ears of the deaf will be unstopped.

The Lord will prepare a highway through the desert, a way called the "way of holiness." It will be so clearly marked that no one can fail to find his way following it. No lions or ravenous beasts will be found there, but the ransomed will walk that road, and they shall come with singing unto Zion, and everlasting joy shall be upon their heads. They shall obtain gladness and joy, and sorrow and sighing shall flee away (35:8-10).

Historical Section: Hezekiah and Judah Face Assyria; Their Deliverance; Hezekiah's Sickness'; Visitors from Babylon (chapters 36-39):

This section is dealt with fully in the text, so we will add no further comment here.

A Series of Visions Setting Forth the Servants of Jehovah through whom He will Deliver Zion and Accomplish His Will Among the Nations (chapters 40-66):

Jehovah Will Deliver Israel: His Incomparable Greatness (chapters 40-48):

Jehovah speaks comfort to His people [*those faithful ones still left among the wicked*]. Isaiah looks forward to a day when the Lord, having chastised Israel will restore her glory. The one who guarantees this future is the Lord. "Behold, the Lord Jehovah will come as a mighty one, and His arm will rule for Him. Behold His reward is with Him, and His recompense is with Him. He will feed His flock like a shepherd, He will gather the lambs in His arm, and carry them in His bosom, and will gently lead those that have their young" (40:10-11).

But who else is like Jehovah? There is none. Can He be compared to a god which a man whittles from a stump? Jehovah sits above the circle of the earth. Isaiah asks, "Why do you not trust in the Lord, O Israel? He gives power to the faint; and to him that hath no might, He increases strength. Even the youths shall faint and be weary, and the young men shall utterly fail: but they that wait for Jehovah shall renew their strength; they shall mount up with wings as eagles; they shall run, and not be weary; they shall walk, and not faint" (40:29-31).

The theme that characterizes this section is: Jehovah assures His people on the basis of who He is — the Mighty Lord. God challenges the idols to foretell the future, or to declare the long ago past, yes, just let them do *anything*! They are nothing. Jehovah is the only Savior men can rely upon. Some of the cleverest satire on idols anywhere is found in these chapters.

Beginning at the last of chapter 44, Cyrus [*the first king of Medo-Persia*] is named by God as His servant, who will "perform all my pleasures, even saying of Jerusalem, 'She shall be built,' and of the temple, 'Thy foundation shall be laid'" (44:28). Cyrus will deliver the exiled people of God from the yoke of Babylon. They will return home, but Babylon will be judged.

Once again, present Israel is rebuked for her dependence upon idols. Nevertheless it is Jehovah who will judge, and He will deliver. Cyrus, whom Jehovah loves, "shall perform His pleasure on Babylon" (48:14).

Jehovah's Suffering Servant Through Whose Sacrifice Israel Shall be Saved (chapters 49-57):

This section begins with the voice of God's Servant, the Christ. Clearly, God's Servant will not be given only for the benefit of Israel, but for Gentiles as well. God speaks these words to Him: "It is too light a thing that you should be my Servant to raise up the tribes of Jacob, and to restore the preserved of Israel: I will also give thee for a light to the Gentiles, that thou mayest be my salvation unto the end of the earth (49:6).

The Lord cheers Zion who feels "the Lord has forsaken me." In beautiful and tender words He comforts His people. Jehovah has not abandoned Israel. He will accomplish His will.

Again and again the voice of God's Suffering Servant speaks: "I gave my back to the smiters, and my cheeks to them that plucked off the hair; I hid not my face from shame and spitting" (50:6).

Perhaps the most famous Messianic passage in the Old Testament is Isaiah 52:13-53:12. This beautiful and sublime passage can be outlined as follows:

The Servant of Jehovah will astonish the nations (52:13-15).
His coming will be very different from what men expect (53:1-3).
He was wounded for our transgressions (53:4-6).
He was oppressed though He had done no wrong (53:7-9).
Through His death He accomplished God's will (53:10-12).

Jehovah continues to comfort His people. He says, "In overflowing wrath, I hid my face from you for a moment" (54:8). He will, however, restore, and the heritage of Jehovah's servants is: "No weapon that is formed against you will prosper" (54:17).

Israel — all of Israel — is encouraged to seek the Lord. Keep His justice and do His righteousness, and Jehovah will bless. Even the eunuch who says, "I am a dead tree," and the foreigners who join themselves to Jehovah will be blessed and will find mercy.

How great has been the forbearance of Jehovah, because His people have become the sons of the sorceress, the offspring of the adulterer and the harlot. They have sinned in every conceivable way. They have sought other gods and have sent their ambassadors everywhere, but they have not turned to God. Yet Jehovah will forgive the contrite heart.

Glorified Zion in a New Dispensation of Universal Redemption in the Spiritual Kingdom of the Seed of David, the Christ (chapters 58-66):

It is difficult to see a clear break between chapter 57 and chapter 58. Yet most scholars begin this last section with chapter 58. Several make the point that the subject matter is basically the same. In some ways it seems that the previous section should extend through chapter 59, and then begin the section dealing with glorified Zion. In fact Keil and Delitzsch say this last section consists of three prophetic visions: (1) Chapter 58, (2) Chapter 59, (3) Chapters 60-66.

In chapter 58 Jehovah rebukes the people for their selfish worship. They worship their way, not His. Is God's idea of a fast for a man to bow his head like a weed, and to spread sackcloth and ashes under him? (58:6). God's idea of a fast is to cut the bonds of wickedness and to do good to others.

Likewise Jehovah says that if they will stop doing what they like on His holy day, the sabbath, and begin to do what He likes, then He will bless them.

In chapter 59 Isaiah says, "Behold, Jehovah's hand is not shortened, that it cannot save; neither His ear heavy, that it cannot hear: but your iniquities have separated between you and your God, and your sins have hid His face that He will not hear" (59:1-2).

110

Isaiah proceeds to confess the nation's sins. "Your hands are defiled with blood." He says, "They hatch adder's eggs, and weave the spider's web: he who eats of their eggs dies, and that which is crushed breaks out into a viper" (59:5). "This is why justice is far from us. We roar like bears and moan like doves, but we have no relief, because our transgressions are multiplied" (59:9-15).

Jehovah, seeing this sinful situation, was displeased, and, since no man arose to do anything about it, He Himself donned His armor and dressed with the garments of vengeance. He will repay His adversaries according to their deeds. "So shall they fear the name of the Lord from the west, and His glory from the rising sun; for He will come as a rushing stream, which the breath of Jehovah drives. And a Redeemer will come to Zion, and unto them that turn from transgression in Jacob, saith Jehovah" (59:19-20). Jehovah's covenant with the redeemed will be that His Spirit and His words will not depart from the mouths of the children of the Redeemer generation after generation (59:21).

In chapters 60-66 the new, glorified Zion is described. Jehovah will preserve and uphold her in the midst of the nations that oppose her. Again the voice of the Messiah is heard telling what His work would be: "to preach good tidings to the meek, to bind up the broken-hearted, to proclaim liberty to the captives, to proclaim the year of the Lord's favor, and the day of vengeance to our God, to comfort all who mourn, to give to all of them that mourn in Zion a garland for ashes, the oil of joy for mourning, the garment of praise for the spirit of heaviness, that they may be called trees of righteousness, the planting of Jehovah, that He may be glorified" (61:1-3).

Zion will no longer be called Forsaken, and her land will not be called Desolate. She shall have a new name. She shall be called Hephzibah (My delight is in her), and her land will be called Beulah (Married).

Jehovah will preserve Zion in the midst of the nations. In times past the Lord looked after His people; He will do so again.

Isaiah calls upon God for help in his day. He once again confesses, "We are all become as one that is unclean...Our iniquities take us away like the wind" (64:6). The prophet says, "We are the clay, and you are our potter...Please do not be extremely angry" (64:8-9).

Jehovah explains that His people have been rebellious. They "provoke me to my face continually, sacrificing in gardens, and burning incense upon bricks" (65:3-4). They say to one another, "You stay over there, don't come near me, for I am holier than you" (65:5). Such are a smoke to God's nose. He will recompense. He will not destroy all; a remnant will be spared.

A new order will be created by God: new heavens and a new earth. The spiritual blessings of this order are set forth figuratively in 65:17-25. Jehovah will judge the wicked. He "will come with fire, and His chariots shall be like the whirlwind to render His anger with fierceness" (66:15). Zion, in contrast, will be enlarged and blessed.

Be alert to the frequent mention of a remnant that will return. It is mentioned over and over in the prophets. We will watch that prophecy come true also.

JUDAH	**ISRAEL**

Jotham — 16 years (good)
(2 Kings 15:5, 32-38; 2 Chron. 26:21; 27:1-9):
Jotham was 25 years old when he began his rule. He did that which was right before

2nd year of Pekah

the Lord. He walked in the ways of Uzziah, except he did not enter illegally into the temple of God.

Idolatry and immorality were by now an inseparable part of the common people. "The people did yet corruptly."

Jotham continued the building of fortifications which his father had started.

Subjugation of the Ammonites
(2 Chron. 27:5-6):

Remember that the Ammonites lived east of Israel, on the fringes of the desert. From the days of the judges, the Ammonites had wanted the rich fields of Gilead. They had troubled Israel through the years.

Jotham made war against the king of the Ammonites and conquered them. The Ammonites were forced to pay Jotham three and three-fourth tons of silver, 62,000 bushels of wheat and 62,000 bushels of barley for three years in a row.

Jotham grew powerful because he walked steadfastly before the Lord his God.

The Prophet Micah
(The Book of Micah)

Micah prophesied in the days of Jotham, Ahaz, and Hezekiah. He and Isaiah were almost exactly contemporary. It is not surprising, therefore, to find many similarities between the two books the prophets wrote; but there were some important contrasts also. Isaiah was the prophet of the court, while Micah was the prophet of the villages. Isaiah addressed himself to political issues; Micah dealt almost entirely with personal religion and social morality. Micah emphasized to Judah some of the same lessons Amos had preached to Israel: condemnation of empty worship from those whose lives were morally and spiritually bankrupt. Yet Micah grieves for his people as Hosea had done.

Notice that the message to Judah sounds very much like the message Amos and Hosea gave to Israel. Unless Judah repents, her judgment is imminent also. Even though Uzziah and Jotham were good kings, and Micah starts his work in the days of Jotham, the people of the land are corrupt. The warning is needed.

Judgment is Pronounced upon Israel and Judah (Chapters 1-3):

The first three chapters pronounce a sharp denunciation and unrelieved doom on both Israel and Judah, with Samaria and Jerusalem as the capitals of the nations. Micah opens his book with a description of a severe judgment coming from the great I AM: "Look! The Lord is coming from His dwelling place. He is treading as a conqueror through the land. The mountains melt before Him, and the valleys split apart, like wax before the fire, like water rushing down a slope." Nothing will stand in His way. And all of this is because of "the transgression of Jacob...and for the sins of the house of Israel."

The proud city of Samaria will be made as a heap in the field. Her idols will be broken in pieces because she has sold herself to other gods as a harlot for hire. The prophet saw no hope for Samaria — "her wound is incurable" (1:9). But Samaria's destruction would not stop there, it would come even to the gates of Jerusalem. Micah went through the streets weeping and wailing in grief. The last part of chapter 1 is a long play on words as the prophet cries out, "Please don't tell it in Tell-town (Gath), weep not in Weep-town (Acco), roll in the dust in Dust-town (Beth Ophrah)..."

These names did not literally mean the interpretation Micah gave them, but as in many plays on words, the words sound like the translation given above. The poetic cry is to keep the horrible news quiet. Don't let all the neighbors hear of Israel's great fall. Don't let them know it has reached Judah also, even to the gates of Jerusalem.

The wicked wealthy class who oppressed the poor is condemned. "Woe to those who plan iniquity, who plot evil upon your beds...for the Lord says, 'I am planning disaster against this people; you cannot escape.'"

The false prophets who were crying peace were condemned. The people who chose to listen to the false prophets rather than the true message from God were rebuked. Have you forgotten what it means to be the house of Jacob? God's attributes are unchanged — He still does good to those who do uprightly, but your sins make it necessary for God to punish.

The prophet calls upon the people to leave Canaan, "Get up, go away! This is not your resting place. You have polluted the land. It is defiled; it is ruined beyond remedy." It was liars who would lie for profit that the people wanted for prophets.

The ruling class was acting as cannibals in their unjust dealings with the people. Reward, hire, money were the beginning and end of their ambition. Yet, they still claimed to lean upon the Lord and expected Him to protect them against any evil. God said He would not respond to their prayers and He would show them no mercy, just as they had shown no mercy to the oppressed.

Your false prophets cry, "Peace," if you only pay them enough money. If there is one who refuses to give you the message you want, then you prepare to wage war against him. Therefore night will come upon your false prophets. There will be no visions. "But I," declares Micah, "am filled with power because God's Spirit is with me, to declare the sins of Jacob."

"Listen, you rulers, who despise justice and distort that which is right, who take bribes, and yet say God is on your side. Because of all your sins, Zion and Jerusalem shall be completely overthrown. The very place of God's presence (the temple) will be plowed as a field."

Future Exaltation of God's People (2:12-13; 4:1-5:15):

Though God's judgment would be fierce, his anger would not burn forever. In the midst of his severe warnings of judgment, the prophet gives a glorious promise of the return of the faithful from all twelve tribes. "I will surely gather all of you, O Jacob; I will surely bring together the remnant of Israel...Their king will pass through before them, the Lord at their head" (2:12-13). Chapter 3 ends with a dark picture of the destruction of Jerusalem; chapter 4 begins with a glorious picture of Jerusalem being exalted above the hills. The expression "in the last days" or the "latter days" in the prophets always refers to the Messianic era. In this "last day" God's government would be restored (the mountain of the house of the Lord shall be established); all nations would flow into it (not just Jews); the law would go forth from Jerusalem; Jehovah would judge all nations and establish a kingdom of peace (one not sustained by warfare); the lame and the halt would become the core of the kingdom, and the Lord would reign over them. God's plan would come to fruition.

The prophet's message returns to his own day. Before the glory of those last days, judgment must come upon the land because of the sins of the people: "Writhe in agony, O daughter of Zion, like a woman in labor, for you must leave the city...you will go to Babylon." But again, God promises that a remnant will return. Then, from this physical remnant, a spiritual remnant will be born through which the Messiah would come. Many nations were gathered against Zion and wanted to see her totally destroyed, but God had another purpose for His people. He would chastise them — but not destroy them. The physical kingdom would be destroyed, but God would establish a new, strong spiritual kingdom.

Notice that Micah said the daughter of Zion (the people of Judah) would go into Babylon, though Assyria is the major enemy on the horizon at the moment. Without God's help, how could Micah know where Judah would be taken captive? Babylon is only a small territory under the control of Assyria as Micah speaks. Watch for the fulfillment of this prophecy.

In chapter 5 Micah turns his attention back to the Messianic hope. A ruler would arise from a lowly birth. Isaiah prophesied that this ruler would be born of a virgin (Isa. 7:14), and now Micah adds the information that He will be born in a village — Bethlehem (5:2). Though He comes from a lowly birth, He will be a great ruler — "One whose origins are from of old," [*that is, though His birth was still in the future here in Micah's day, His existence was from ancient time*]. All enemies will be defeated; no power will stand against Him. Wickedness and idolatry will be cut off. Vengeance will be meted out.

This prophecy was fulfilled under Christ. There is no future kingdom of Israel to be set up as the millenialists try to claim.

Jehovah and Israel in a Controversy (lawsuit); The Way of Salvation (chapters 6-7):
The Lord calls upon the mountains to witness in a lawsuit against the people. The mountains had endured, and would endure, so they could testify to the wickedness of the nation. The court convenes and the trial begins. God speaks first:

My people, what have I done to you? How have I burdened you? I brought you out of Egypt; I redeemed you from slavery; I sent Moses, Aaron, and Miriam to lead you; I kept Balaam from cursing you when King Balak of Moab hired him to do so; I led you from Shittim into the land of Canaan, so that you might know the righteous acts of God.

The people answer:
What do you want from us? Shall I bring a burnt offering when I come before you? Would you be happy if I brought a thousand rams and ten thousand rivers of oil? Maybe you would like for me to offer my firstborn son for my sins. We don't know how to please you, O God. We have observed all the rituals faithfully.

| **Judah** | **Israel** |

The prophet speaks:

He has showed you, O man, what He wants. What does the Lord require of you? He wants you to act justly, and to love mercy, and to walk humbly with your God.

God speaks again:

Listen, O city! Heed the rod of correction! Am I to forget all your ill-gotten treasures, and your false weights and measures by which you cheat your brethren? Am I to forget your violence and your lies? No! I have begun already to destroy you: you will eat, but not be full; you will store up for yourselves, but all you save will be taken by the enemy; you will plant, but not harvest — because of all your sins. Therefore I will give you over to ruin. You will be the laughing stock of the nations.

The prophet closes his book by confessing the sins of the people. There were no righteous left; all were wicked. But a few, a spiritual remnant, looked to the Lord for salvation. God would hear these few and would allow them to rise again. Then the prophet offers a final prayer for God's blessings upon the remnant that would return: "Let them feed in the rich fields of Carmel, Bashan and Gilead as they did when they first came from Egypt."

"Who is a God like unto thee?" God had every right to destroy the people, but He was going to show mercy upon them and allow a remnant to return. He would keep His covenant with Abraham and Jacob.

About 100 years pass, and Judah is still standing in Jeremiah's day — though the kingdom is crumbling at that time. Jeremiah is crying out against his people, and his listeners become so angry they are ready to kill him. This time some of the officials step in and save the prophet. They tell the mob, "This man should not be put to death! He has spoken to us in the name of the Lord our God. Micah of Moresheth prophesied the same thing in the days of King Hezekiah. Micah prophesied, 'Zion will be plowed like a field, Jerusalem will become a heap of rubble, the temple hill a mound overgrown with thickets.' But Hezekiah did not kill Micah. Instead, he listened to Micah's warning, and sought the favor of God, so that God relented and did not bring the disaster pronounced. If we harm Jeremiah and do not listen to what he is saying, we will bring terrible disaster upon ourselves!" (see Jer. 26:17-19; Micah 3:12).

At this point in our history, we have not yet introduced Hezekiah on the throne. Let us watch and see how he responds to the warnings of the prophets. Just as punishment was postponed for the Assyrians when they listened to Jonah, so Judah's punishment is postponed when Hezekiah leads his people back to God for a time. But first, before Hezekiah, there will be another wicked king, Ahaz.

| **JUDAH** | **ISRAEL** |

Jotham, the son of Uzziah, continues to reign in Judah.

The Beginning of Captivity for Israel (1 Chron. 5:25-26):

In the days of Pekah, Tiglath-pileser III came and took captives from Gilead (the east side of the Jordan). This was the area where the tribes of Reuben, Gad, and half of the tribe of Manasseh had settled.

There is evidence that Pekah may have ruled as a rival to Menahem and Pekahiah. If so, then this invasion of Tiglath-pileser's forces came earlier than the one mentioned in 2 Kings 15:29 which affected northern Israel on the west side of the Jordan.

The Bible specifically says that God stirred up the spirit of Tiglath-pileser against Israel because they had gone astray after the gods of the people the Lord had destroyed before them.

War Between Jotham, Rezin, and Pekah
(2 Kings 15:37)

Before the end of Jotham's reign in Judah, Pekah king of Israel and Rezin king of Damascus began to afflict Judah. That is all the information given at this point. More will be given a little later.

Ahaz — 16 years (wicked)
(2 Kings 16:1-20; 2 Chron. 28:1-27; Isaiah 7):

When Jotham died he was buried in the City of David. He was succeeded by his son Ahaz.

Character of Ahaz (2 Kings 16:2-4; 2 Chron. 28:1-4):

Without question, Ahaz was the most wicked king Judah had seen. In fact he did things that not even Ahab had done. He worshiped Baal and offered his children as sacrifices to the false gods. This is the first mention of such worship by any king of Israel or Judah. It is also the first mention of the valley of the son of Hinnom as the place where this worship was conducted.

17th year of Pekah

Chronological Note:

Chronology continues to be a problem in this period. The situation with regard to the reigns of Jotham and Ahaz in Judah and the reigns of Pekah and Hoshea in Israel is complicated by a number of questions and we can only give possible solutions.

According to 2 Kings 15:30, Hoshea slew Pekah in the 20th year of Jotham, yet Jotham only reigned 16 years. Pekah ruled 20 years in Israel and Ahaz the son of Jotham began ruling in Judah in the 17th year of Pekah (2 Kings 16:1). This would have been the 16th year or last year of Jotham. Many argue that Jotham ceased reigning in this 16th year but lived four more years making the 20 years required by 2 Kings 15:30. Other explanations are given, however.

According to 2 Kings 17:1, Hoshea began ruling in the 12th year of Ahaz. Yet Hoshea smote Pekah in the 3rd year of Ahaz. Some would explain this by saying there was a nine

War Between Ahaz, Pekah of Israel, and Rezin of Syria
(2 Kings 16:5-6; 2 Chron. 28:5-15; Isa. 7:1-17)

We have already noted that hostilities had begun between the forces of Rezin king of Syria and Pekah king of Israel on the one hand and those of Jotham on the other (2 Kings 15:37). This conflict continued with Ahaz the son of Jotham.

A coalition had been formed between Rezin and Pekah almost certainly to protect themselves against the Assyrian threat which was very great at this point. The most likely reason for the conflict with Ahaz was because he would not agree to join their coalition, although these details are not made clear in the scripture. It seems that Rezin and Pekah intended to kill Ahaz and put a man on the throne in Judah who would support them in their coalition (see Isa. 7:6).

When Ahaz (king of the house of David) heard of the coalition of Rezin and Pekah, he was very frightened and worried. Isaiah asked Ahaz to meet him outside of Jerusalem. There the prophet told Ahaz that he need not worry about Rezin and Pekah. The kings were no more than smoldering stubs of firewood. The kings and their kingdoms were going to fall soon. Isaiah told Ahaz to rely upon God for deliverance. "If you do not stand firm in your faith, you will not stand at all" (Isa. 7:9b).

Isaiah told Ahaz to ask for a sign from Jehovah to strengthen his faith. Ahaz refused to do so. Therefore, God declared He would give a sign to the house of David. Before a virgin could conceive a child, give birth to him, and that child have time to grow to the age of discernment, the lands belonging to Rezin and Pekah would be forsaken (Isa. 7:13-17).

Ahaz would not listen to Isaiah and would not put his trust in Jehovah. Soon the forces of Rezin and Pekah attacked and did much damage in Judah. There seems to have been more than one campaign by the coalition against Judah. At one point the text says that Rezin and Pekah marched against Jerusalem but could not overpower Ahaz. But the efforts continued, and Rezin took Elath away from Judah and took control of it. Then Rezin defeated Ahaz and carried a great number of captives to Damascus. Pekah also won victories. He slew 120,000 valiant men in one day and took 200,000 captive to Samaria. They were able to defeat Ahaz "because Judah had forsaken the Lord, the God of their fathers."

A prophet named Oded met the army of Pekah with their captives and he said, "Because Jehovah was angry with Judah He gave them into your hand, and you have slaughtered them with a rage that had reached unto heaven. Now you apparently intend to make the men and women of Judah your slaves, but are you not also guilty of sins before the Lord your God? Listen to me, therefore, and send back the captives you have taken from your own brethren, because God's fierce wrath is upon you."

Some of the leaders in Ephraim confronted those who were coming back from the war. They said, "You will not bring those captives in here. You are about to commit a transgression which will bring the wrath of Jehovah upon us. Do you intend to add to our sin and our guilt?"

The soldiers gave up their captives before the officials and the whole assembly. The leaders of Ephraim took food and clothing from the plunder and fed and clothed the captives. They administered first aid to the injured and found donkeys for the weak to ride. Then they took them back to the city of Jericho and returned them to their brethren in Judah.

JUDAH	**ISRAEL**

Invasion by the Edomites and Philistines (2 Chron. 28:17-19):

At some point in this hectic period, Edom and Philistia also invaded Judah and carried away captives. Obviously, Judah was suffering enormous setbacks at this time. It should be equally obvious that this was because of the sins of Judah and of Ahaz (2 Chron. 28:19).

Ahaz asks Help from Tiglath-Pileser (2 Kings 16:7-10; 2 Chron. 28:16, 20-21):

Ahaz had refused to seek help from Jehovah, or to join a coalition against Assyria. Now he sent messengers to Tiglath-pileser saying, "I am your servant. Please come and help me against the kings of Syria and Israel who are attacking me."

Ahaz took gold and silver from the temple and palace treasuries and sent it as a gift to the Assyrian monarch. Tiglath-pileser must have been glad to receive money to attack an area he already wanted.

Pekah continues to reign in Israel.

Historical Note — Raids across Canaan:

Tiglath-pileser made three raids across Canaan in three successive years (734-732 B.C.). He marched to the sea, turned south along the shore and conquered the Philistines. He left troops on the border of Egypt, but did not invade there. Then he turned back and dealt Israel a direct blow. The Assyrians took Ijon, Abel-beth-maacah, Janoah, Kedesh, Hazor, Gilead, and Galilee (2 Kings 15:29). The Assyrians not only took control of the area, they burned the cities to the ground and took the people captive.

If you will find these places on your map you will see that the whole northern portion of Israel was taken. So was the entire eastern portion and the coastal plain. The only portion left to Israel was the territory right around

Samaria. Possibly even this portion would have been taken if the Israelites themselves had not removed Pekah from the throne and agreed to pay taxes. The Bible says a man named Hoshea conspired against Pekah and killed him.

Megiddo is not named as one of the cities burned, but there is evidence that it fell also. The city was burned, and a new city was built with Assyrian style architecture. It became the administrative center for the new Assyrian province made up of all Canaan north of Samaria and west of the Jordan. Isaiah spoke of the region as "Galilee of the nations" (Isa. 9:1).

Isaiah gives a Glimpse of Hope
(Isa. 9:1-2):

The portion taken in this raid was the territory that had been allotted to Zebulun and Naphtali originally. Now the cities were destroyed and the people were deported to Assyria.

This invasion moved Isaiah to speak these words by inspiration: "But there shall be no gloom to her that was in anguish. In the former time he brought into contempt the land of Zebulun and the land of Naphtali; but in the latter time hath he made it glorious, by the way of the sea, beyond the Jordan, Galilee of the nations. The people that walked in darkness have seen a great light: they that dwelt in the land of the shadow of death, upon them hath the light shined" (Isa. 9:1-2)

Tiglath-Pileser Destroys Damascus
(2 Kings 16:9):

The Assyrian armies came again. This time they took Damascus. Rezin was killed, and the people of Syria were taken captive. The area was made into another Assyrian province. Isaiah's prophecy about the fall of Israel and Syria was coming true.

Ahaz continues in his Wickedness
(2 Kings 16:10-18; 2 Chron. 28:22-25):

Ahaz was so pleased that Tiglath-pileser had made his attacks, he went to Damascus to meet him. The Bible states that the relationship did not help Ahaz, however.

Even though Zebulun and Naphtali had been devastated by Tiglath-pileser, Isaiah was giving a glimpse of hope concerning a time when that same territory would be glorified by a great light. It was that same area where Jesus later did so much of His work (see Matt. 4:12-16).

While Ahaz was in Damascus, he offered sacrifices to the gods of the Syrians. He said, "Since the gods of the kings of Syria helped them defeat me, I will offer a sacrifice to them so that maybe they will help me." Instead, the gods proved to be one more step in Ahaz's downfall.

Ahaz liked the altar to the false god so much he sent a pattern of it to Urijah the priest in Jerusalem. Urijah had a replica of it made. It was ready for Ahaz when he returned. Ahaz had the brazen altar of the Lord moved from in front of the temple to the north side. Ahaz then told Urijah to offer the various sacrifices on the new altar, but to save the old altar of Jehovah for him to inquire of God by. He then proceeded to offer sacrifices to the gods of Damascus.

Ahaz continued to set aside the worship of Jehovah. He dismantled the brazen lavers and took the bronze sea off the bronze oxen upon which it sat. He finally shut the doors of the house of Jehovah.

12th year of Ahaz

Death of Ahaz (2 Kings 16:19-20; 2 Chron. 28:26-27):

About three years into the reign of Hoshea, Ahaz died and was buried in Jerusalem but not in the sepulchers of the kings.

Here is another wicked king who was not buried in the sepulchers of the kings.

Hezekiah — 29 years (good)
(2 Kings 18:1-20:21; 2 Chron. 28:27-32:33; Isaiah 36-39):

****

Hoshea — 9 years (wicked)
(2 Kings 15:30; 17:1-18:1; 18:9-12)

Hoshea made a conspiracy against Pekah and slew him. Hoshea reigned for nine years, but it was an exceedingly tumultuous nine years. Hoshea was evil but not as bad as the kings that were before him.

In the Assyrian records, Tiglath-pileser claims to have placed Hoshea on Israel's throne. Although the Assyrian king did not kill Pekah when he defeated him, his vassal Hoshea did it for him and with his approval.

3rd year of Hoshea

Character of Hezekiah (2 Kings 18:3-7; 2 Chron. 29:2):

Hezekiah was the best king Judah had seen since the days of David. He removed the high places, smashed the sacred stones and cut down the Asherah poles. He also broke in pieces the brazen serpent which Moses had made many years earlier in the wilderness (Num. 21:4-9), because the people had been burning incense to it. He called it Nehushtan which means "a thing of brass," to emphasize it was no god.

Hezekiah trusted in Jehovah and served Him like no king before or after. He kept the commandments that the Lord had given Moses so that the Lord was with him and he was successful in everything he undertook.

Cleansing of the Temple (2 Chron. 29:3-19):

Remember that Ahaz had completely abandoned the temple. In the very first month of the very first year of his reign, Hezekiah opened the doors of the temple and repaired them.

He assembled the priests and Levites and said, "Listen to me, Levites. Consecrate yourselves and consecrate the temple of Jehovah. Remove all defilement from the sanctuary. Our fathers were unfaithful; they forsook the Lord and turned away from His dwelling place; they shut the doors of the temple and put out the lamps. Therefore the wrath of Jehovah has fallen upon Judah and Jerusalem. This is why our fathers have fallen by the sword, and why our sons and daughters and our wives are in captivity. I intend to make a covenant with the Lord our God so that His fierce anger will turn away from us. Do not be negligent now because the Lord chose you to stand before Him and to serve Him and to burn incense."

Are you noticing that Hezekiah has gotten the point that the prophets have been making?

He says, "We are wicked — so we are being punished. The only hope is to turn back to Jehovah." The covenant had not been renewed since the days of Jehoiada when the child Joash was made king (2 Kings 11:17-20; 2 Chron. 23:16-21).

The Levites got busy and started purifying the temple. The priests went into the temple and brought the unclean things out into the courtyard. The Levites took them from there and dumped them into the Kidron Valley. It took them sixteen days to complete the work.

Then they went to Hezekiah and reported: "We have purified the entire temple of the Lord, the altar of burnt offering with its vessels, and the table for the shewbread with its vessels. We have prepared and consecrated all the things that King Ahaz removed in his unfaithfulness. They are in front of the altar."

Temple Re-Dedicated (2 Chron. 29:20-36):

The very next morning after the purifying work was finished, King Hezekiah gathered the officials of the city together and sacrifices were offered, and ceremonies were held which set the temple worship back in operation. Then the assembly brought sacrifices. So the service of the temple was restored. Hezekiah and the people rejoiced at how God had blessed their work because it was done so quickly.

Hezekiah Prepares a Passover Feast To Which He Invites both Israel and Judah
(2 Chronicles 30:1-12)

The Passover Feast was due to be celebrated in the first month of each year, but there were not enough priests consecrated, nor had the people been assembled. They were in the process of cleansing the temple in the first month. Therefore Hezekiah and his officials decided to celebrate the feast in the second month, which was exactly how the law specified it was to be done if someone were unable to partake of it in the first month (see Num. 9:10-11). They also decided to send invitations throughout all Israel, from Dan to Beersheba, inviting all Israel to share in the Passover. The Passover had not been observed for a long time. The decree said:

People of Israel, turn to the Lord, the God of Abraham, Isaac, and Israel, that He may return to you who are left, who have escaped the hands of the Assyrians. Do not be like your fathers and brothers, who were unfaithful to Jehovah so that He made them desolate, as you can see. Come to His sanctuary. Serve the Lord so that His fierce anger will turn away from you.

Messengers went through Ephraim and Manasseh, even to Zebulun, but the people ridiculed them. There were some, however, from Asher, Manasseh, and Zebulun who humbled themselves and went to Jerusalem. Also the hand of God moved Judah to act with one heart to do the commandment of the king and of the princes, following the word of the Lord.

The Keeping of the Passover
(2 Chronicles 30:13-27)

A very large crowd gathered in Jerusalem to keep the feast of unleavened bread (the Passover). They removed the altars of the false gods and the incense altars and threw them into the Kidron Valley.

The priests and Levites were ashamed of their negligence and hurried to consecrate themselves and offered burnt offerings. Then they filled the places prescribed for them in the law of Moses.

Many in the congregation were not consecrated, so the Levites slew the Passover lambs for those who were ceremonially unclean. Most of the people from Ephraim, Manasseh, Issachar, and Zebulun had not purified themselves. They ate the Passover anyway because Hezekiah prayed to God on their behalf, saying, "May the Lord, who is good, pardon everyone who sets his heart on seeking God even if he is not clean according to the rules of the sanctuary." Jehovah heard the prayer and healed the people, and there was great rejoicing.

After the seven days prescribed by the law for the feast, the whole assembly adopted the extraordinary measure of continuing the festival seven more days. Hezekiah himself provided a thousand bulls and seven thousand sheep and goats. His officials added another thousand bulls and ten thousand sheep and goats. A great number of priests consecrated themselves. The entire assembly rejoiced, both those from Judah and those from Israel, for there had been nothing like this since the days of Solomon.

The priests and Levites blessed the people, and God heard them, for their prayer reached unto heaven, His holy dwelling place.

The Assembly Destroys Idols of the Land
(2 Kings 18:4; 2 Chronicles 31:1)

When the feast was over, all the Israelites went out into the towns of Judah and Benjamin and even into Ephraim and Manasseh. They destroyed the sacred stones, the Asherah poles, the various high places, and altars that were throughout the land. Then they returned to their own houses.

<table>
<tr><td>

JUDAH

Hezekiah's Further Religious Reforms
(2 Chron. 31:2-21):

The particular reforms mentioned in this passage were matters concerning the temple service, the priestly responsibilities, and the offerings. God had ordained the priests' work as essential to the spiritual life of Israel. The temple, the priests, and the offerings were all a necessary part of their spiritual welfare.

After getting the temple consecrated, Hezekiah set the priests in their divisions and assigned their duties. The king contributed from his own possessions to get the regular sacrifices started. Then he commanded all Judah to begin bringing in the offerings required by the law.

As soon as the order went out, the people contributed generously of the firstfruits of their crops and a tithe of all they possessed. In fact, they gave so much they piled it in heaps. They began their contributions in the third month and continued until the seventh month. Hezekiah and the officials praised God and blessed the people when they saw the amount contributed.

Hezekiah inquired of the priests about the heaps and Azariah the high priest answered, "Since the people began bringing their contributions to the temple of the Lord, we have enough to eat and to spare. The Lord has blessed the people, and this great amount is left over."

Hezekiah gave orders for store rooms at the temple be prepared for the surplus, and the priests and Levites carefully stored the gifts while the people continued to give liberally.

Thus Hezekiah began his rule with a very vigorous effort to bring the people back to God. His zeal inspired the people to serve God faithfully for a while, even though they had not been serving God for many years — even with good

</td><td>

ISRAEL

Hoshea continues to reign in Israel.

Historical Note - Tiglath-Pileser Dies:
Tiglath-pileser III died in the year 727 B.C., and was succeeded by his son Shalmaneser V.

The Fall of Samaria **(2 Kings 17:3-6):**
Hoshea became a vassal to Shalmaneser V; but then he decided to rebel, thinking it would be better if he joined an alliance with

</td></tr>
</table>

124

Judah	Israel

kings on the throne (such as in the days of Jotham).

Samaria fell in the 6th year of Hezekiah (2 Kings 18:10).

Egypt. Egypt was not able, however, to give any help.

When Hoshea ceased paying tribute to Shalmaneser, the Assyrian king came down, seized him, and put him in prison (17:4).

It was in Hoshea's seventh year that Shalmaneser invaded the land and besieged the city of Samaria. The city held out for three long years before collapsing. Thus all Israel was in ashes. It was 721 years before Christ was born.

*Shalmaneser died before the task of taking Samaria was completed. A man named Sargon II came to the throne (see Isa. 20:1). His records telling about the fall of Samaria were found in the mid-1800's. "At the beginning of my rule, in the very first year I reigned…I set siege to and conquered Samaria…I carried away into captivity 27,290 persons who lived there; I took 50 fine chariots for my royal equipment" (*Documents From Old Testament Times*, edit. by D. Winton Thomas; ed. 1958, p.59).*

Samaria, An Assyrian Province (2 Kings 17:6, 24-41):

The king of Assyria removed the people of Israel to Assyria and settled them in Halah, in Gozan on the Habor River, and in the towns of the Medes.

Tiglath-pileser was the ruler who started the policy of mass deportation of people from conquered areas. When conquered people were removed far from their homeland and scattered in foreign cities, it broke down all sense of national resistance. Thus Assyria could constantly move on to new territories to conquer without having to worry about lands already conquered.

Then the Assyrian king brought in captives from Babylon, Cuthah, Avva, Hamath and Sepharvaim and settled them in the towns of Samaria to replace the Israelites. At first these people made no effort whatsoever to worship Jehovah, so He sent lions among them and killed some of the people.

When this was reported to the Assyrian king, he gave order saying, "Have one of the priests you brought from Samaria go back and teach the people what the god of the land requires."

Ironically, one of the priests of Bethel was sent back to teach them how to worship Jehovah! After that, the people worshiped the Lord, but they worshiped their gods as well.

These people intermarried with the very poor Israelites left in the land and became the hated mixed race known as Samaritans in Jesus' day.

Reason for Israel's Fall
(2 Kings 17:7-18)

God's word has come true. The kingdom of Israel is fallen, never to be rebuilt. Her people are scattered to the four winds of the empire. God waited until His people had turned their backs entirely upon Him. Then, judgment was inevitable — just as the prophets had warned. Look to 2 Kings 17:7-18 for an inspired analysis of why the kingdom fell.

Israel fell because they worshiped other gods and followed the ways of the nations whom the Lord drove out before them. They also followed the evil ways introduced by their own kings of Israel. They worshiped sacred stones, Asherah poles, the golden calves, and idols of every sort.

They steadfastly ignored and rejected every prophet the Lord sent them to warn of impending judgment. They rejected God's commands and *the covenant He made with their fathers.*

Jehovah placed special blame upon Jeroboam the son of Nebat, the very first king of Israel. He led Israel astray because he was the one who introduced the golden calves and started them down the path of idolatry.

Therefore, Jehovah was angry with Israel and removed them from His presence. Only Judah was left, and even Judah had not kept the commandments of the Lord as they should.

THE END OF THE DIVIDED KINGDOM

Judah Alone

We are back to one kingdom in our history, not because the two kingdoms have decided to settle their differences and become one again, but because the northern kingdom of Israel no longer exists. The cities have been burned and the people have been carried into Assyrian captivity. Only the very poorest people have been left. Foreigners have been brought in to fill the vacuum. The foreigners mixed with the poor Israelites left and became known as the "Samaritans."

By now all the little countries in Palestine had been affected by the Assyrian scourge. Syria was gone, and the territory around Damascus was an Assyrian province. The city of Tyre still stood, but most of Phoenicia was gone. A few Philistine cities still stood. Moab, Edom, and Ammon still had their own kings, but they were paying enormous tributes to Assyria.

The little kingdom of Judah felt the heavy hand of Assyria also. If all their kings had been as wicked as Ahaz, who died only five or six years before Israel fell, then Judah would likely have fallen at the same time. But, fortunately, Hezekiah came to the throne in Judah and began extensive reformations. We have already noted those reformations in our study of the last years before the fall of the city of Samaria. He destroyed idols in the land; he cleansed the temple and re-started the regular worship at the temple; he proclaimed a Passover feast and invited all the people from Dan to Beersheba to participate; he organized the priests and Levites to do their proper work; and he led his people in renewing their covenant with Jehovah. Therefore, Judah was allowed to stand.

Judah was a very tiny, sick little kingdom by this point, however. Take a new map of Canaan and show the kingdom of Judah. Label your map "Judah, After the Fall of Israel." Draw in Judah, label Jerusalem as the capital, and color the territory. Label Moab, Ammon, and Edom and color each a separate color. Label Tyre as the main Phoenician city left, and label Ashdod and Gaza as the main Philistine cities left. Label the Assyrian provinces of Galilee, Dor, Samaria, and Damascus. Color all those provinces one color to indicate they are totally under the control of the Assyrians. Now compare this map with the map showing the land as God intended it to be, back in the days when the Israelites had first conquered the land, and it had been divided among the twelve tribes. Why is it so different? Is it God's fault that the Israelites have not been able to hold the land?

The name Jew came into use about this time. The first time we find it in the Bible is in 2 Kings 16:6. There it refers to the people of Judah. Since the kingdom of Judah is the only one left at this point, the name began to be used more and more.

Hezekiah, continued — 29 years (good)
(2 Kings 18:1-20:21; 2 Chron. 28:27-32:33; Isa. 36-39)

The fall of Samaria was in the sixth year of Hezekiah (2 Kings 18:10). Since Hezekiah ruled for a total of twenty-nine years (2 Kings 18:2), he ruled for twenty-three years after the fall of Samaria. Since Samaria fell in 721 B.C., Hezekiah began his reign in about 727 B.C. During the remainder of his reign he was primarily occupied with dealing with the Assyrian threat to Judah. There are three main episodes told about during those years: an invasion by the Assyrians, a serious illness of Hezekiah's, and a visit of emissaries from Merodach-baladan of Babylon.

There are major problems in trying to correlate the Bible record of Hezekiah's dealings with Sennacherib with Assyrian records. There is much disagreement among scholars about the meaning of Assyrian documents, so there is no certain Assyrian chronology to go by. Therefore, first, we will set forth the events according to the Bible. Then we will look at what Assyrian records say. At this point, there is no way to know how the two records harmonize. Our feeling is that the reputation of the Bible as a reliable historical record is well-established. Future study in archaeology may help to see how Assyrian records fit into the Bible order of events. Beware of books which will tell you blow-by-blow exactly how it was, when what they are really doing is going solely by Assyrian and Babylonian records, giving no credence at all to the Bible facts.

During the years following the fall of Samaria, Assyria was the threat most on the minds of Hezekiah and the people of Judah. Opportunities to rebel were eagerly sought. The secret weapon Hezekiah counted on for success was Egypt. Egypt wanted a buffer state between herself and Assyria and, therefore, encouraged the little nations in Canaan to rebel. There were rival factions in Jerusalem over the matter: One group contended strongly for rebelling. They said Egypt would help them, and they could successfully defeat Assyria. Another group, led by Isaiah the prophet, argued that Judah should put their reliance upon God, that Egypt could not be depended upon.

Jehovah Himself warned about the futility of depending upon Egypt (Isa. 18:1-7; 19:1-15; 30:1-14; 31:1-3). The Lord wanted His people to repent and to rely upon Him. If they would be righteous and serve Him, they did not need to worry about how they could be delivered from their enemies. But, for a time, Hezekiah and Judah refused to heed this advice (Isa. 30:8-18). Therefore, it was to be expected that the Assyrian forces would come again to put down the rebellion.

Preparation for the Assyrian Invasion
(2 Kings 20:20; 2 Chron. 32:1-8, 30; Isa. 22:11):

Hezekiah made careful preparations to protect his land from the Assyrians. Fortifications were made, garrisons were provisioned, and the army prepared. Some of these things could have been done, and probably were done, after Sennacherib's forces were already in the area. But one of the things Hezekiah did before Sennacherib arrived was to dig an extensive tunnel called the Siloam Tunnel.

Judah Alone

A spring called Gihon (also called the Virgin's Spring) flowed out of a cave just outside of the city wall of Jerusalem and down the mountain side into the Kidron Valley. From the days when the Jebusites lived in the city, there was a vertical shaft dug down through the rock so that, from inside the city walls, buckets could be lowered through the shaft and water drawn up from the pool formed by the spring. Hezekiah closed the cave opening and caused the spring waters to be diverted through a tunnel 1,777 feet long to the Pool of Siloam inside the city of Jerusalem. By such a move, not only did Jerusalem have access to a never-failing source of water during siege, but the Assyrians were thus deprived of water outside the city. The tunnel was dug through rock with hammer, chisel, and pickaxe. One party started from the spring and another from the pool. They met, and the water flowed. In 1880, an inscription was found inside the tunnel, not far from the Pool of Siloam. Dating from Hezekiah's day, the inscription tells of the digging of the tunnel. The water still flows through the tunnel today.

The Invasion of Sennacherib
(2 Kings 18-19; 2 Chron. 32:1-22; Isa. 36-37):
Isaiah's account of this event is just like the one given in 2 Kings 18-19.

While Sennacherib was besieging Lachish, Hezekiah sent messengers to him saying, "I have done wrong. Withdraw from me and I will pay whatever tribute you ask."

Sennacherib demanded eleven tons of silver and about one ton of gold. To find the money, Hezekiah raided the temple treasury and his own royal treasury as well. He also stripped off the gold with which he had plated the doors and doorposts of the temple. According to Assyrian records, Hezekiah sent many other things in tribute as well, even including some of his own daughters.

Sennacherib sent a great army to Jerusalem under the leadership of officers whose titles were Tartan, Rabsaris, and Rabshakeh. Hezekiah did not go out to meet the officers, but sent his own high-ranking officials to parley — Eliakim the son of Hilkiah who was over the household, Shebnah the scribe, and Joah the son of Asaph who was the chronicler.

The speech which Rabshakeh (chief cup-bearer) made was deliberately insulting. In the name of the Assyrian king, he said:

What are you depending upon? You claim to have plans and military strength, but you speak empty words.

You may say that you are depending upon Egypt. But Pharaoh king of Egypt is no more than a splintered reed which pierces a man's hand if he leans upon it to all who would depend upon him.

And if you say to me, "We are depending on the Lord our God," isn't He the one whose high places and altars Hezekiah has removed, telling Judah and Jerusalem, "You must worship before this altar in Jerusalem"? When Hezekiah says, "The Lord our God will save us from the hand of the king of Assyria," he is deceiving you to let you die of hunger and thirst.

Do you not know what I and my fathers have done to all the peoples of other lands? Have any of their gods been able to save them? Do not let Hezekiah mislead you. No god has been able to deliver his people from my hand or the hand of my fathers. How much less will your god deliver you from my hand.

Furthermore, have I come to attack and destroy this place without word from Jehovah?

Judah Alone

Jehovah Himself told me to march against this country and destroy it!

The servants of Sennacherib were speaking in Hebrew. Eliakim, Shebna, and Joah said to the field commander, "Please speak to us in Aramaic, since we understand it. Do not speak to us in Hebrew in the hearing of the people on the wall."

The Assyrian became even more insolent, and refused to speak in Aramaic. He said, "Was it only to your master and to you that my master sent me to say these things and not to the men stationed on the wall — who, like you, will have to eat their own filth and drink their own urine?"

It is obvious that the Assyrians were planning a siege of Jerusalem, and such horrible things happened when a city was starving.

Once again Rabshakeh shouted that the people of Judah should not let Hezekiah deceive them. Then, abruptly, he changed tactics and said, "The king of Assyria says, 'Make peace with me and come out to me. Then each one of you will eat from his own vine and fig tree and drink water from his own cistern until I come and take you away to a land like your own, a land of grain and new wine, a land of bread and vineyards, a land of olive trees and honey. Choose life and not death!'"

Rabshakeh returned to his main theme: "Do not listen to Hezekiah. No god has been able to stop us. Where are the gods of Hamath and Arpad? How then can Jehovah deliver Jerusalem from my hand?"

Of course, the entire performance of Rabshakeh was for the purpose of propaganda. His words were calculated to make the men who were guarding the walls afraid so that they would give up and not resist. The Assyrians spoke about the God of Jerusalem as they did about the gods of the other peoples of the world — the work of men's hands.

The men of Judah had been given orders to say nothing in reply to the commander's taunts so they remained silent. Eliakim, Shebna, and Joah went in to Hezekiah with their clothes rent. When he heard their report, Hezekiah sent his servants and chief priests, all wearing sackcloth, to ask Isaiah about the Assyrians' threats.

They brought this request to Isaiah: "Thus says Hezekiah: 'This day is a day of distress, as when children come to the point of birth, and there is no strength to deliver them. It may be that the Lord your God has heard the words of the field commander which his master has sent to ridicule and insult the living God and that He will rebuke him for these words. Therefore pray for the remnant which survives.'"

Isaiah replied with a message from Jehovah: "Tell your master that this is what the Lord has said: 'Do not be afraid of what you have heard, the blasphemous words with which the underlings of the king of Assyria have blasphemed me. Listen! I am going to put such a spirit in him that when he hears a certain report, he will return to his own country, and there I will have him cut down with the sword.'"

Meanwhile the commander of the Assyrian army heard that Sennacherib had left Lachish. He withdrew the army from Jerusalem and joined the king who was fighting against Libnah. It was not long before Sennacherib received a report that Tirhakah the Ethiopian was leading an Egyptian army against him. So he moved his army to Eltekeh to meet Tirhakah, where he defeated the Egyptian forces decisively according to Assyrian records.

130

Before he went to battle, however, he sent a letter to Hezekiah. The gist of the entire letter was "Do not let the god you depend on deceive you when he says, 'Jerusalem will not be handed over to the king of Assyria.' Surely you have heard what the kings of Assyria have done to all the countries, destroying them completely. What makes you think it could possibly be any different with your god?"

Hezekiah read the letter, and then he went up to the temple of the Lord and spread it out before God. This action of Hezekiah shows the very strong faith he had in God and is one of the most beautiful episodes in the life of any Israelite king. He prayed:

O Lord, God of Israel, enthroned between the cherubim, you alone are God over all the kingdoms of the earth. You have made heaven and earth. Give ear, O Lord, and hear; open your eyes, O Lord, and see; listen to the words Sennacherib has sent to insult the living God.

It is true, O Lord, that the Assyrian kings have laid waste these nations and their lands. They have thrown their gods into the fire and destroyed them, for they were not gods but only wood and stone, fashioned by men's hands. Now, O Lord our God, deliver us from his hand, so that all kingdoms on earth may know that you alone, O Lord, are God.

Jehovah gave His answer to Hezekiah's prayer through Isaiah:

Jerusalem can afford to be scornful toward the Assyrian threats, because the Assyrians have dared to insult and blaspheme Jehovah, the Holy One of Israel.

The Assyrians are filled with pride, thinking that they are responsible for their power and for their successes. God asks the Assyrians, "Have you not heard? I ordained it long ago. In days of old I planned it; now I have brought it to pass." The Assyrians have succeeded where it has pleased God to *let* them succeed.

But now the Assyrians rage against Jehovah Himself, so He says: "Because you rage against me, and your insolence has reached my ears, I will put my hook in your nose and my bit in your mouth, and I will make you return by the way you came."

Then God made Hezekiah and Jerusalem this firm promise: "Concerning the king of Assyria, the Lord says, 'He will not enter this city or shoot an arrow here. He will not come before it with shield or build a siege ramp against it. By the way that he came he will return; he will not enter this city. I will defend this city and save it, for my sake and for the sake of David my servant.'"

That night the angel of the Lord went out and put to death 185,000 men in the Assyrian camp. When the soldiers awoke the next morning, there were all the dead bodies. So Sennacherib king of Assyria broke camp and went home.

Sennacherib was slain by two of his sons, Adrammelech and Sharezer, while he was worshiping in the house of his god Nisroch. He was succeeded by his son Esarhaddon (Isa. 37:38).

The Sickness of Hezekiah
(2 Kings 20:1-11; 2 Chron. 32:24; Isa. 38:1-22):

This story is told in the Bible immediately after the previous account, but it probably happened during, or immediately before, the events just described (see Isa. 38:6). God added fifteen years to Hezekiah's life, so that would make his illness in his fourteenth year, the same year as Sennacherib's

Judah Alone

invasion (Isa. 36:1).

It was a bad time for Hezekiah to be sick, with the Assyrians threatening. The sickness was from a boil which he had (Isa. 38:21).

Jehovah sent Isaiah to tell Hezekiah: "Set your house in order; for you will die, and not live."

Hezekiah turned his face to the wall and prayed to God: "Remember, O Lord, how I have walked before you faithfully, and with wholehearted devotion, and have done what is good in your eyes." And he wept bitterly.

Before Isaiah had left the middle court, God spoke to him, saying, "Go back and tell Hezekiah, the leader of my people, this is what the Lord, the God of your father David says: 'I have heard your prayer and seen your tears; I will heal you. On the third day from now, you will go up to the temple of the Lord. I will add fifteen years to your life, and I will deliver you and this city from the hand of the king of Assyria.'"

Hezekiah asked, "What shall be the sign that the Lord will heal me, and that I will go up to the temple of the Lord on the third day from now?"

Isaiah replied, "This is the Lord's sign that He will do as He has promised: Shall the shadow go forward ten steps, or shall it go back ten steps?"

It seems Isaiah was speaking of degrees on what is thought to have been a sun-dial which King Ahaz had made (Isa. 38:8).

Hezekiah said, "It is a simple matter for the shadow to go forward ten steps, so have it go backward instead." Isaiah called upon the Lord, and He made the shadow go backward ten steps on the dial.

Then the prophet commanded that a poultice of figs be applied to the boil. This was done and Hezekiah recovered.

In gratitude to God Hezekiah wrote a song in which he tells of his suffering and his despair. He praised God for delivering him from death:

I said, In the prime of life, I am going to the gates of death.
The remainder of my years is taken away from me.
I will not see Jehovah, or man, anymore in the land of the living.
My life is to be folded up and put away like a shepherd's tent.
Through the night I thought, As a lion He crushes my bones.
I chattered like a bird, and moaned like a dove; my eyes give out from looking upward.
O Lord, I am oppressed; I will depend upon you.

What shall I say? He has both spoken to me and He Himself has answered my prayer.
I shall live my life deliberately, step by step, because of how close I came to death.
O Lord, by your gracious deeds men live, and in your kindness to me is the life of my spirit.
Behold, it was for the loss of my peace I was so bitter, but you have loved my soul and have
    saved it from the pit of destruction.
Those who are dead cannot praise thee, but the living can, as I do this day.

The Lord stands ready to save me. Therefore, I will sing my songs with stringed instruments,
    all the days of my life in the house of the Lord.

Messengers from Babylon
(2 Kings 20:12-19; 2 Chron. 32:25-31; Isa. 39:1-8):

Merodach-baladan of Babylon heard that Hezekiah had been ill and had recovered, so he sent him letters and a gift.

Merodach-baladan had led a rebellion against Assyria, and had set up an independent state in Babylon for a few years. He was driven out in about 710 B.C. About 703, he tried again to set up a kingdom. Finally, in 700 B.C., he fled from the Assyrians by sea. He left his family behind, but took with him his national gods and the bones of his ancestors (Joan Oats, Babylon, p. 116-117). He actively cultivated the friendship of anyone he thought might support him against the Assyrians.

The text says that when the envoys came from Babylon, the Lord left Hezekiah alone, to test him, to know everything that was in his heart. Hezekiah failed the test! His pride was lifted up, and he showed the messengers from Babylon all his wealth — the silver, the gold, the spices and fine oil, his armory, and everything found among his treasures. There was nothing he did not show them.

Then Isaiah went to King Hezekiah and asked, "What did those men say, and where did they come from?"

"From a distant land," Hezekiah replied. "They came from Babylon."

Isaiah asked, "What did they see in your palace?"

"They saw everything in my palace," Hezekiah said. "There is nothing among my treasures that I did not show them."

Then Isaiah said to Hezekiah, "Hear the word of the Lord: 'The time will surely come when everything in your palace, and all that your fathers have stored up until this day, will be carried to Babylon. Nothing will be left. And some of your descendants, your own flesh and blood, that will be born to you, will be taken away, and they will become eunuchs in the palace of the king of Babylon.'"

Hezekiah was not unduly troubled by this news because he thought, "Will there not be peace and security in my lifetime?" Remember this prophecy, however. We will watch as events unfold, and we will see it fulfilled.

An Interesting Prophecy:

As we stated earlier, Isaiah was the greatest of the Messianic prophets. There are more prophecies about Christ in Isaiah than in any other book. Christ is presented as the ideal servant of Jehovah who would come and fulfill all of God's purposes. Nothing — the wickedness of God's people, the Assyrian armies, the Babylonian armies, nor any other force — would stop God in accomplishing His purposes nor those of His ideal servant, the Christ.

Isaiah predicted other servants of God also. For example, Assyria served as a tool of God by punishing wicked Israel. Isaiah warns that Babylon will serve as a similar tool in punishing Judah. God had intended that Israel be His tool for good in the world to keep the knowledge of Jehovah alive, but Israel had not cooperated and had ignored the blessings from God and had turned away from Him. Therefore Israel and Judah must be chastised. But God's purpose for His people was not complete. He promises that they will be restored after their chastisement — not because of their righteousness, but because of His mercy.

Then comes a very interesting, very detailed prophecy. Remember that when Isaiah was doing his work in Jerusalem, the city was still standing. In fact, the Assyrian forces had not succeeded in entering the city at all. They had not even besieged it. But Isaiah predicts that God would give the decree that the city be "rebuilt" and even gives the name of the one who would do so — Cyrus. Isaiah says:

> God is the one who says of Jerusalem, 'It shall be inhabited,' of the towns of Judah, 'They shall be built,' and of their ruins, 'I will restore them,' who says to the watery deep, 'Be dry, and I will dry up your streams,' who says of *Cyrus*, 'He is my shepherd and will accomplish all that I please;' he will say of Jerusalem, 'Let it be rebuilt,' and of the temple, 'Let its foundations be laid.'" (See Isa. 44:24-45:7.)

Isaiah did his work in the years from 740 to about 700 or 690 B.C. The man Cyrus did not come on the scene of history until about 562 B.C., and he did not give the edict for the city of Jerusalem to be rebuilt until 538 B.C. That means this prophecy naming a specific man and his work was made nearly 200 years before it came to pass. Remember this prophecy. We will watch for its fulfillment.

Death of Hezekiah
(2 Kings 20:20-21; 2 Chron. 32:32-33):
Hezekiah lived the rest of his days in honor. When he died he was buried in the tombs of David's descendants (the kings). All Judah and the people of Jerusalem honored him.

Historical Note — The Assyrian Record:
At the first of the story of Hezekiah's struggles with Assyria, we said there were conflicts between the Bible account and the Assyrian account of the same struggles. We have looked carefully at the Biblical account in the information above, but before we leave the history, let us look briefly at what the Assyrian accounts say. Perhaps more archaeological research will help unravel the puzzle someday.

Sargon II ruled Assyria from 722-705 B.C. He took Israel away into captivity in 721 B.C. In the very next year (720 B.C.), he came back to put down a rebellion led by the king of Hamath. This revolt included those living in Damascus, Samaria, Gaza, and Egypt. The armies swept down the coastal plain and put a quick stop to an Egyptian force that met them at Gaza.
A few years passed, and in 715 B.C. (some say 711), Ashdod and Egypt tried another coalition. According to Assyrian records Judah, Edom, and Moab gave tentative support to this coalition, but they withdrew quickly when they saw the Assyrians approaching. This time Ashdod and neighboring towns fell, and old Philistia became an Assyrian province called Ashdod (see Isa. 20:1). Sargon claims to have been the "subjugator of the land of Judah" on this raid, but there is no evidence, either from the Assyrian records or the Bible, that he actually made any invasion of Judah. Hezekiah seems to have wisely given heed to the prophet Isaiah and others who warned not to join the rebellion.

One of the problems with chronology can easily be seen at this point by remembering that Sennacherib is said by the Bible to have invaded Judah in the fourteenth year of Hezekiah (2 Kings 18:13). But if Hezekiah began his reign in 727 B.C., then Sennacherib would have invaded in about 713. But historians are practically unanimous in dating the invasion of Sennacherib into Judah at 701 B.C. Such a date raises all kinds of problems. First, 701 was certainly not the fourteenth year of Hezekiah. Secondly, since the illness of Hezekiah coincided with the invasion of Sennacherib (Isa. 38:6), then he lived fifteen years after this conflict with the Assyrian king (Isa. 38:5). If we say that obviously Sennacherib's invasion was in 713 B.C., then we have the problem that according to Assyrian records, Sennacherib did not become king until 705 B.C. when his father Sargon died.

The death of Sargon was a signal for widespread rebellion among the countries under Assyria's thumb, including Judah (2 Kings 18:7). As the Assyrian accounts tell the story, their army came into the territory of Palestine and destroyed the mainland city of Tyre, and then Joppa, as they came down the coast. They met and defeated an Egyptian army that tried to stop them and then laid siege to Judah's walled cities. One branch of the army swept northeast toward Bethel, took all the cities still standing in the area, and turned south and shut up Jerusalem "like a bird in a cage." Another branch of the army devastated the countryside. They took a total of forty-six cities.

There is strong, though by no means conclusive, evidence from Assyrian records that there were two invasions of Sennacherib. According to this theory, the Assyrians defeated the Syrian, Philistine, and Egyptian allies, devastated the towns and villages of Judah, and surrounded Jerusalem long enough to force Hezekiah to pay tribute in the year 701 B.C. (2 Kings 18:13-16; 2 Chron. 32:1-8). Then, in another campaign, about fifteen years later, Sennacherib came again and suffered a crushing defeat shortly before his death — to which defeat no reference whatever is made in the Assyrian records, but which is recorded in the Bible (2 Kings 18:17-19:36). In the account given in 2 Kings, scholars think they find evidence for two invasions by comparing 18:13-16 and 18:17-19:36. In the first passage Hezekiah submits to Sennacherib and agrees to pay him tribute. In the second, Sennacherib is determined to force Hezekiah to submit. Since he had already submitted in 18:13-16, it is argued that this latter instance was a second invasion. On the other hand, it is entirely possible that when Sennacherib saw how completely he had things in hand, he decided to go ahead and bring Jerusalem under his power in spite of the tribute Hezekiah had paid.

If the events just described happened in 701 B.C., then it was about twenty years later that the death of Sennacherib, as described in 2 Kings 19:37 and Isaiah 37:38, occurred because he was slain according to the Babylonian Chronicle in 681 B.C. If there were two invasions, then Sennacherib's defeat occurred in about 686 B.C., only five years before his death. For further discussion, see Israel and the Nations by F.F. Bruce and Documents from Old Testament Times, edited by D. Winton Thomas.

Manasseh — 55 years (wicked)
(2 Kings 21:1-18; 2 Chron. 33:1-20)

Manasseh was only twelve years old when he began to rule. That means he had not been born at the time Hezekiah almost died, and the Lord added fifteen years to his life. That sounds as if the lineage of David was nearly broken when God said Hezekiah would die, but God does not forget His promises, nor does He become confused about whether the timing is right for an event to occur. God said Hezekiah was going to die before Hezekiah prayed; and yet God had said there would always be a son of David available to rule on his throne (2 Sam. 7:11-16). Therefore, there must have been an heir to the throne living when Hezekiah got sick. We have no idea what this heir's name was, nor what happened that made it necessary for a child of twelve to be made king.

Wickedness of Manasseh
(2 Kings 21:2-9; 2 Chron. 33:2-9):

Manasseh worshiped virtually every idol he could find. He followed all the practices of the nations which the Lord had driven out before the Israelites. He rebuilt the high places which Hezekiah had destroyed; he erected altars to Baal and even made an Asherah pole as Ahab the king of Israel had done; he worshiped the stars and put pagan altars in the temple where God had said He would put His Name. Manasseh even burned his own sons in the fire as an idolatrous sacrifice in the valley of the son of Hinnom. He practiced sorcery and divination.

God's promise had been given to David and to Solomon: "In this house and in Jerusalem, which I have chosen out of all the tribes of Israel, I will put my Name forever. I will not again make the feet of the Israelites wander from the land I gave their forefathers, *if only they will be careful to do everything I commanded them and will keep the whole Law that my servant Moses gave them*" (2 Kings 21:7-8). But neither Manasseh nor the people would listen.

Jehovah's Message Through His Servants, the Prophets
(2 Kings 21:10-15; 2 Chron. 33:10):

As He had always done, Jehovah sought to warn, to plead, to turn Judah back from the course leading to destruction, but they paid no heed. So Jehovah spoke through His prophets, saying: "Manasseh, king of Judah, has committed every abomination and has sinned more than the Amorites who were before him. He has led Judah into sin with his idols. Therefore I am going to bring such disaster upon Jerusalem and Judah that it will make the ears of everyone who hears it to tingle. I am going to measure Judah by the same standard I used against Samaria and against the house of Ahab. I will wipe Jerusalem as one wipes a dish, wiping it and turning it upside down. I will abandon the remnant of my inheritance and hand them over to their enemies. They will be looted and plundered by all their enemies, because they have done evil in my eyes, and have provoked me to anger from the day their forefathers came out of Egypt until this day."

Manasseh had crossed the line of God's patience. From this day forward, judgment upon Judah was inevitable. Even as late as the days of Jehoiakim, when the bands of the Chaldeans, Syrians, Moabites, and others were raiding Judah, the comment is made: "Surely at the commandment of Jehovah came this upon Judah, to remove them out of His sight, for all the sins of Manasseh, according to all that he did, and also for the innocent blood that he shed; for he filled Jerusalem with innocent blood: and Jehovah would not pardon" (2 Kings 24:2-4). Tradition has it that one of the innocent ones whose blood Manasseh shed was Isaiah. The Bible does not say. Certainly anyone who opposed Manasseh's sins was dealt with ruthlessly (2 Kings 21:16).

Manasseh's Captivity and Repentance
(2 Chron. 33:11-13):

Manasseh's reign of fifty-five years was the longest of any king in Israel or Judah, but we are told almost nothing about his history. Remember, this is a religious history of the nation. Therefore, whatever things he accomplished were of very little value, because he was so wicked he could not prosper in God's eyes.

Because of his wickedness, the commanders of the Assyrian army came and took Manasseh prisoner. They bound him with bronze shackles, put a hook in his nose, and led him away to prison in the city of Babylon.

This is all we are told about this story. No date is given, nor the name of the Assyrian king who took him. There were two kings it could have been. Esarhaddon succeeded his father Sennacherib to the throne in 681 B.C. and ruled until 669 B.C. when he was succeeded by his son Ashurbanipal. Manasseh ruled during the entire reign of Esarhaddon and well into the reign of Ashurbanipal, so it could have been either one. Both Assyrian kings mention Manasseh in their records, but only as a tributary, not as a captive. Neither does it help to know that he was taken to Babylon instead of Nineveh. Esarhaddon treated Babylon as a second capital. It continued to be an important city to the Assyrians during the reign of Ashurbanipal. It must be that Manasseh refused to pay the required tribute at some point and, therefore, angered the Assyrian ruler. Manasseh was carried away with hooks and fetters. A hook or ring was often placed in the lips or nose and fetters placed on the hands and feet.

In his trouble, Manasseh repented of his sins. The Bible says he "humbled himself greatly" before God and sought help from the Lord. God heard his prayer and brought him again to Jerusalem. Then Manasseh knew that Jehovah was truly God.

Do you see God's mercy once more? Manasseh was more wicked than all the kings of Judah that had preceded him. God was determined to punish the land for the wickedness that filled it at Manasseh's instigation. Manasseh had treated innocent men as cruelly as he himself was being treated at the hands of the Assyrians. Yet, when this man humbled himself and sought Jehovah, his prayer was heard and God's mercy was shown to him.

Manasseh's Efforts at Restoration
(2 Chron. 33:14-17):
Manasseh was allowed to return to Judah and to his kingdom. He added an outer wall to the city of David and strengthened the defenses of Jerusalem and of all the walled cities of Judah.

Much more importantly, Manasseh took away the strange gods, and the idol out of the house of the Lord, and the pagan altars which he had placed on the temple grounds and throughout Jerusalem. He built up the altar of the Lord and offered sacrifices upon it, and commanded Judah to serve Jehovah, the God of Israel.

The people continued to worship at the high places, but they worshiped only Jehovah. By this time, the people found it very easy to just change the name of the god they worshiped, and not miss a beat with their rituals. Needless to say, Manasseh did not effect any permanent overthrow of the evils he had introduced into Judah.

Amon — 2 years (wicked)
(2 Kings 21:19-26; 2 Chronicles 33:21-25)

Amon was twenty-two years old when he succeeded his father Manasseh. He reigned two years. He was very wicked and swiftly turned to the worship of idols. The Bible says he was just like Manasseh, except that he did not humble himself before the Lord as Manasseh had.

The servants of Amon conspired against him and slew him in his own house. He was buried in a sepulchre in the garden of Uzza. The people then executed the conspirators and placed Amon's son Josiah upon the throne.

It is so strange that one king could be as faithful as Hezekiah, and his son could be as wicked as Manasseh. Or a man like Manasseh could try to reform the evil he himself had introduced into the land, and yet his own son would follow and immediately lead his people right back into idolatry. How could such things happen?

Of course, there were many reasons. One is that the wives of kings lived in harems, or in separate houses, with their children. The kings did not have an intimate part in directing their children's education. Therefore, their own beliefs were not always taught to their children. By this time there were always very strong wicked influences all over the land. The heirs to the throne came nearer reflecting the views of their nurses and early tutors than of their fathers.

Josiah — 31 years (good)
(2 Kings 22:1-23:30; 2 Chron. 34:1-35:27)

Josiah was an outstanding king, perhaps the best king Judah ever had. He was only eight years old when he began to rule.

Josiah Begins to Purge the Land of Idolatry
(2 Chron. 34:1-7):

Someone had a marvelous influence upon this eight year old boy. In the eighth year of his rule, when he was only sixteen years old, he began to seek the God of David. Throughout his life he never varied from the ways of David his ancestor.

In the twelfth year of his reign, when he was twenty, he began to purge the country and Jerusalem itself of idolatry. The Asherah poles and altars of the Baalim had multiplied. Josiah destroyed them, plus the sun-images, and all the graven and molten images he could find. These images were broken up, ground to powder and sprinkled on the graves of those who had sacrificed to them. Josiah carried his campaign far afield from Judah, destroying altars and images even in the territories of Manasseh, Ephraim, Simeon, and even into Naphtali.

The Prophet Zephaniah
(The Book of Zephaniah)

At about this point, another prophet arises on the scene. Zephaniah arises to pronounces doom upon the wicked nation of Judah. God has already stated that judgment is inevitable because of the wickedness of Manasseh (2 Kings 21:10-15). Now Zephaniah says the same thing.

Zephaniah introduces himself by giving his lineage back four generations to Hezekiah. Since it was unusual for a prophet to give more than his father's name, it seems logical to assume that the Hezekiah listed was the good king Hezekiah. If so, then Zephaniah was of royal blood and a cousin of the young king Josiah. Zephaniah also says that he did his work during the reign of Josiah. That would place him during the years 640 to 609 when Josiah was ruling. His work likely started early in Josiah's reign, immediately after the wicked reigns of Manasseh and Amon, and before Josiah started his reformations in the land, because Zephaniah's message is one of doom. Judgment is coming! The chastisement will be severe!

Zephaniah has been called the hottest book in the Bible. There are calls to repentance, but even such calls were to give hope for refuge in the time of judgment, rather than hope for the avoidance of judgment. For example, look at 2:3. The prophet says: "Seek ye the Lord, all ye meek of the earth, which have wrought his judgment; seek righteousness, seek meekness: it may be ye shall be hid in the day of the Lord's anger." It seemed too late for reformation; the day of Jehovah's wrath had arrived.

Judgment upon the Whole World, Judah in Particular (1:1-18):

The prophet begins with a pronouncement of severe judgment upon the whole world: Everything will be utterly swept away. Every civilization of man will be brought to nought.

Then God turns to Judah and Jerusalem, and pronounces their doom also. They had sinned and God was about to send His judgment. Their sin was religious apostasy. The Baal worship, the star worship, the Molech worship, and the false, ritualistic Jehovah worship would all be cut off. "The day of the Lord is at hand. The Lord has prepared His sacrifice and has invited His guests to come." All classes of people will be punished. Neither rank nor riches would protect them from God's judgment. Even the complacent would fall under the scourge. There were some in Judah saying, "The Lord does not care. He will do nothing, either good or bad," but that group would fall also.

Verses 14-18 of chapter 1 give one of the most striking descriptions of the day of the Lord to be found in the prophets. "That day will be a day of wrath, a day of distress and anguish, a day of trouble and ruin, a day of darkness and gloom, a day of clouds and blackness, a day of trumpet and battle cry against the fortified cities and against the corner towers. I will bring distress on the people and they will walk like blind men, *because they have sinned against the Lord.* Neither their silver nor their gold will be able to deliver them in the day of Jehovah's wrath. The whole land will be devoured by the fires of His jealousy." How chilling such a message should have been to the right-thinking people in Judah!

Remember that "the day of the Lord" always refers to a day of judgment in the prophets. In this case, it is primarily judgment upon Judah, but in addition, judgment to all the wicked nations.

Exhortation to Repentance and Perseverance (2:1-3:8):

Therefore the call goes out to gather to seek the Lord. Gather before the appointed time arrives, before the fierce anger of Jehovah comes upon you. Seek the Lord, all you humble of the land. Perhaps God will hide you when the time of judgment comes.

Then the prophet turns again to the nations around. Philistia will be destroyed; none will be left. Moab and Ammon will be destroyed, because God has been listening to the insults they have hurled against His people through all the preceding years. The remnant of God's people will dwell in these lands. Ethiopia (or Cush) will fall by the sword. Even mighty Nineveh and the Assyrians will fall. God will stretch His hand out over the north, and Nineveh will be left utterly desolate and dry as the desert. Nineveh was so proud she thought she could not be brought down, but she would become no more than the lair of wild animals, so that all who pass by will scoff at her.

Now the message returns to Jerusalem, that wicked city of oppressors, rebellious and defiled! "Woe to her that is rebellious and polluted." She had refused to obey the voice of God and had turned in the opposite direction. Judah's civic and spiritual leaders — the priests, the judges, and the prophets — had led in the wickedness. They had watched Jehovah cut off the nations around them; they had seen strongholds fall. God had hoped Judah would learn the lessons from the surrounding destructions and would turn back to Him. He said, "Surely you will fear me and accept correction!" Then her dwelling would not be cut off and God's punishments would not come upon her — but they did not learn. They were still eager to act corruptly in all they did.

"Therefore wait for me," declares the Lord, "For the day of judgment has come. I will assemble the nations and gather the kingdoms to pour out my fierce wrath upon them. The whole world will be consumed by the fire of my jealous anger."

After the Judgment, Salvation and Glorification for the Remnant (3:9-20):

But here in the midst of such dark predictions, there is a ray of hope for God's people. Judgment is coming upon all wickedness, but God will have a remnant of faithful people. God declares He will purify the lips of all those who call upon Him and who serve Him. The day will come when He will call His faithful remnant, and will bring them back to His holy hill. The haughty and wicked will be purged, but the meek and humble will be left to inherit. Sing, shout aloud, rejoice, you remnant. The Lord has turned back your punishment, and you will live secure once more. The Lord is mighty to save and He will take great delight in you.

In each of the prophets, there is a similar promise of a remnant who would return to the land. This would be the group who learned the lesson of God's judgment and turned back to Him in faithful service. We will watch as the history progresses, and in the next book of the series, we will see that remnant return after the captivity.

God promised great blessings to that remnant that He could not carry out to their fullest extent, because even that remnant did not serve Him as they should. Therefore, from that physical remnant God had an even smaller remnant that He could bless — a spiritual remnant of those who would truly serve Him and accept His rulership. That is the spiritual Israel spoken of in the New Testament. All the faithful since the days of Christ fall into this spiritual remnant. No group of Jews has any right to hope to return to their homeland as a fulfillment of these prophecies. The Jews were punished as the prophets foretold; then a remnant was allowed to return as predicted; and from that group the Christ came and offered all mankind the right to be part of the spiritual remnant. That spiritual remnant will be God's inheritance out of all the universe.

The Prophet Jeremiah
(The Book of Jeremiah)

Jeremiah is more historical than any other prophetic book. Not only is his book filled with historical notes, the message itself is completely interwoven with the history of the country. Therefore, we need to give Jeremiah's book more attention than we have given the other prophetic books. We are giving a very brief outline of the whole book, then we will summarize the first twenty chapters here. The rest of Jeremiah will be dealt with in its historical context.

Again — A Warning:

Just before the summary of the book of Isaiah, we gave a warning to be careful not to lose your perspective in the study. This is a study of the *history* of the divided kingdom. Israel has fallen, and now Judah is about to fall. It is very important to understand that the prophets fit into this period of history. One cannot truly understand the history itself without understanding the messages that the prophets were bringing from God, and one cannot understand the prophets without knowing the conditions of the people around them. *But to interrupt the study here for a detailed study of any one of the prophets, would make you lose sight of the primary thread of your study!* Use this introduction to the book of Jeremiah as a foundation, a skeleton, for a later detailed study of the book. It is the over-all picture of Bible history that we have missed too many times in our Bible classes.

The Prophet Himself:

Jeremiah was a priest, the son of Hilkiah. There is a priest named Hilkiah who plays a prominent role in the story of Josiah, probably as the High Priest of his day. Almost certainly, Jeremiah is his son, though it could not be definitely proven. His home was Anathoth, a few miles northeast of Jerusalem.

The personality of Jeremiah comes shining through his writings. He was a truly good man who cared deeply for the ways of his God, and for the welfare of his people. He was a man of great sensitivity, very meek, but possessed of great courage.

Jeremiah was given what must have been one of the most difficult tasks anyone ever had. When his nation was being ground under the foot of Babylon, his task was to tell the people: "Do not resist the Chaldeans; you cannot win. Jehovah says for you to give up and submit to the king of Babylon." He had to preach a message which made him appear a traitor to his people. That he was right meant nothing to the wicked of Judah, and offered scant comfort to Jeremiah.

Be alert to the interchangeable use of the names "Chaldean" and "Babylonian." Both names refer to the same kingdom, the same people.

Outline of Jeremiah:

I. Prophecies regarding Judah and the kingdom of God (chapters 1-45):
    A. The prophet's call (chapter 1)
    B. Condemnation of Judah and Jerusalem (chapters 2-29)
        1. Discourses and visions regarding Judah and Jerusalem (chapters 2-20)
        2. Charges against the rulers (chapters 21-24)
        3. Sentence described (chapters 25-29)
    C. Promise of restoration (chapters 30-33)
    D. Penalty inflicted (chapters 34-45)
        1. Last years of the kingdom (chapters 34-38)
        2. Destruction of Jerusalem (chapter 39)
        3. Wretched remnant (chapters 40-45)

II. Judgment against the nations (chapters 46-51)
    A. Egypt (chapter 46)
    B. Philistines (chapter 47)
    C. Moab (chapter 48)
    D. Ammon (49:1-6)
    E. Edom (49:7-22)
    F. Damascus (49:23-27)

    G. Kedar and Hazor (49:28-33)
    H. Elam (49:34-39)
    I. Babylon (chapters 50-51

III.   Captivity of Judah (chapter 52)

Summary of Jeremiah 1-20

The Prophet's Call (chapter 1):

Jehovah called Jeremiah to preach in the thirteenth year of King Josiah. God continued to speak through the prophet until Jerusalem was carried away into captivity, a period of about forty years. Before Jeremiah was born, God planned a special task for him: "I have appointed you a prophet unto the nations."

Jeremiah said, "I don't know how to speak, for I am a child."

The Lord replied, "Do not say, 'I am a child,' because you will go where I send, and you will say what I give you. Do not be afraid, because I will be with you to deliver you from danger."

The Lord reached His hand out and touched Jeremiah's mouth, and said, "Look, I have put my words in your mouth. I have set you over the nations to destroy and to overthrow, to build and to plant."

The Lord asked Jeremiah: "What do you see?"

Jeremiah answered, "I see an almond tree (a *shaked*, pronounced shah ked)."

Making a play on words, the Lord said, "Yes, and I will watch (*shoked*, a different word but pronounced shah ked) my word to see that it is done."

The second time the Lord said, "What do you see, Jeremiah?"

This time Jeremiah saw a boiling cauldron, and it was set to pour out its scalding contents from the north. Jehovah said, "Out of the north, I will bring calamity on the land of Judah and the city of Jerusalem, because they have forsaken me and have worshiped other gods."

God told Jeremiah, "Do not be dismayed when the people oppose you, for I will be with you."

Israel Forsook God, as a Bride Her Husband (2:1-3:5):

The Lord said, "Tell the people of Jerusalem, that I remember the former days of Israel when, as a bride very much in love with her husband, you followed me."

Jehovah wants to know, "What unrighteous thing have I done to make you leave me?" After all God did for Israel in those early days, yet they sought Him not and turned aside to idols.

Therefore the Lord will contend with His people. He says, "Look around from the desert to the far islands of the sea: has any nation ever changed its gods? But my people have done two evil things: they have abandoned me, and have hewn them water tanks in the rocks, tanks which are cracked and can hold no water [idols]." The Lord says, "Do you know why everyone is seeking to harm you? You have brought it upon yourselves, by abandoning me. Your kings, your priests, and prophets have brought shame upon you; they say to a stump: 'You are my father,' and to a rock: 'You brought me forth.'"

Judah had persisted in seeking help from Egypt and in negotiating with Assyria. But there is no help for them as long as they remain polluted and sinful.

Though a woman put away from a man, a woman who has since taken other lovers, cannot return to her husband (Deut. 24:1-4), yet God offers to take Israel back. He beseeches her to return, but she has a "harlot's forehead." Israel has made her choices.

Judah's Conduct Worse Than Israel's (3:6-4:2):

In the days of Josiah, God told Jeremiah to observe what had happened to Israel: "She has played the harlot, and I hoped she would return to me, but she did not. I had to put her away and give to her a bill of divorcement. Treacherous Judah saw what happened, and went right on and became worse than Israel."

The Lord called upon Judah to return. He said He would give them shepherds who would lead them properly. Jerusalem would be called the throne of Jehovah. Judah would walk with Israel from the north, and return to the land God gave their fathers for an inheritance.

Judah had not fit with the plans God made for them. They had dealt treacherously with Him. Jeremiah voices his confession for his people, but, unfortunately, it was a chorus of only one voice.

Threat of Overwhelming Punishment if Judah Does not Repent (4:3-6:30):

Jehovah warns Judah to repent, or else His wrath will go out against them. Calamity is on its way from the north. The lion has left his thicket. A wind is blowing toward Jerusalem, not to winnow or to cleanse, but to destroy. "Your deeds have brought these things upon you."

The whole land will be a wreck. "When you are desolate, what will you do? Put on your make-up to attract your lovers? They will despise you."

"Quickly, run through the streets of Jerusalem, and find a man who does what is right and who speaks the truth so I can forgive the city."

Jeremiah found no one. Then he said, "These are the poor who do not know the way of Jehovah. I will seek among the great," but he found that no one obeyed God.

Do you remember that only ten righteous souls could have saved Sodom and Gomorrah from destruction (Gen. 18:16-32)? But the ten could not be found. Now, God is asking for only one — and Jeremiah cannot find that one — whether among the common people or among the great.

Because of the sins of Judah God says, "I will make my words in your mouth fire, and this people wood, and it shall burn them up."   After painting a picture of Judah's guilt, the Lord says, "An unbelievable, horrible thing has happened in the land: the prophets prophesy falsely, and the priests rule as they are paid — and my people love it that way."

The siege of Jerusalem is predicted. The enemy will thoroughly glean Judah. Jeremiah says, "To whom can I tell these things? No one will listen. I am full of the wrath of Jehovah; I am tired of holding it in. The whole land is corrupt, from the prophet to the priest, who say, 'Peace, peace,' when there is no peace. When they committed abomination, were they ashamed? No, not at all. They could not even blush."

Jeremiah calls upon the people to seek the old ways and walk in them, but the people say, "No, we will not walk in them." Therefore punishment is on its way. "Men gather their weapons; they are cruel, and they ride against you, O daughter of Zion."

Jeremiah Commanded to Speak to the Worshipers at the Temple (7:1-10:25):

God told Jeremiah to go to the gate to the Lord's house and tell them: "Listen, you who worship Jehovah: change your ways, and I will cause you to stay here. But do not think, 'The temple of Jehovah is among us. That will not save you.' Only if you repent, will I let you stay in the land."

God warns His people not to trust in lying words uttered by false prophets. Their idolatry and stubbornness would be punished. And if they thought merely having the temple among them would save, then take a look at Shiloh where the tabernacle was first located in the land. "I will cast you out of my sight, as I have cast out all your brethren, even the whole seed of Ephraim."

Shiloh was the place where the tabernacle was set up when the Israelites conquered the land under Joshua (Josh. 18:1). It remained the center of their worship until the days of Eli (1 Sam. 1:3). The people of Eli's day were wicked, and God allowed the Philistines to defeat the Israelites, and to capture the ark of the covenant (1 Sam. 4:1-11). Though Shiloh was not destroyed at that time (see 1 Sam. 14:3), it was never again the gathering place for the people. The history does not tell of Shiloh's destruction, but it is evident from this passage in Jeremiah that it met its end by the plan of God.

God tells Jeremiah, "Do not pray in behalf of this people; I will not listen." They must repent and learn again to obey. "Making burnt offerings is not what makes you my people, but obeying my voice."

After telling of the treachery and brazen, shameless disobedience of Judah, Jeremiah says, "Oh that my head were waters, and mine eyes a fountain of tears, that I might weep day and night for the slain of the daughter of my people."

In chapter 10, the false gods are contrasted with Jehovah. Men will pick out a tree, and cut it and shape it. Then they plate it with silver and gold. It is still a stump. In contrast, God made the world and sustains the creation.

Jeremiah cries to God, and says, "O Jehovah, I know that the way of man is not in himself. It is not in man who walks to direct his own steps." He asks God to correct him by measure, not in anger, lest he be brought to nothing.

A Conspiracy Against God and Against Jeremiah (chapters 11-12):

The Lord says Judah has not kept the covenant God made with them when He brought them out of the burning furnace of Egypt. At that time He said, "Obey my word, and do all that I command you, and in this way you will be my people, and I will be your God" (see Exod. 19:5-6). But a conspiracy is found among the men of Judah. They have turned back to the iniquities of their ancestors and have broken the covenant I made with their fathers.

Therefore God tells Jeremiah not to pray for them, because He will not hear. They no longer belong in God's house because they are polluted through sin.

Jehovah warned Jeremiah of a plot against his life, one planned by the men of Anathoth — Jeremiah's own town — because of his condemnation of the priests. God says, "I will see your vengeance taken upon them." God says there will be no remnant of them.

One of the reasons Jeremiah was hated so badly was that he was one of the priests, yet he condemned the priests so graphically. As a priest he was well acquainted with the practices and teachings of the priests, and he was well known among them and to the king.

In chapter 12 Jeremiah asks about the prosperity of the wicked. "How long," he asks, "will the wicked dwell in the land?"

God replies that calamity was already coming, but it would not compare with what was yet to come. God would pluck up Judah's evil neighbors as well as Judah. Then He would give each one the chance to learn His ways. Otherwise, if they did not, then that nation would be destroyed.

Judah Alone

The Marred Girdle (chapter 13):

God told Jeremiah to buy a girdle or sash. He wore it for a time, but did not wash it according to God's instructions. Then God had him to go to the Euphrates and hide it in the crack of a rock and leave it. Many days later Jehovah told Jeremiah to go get the girdle from its hiding place. When he did, he found it was fit for nothing. [*Of course, the Euphrates was chosen, because that is where the Babylonian kingdom was.*]

Jehovah said, "I took this people to cleave to me as a sash for their praise and glory, but they would not hear. Therefore I will mar their pride and glory as this sash."

Drought and a Prayer for Mercy; Jehovah Says No (chapters 14-15):

A time of terrible drought came upon Judah, and Jeremiah set out to pray and beseech God for mercy. The Lord answered, "Do not pray for this people, for I plan to consume them, by the sword, and by the famine, and by the plague."

Jeremiah said the false prophets were telling the people, "You won't see the sword; you won't have famine. You will have peace from God."

But Jehovah said, "Yes, but they lie. I have not spoken to them. Moreover, by sword and famine will those prophets be consumed."

Jeremiah eloquently pressed his case for God's mercy. But God replied, "Even if Moses and Samuel stood before me, I would not be favorable to this people. I will cause them to be scattered far and wide because of what Manasseh the son of Hezekiah did."

Jeremiah Commanded Not to Marry (chapters 16-17):

Jehovah commanded Jeremiah not to marry because of the distress that would come upon the children of the people. "They shall die grievous deaths."

"Do not go to mourn or lament. I have taken peace away from this people. There will be so much death, there will be no opportunity for lamenting. Neither will there be feasting or mirth."

A time of restoration is mentioned, but first must come chastisement because of iniquity and sin.

The sin of Judah is written with a pen of iron and the point of a diamond upon the tablets of their hearts, as they remember their altars and their groves.

Foolish are those who depend upon themselves. Only the Lord can be depended upon.

Jeremiah prayed to God, "Save me, Lord, because you are my praise. The people say to me, 'Where is the word of the Lord? Let it come now.' Let them be put to shame who persecute me, but let me not be ashamed."

The Lord told him to go stand in the gates where the king and the people went in and out, and tell them that the sabbath must be kept. If they obey, they will be blessed; if not, "I will kindle a fire which shall devour the palaces of Jerusalem."

The Potter's Vessel (chapter 18):

The Lord told Jeremiah to go to the potter's house, and there He would give him a message. So Jeremiah went to the potter and watched him at work. The potter would put a lump of clay on the wheel and work it with his hands. He might start out to make a pretty vase. If he messed it up, he would simply wad the clay back up and mold it into another vessel, a pot or something else.

The Lord said, "O house of Israel, can I not do with you as this potter? As clay in the potter's hand, so are you in my hand, O Israel." The Lord could do as He wished. If a nation were evil, He could destroy it, but if it repented, then, like the potter, God could change His mind and do something else with it.

Judah Alone

The Broken Vessel; Pashhur's Reaction (chapters 19-20):

Jehovah had Jeremiah to buy a pottery vessel and gather the elders of the people and of the priests to Topheth. There Jeremiah was to tell them: "This is what Jehovah says: 'I am going to bring calamity upon this place because Israel has forsaken me and worshiped Baal, and have burned their sons in the fire for burnt-offerings to Baal. Therefore the day will come when this place will not be called Topheth, or the valley of the son of Hinnom, but the valley of Slaughter. I will give the dead bodies of the people of this city to feed the birds. I will cause this people to eat their sons and daughters during the siege."

God told Jeremiah that at that point he was to break the bottle and say, "Even so will I break this people and this city, so that no one can put it together again, and they will bury in Topheth till there is no place to bury."

After doing these things, Jeremiah came to the court of the temple and said, "Jehovah says He is going to bring all the calamity He has spoken of upon this city and upon all of the towns in the land, because the people are stubborn and will not hear."

Pashhur, son of Immer the priest, chief officer in the temple, heard Jeremiah, and put him in the stocks near the temple. He left him overnight. The next day, when Pashhur released him, Jeremiah said, "Jehovah has not called your name Pashhur [*Free*] but Magor-missabib [*Terror on every side*]." Jeremiah proceeded to tell Pashhur that he and everything he had would be carried to Babylon. He said, "You will go to Babylon, and there you will die, and there you will be buried, you and all your friends to whom you have prophesied falsely."

Following this is one of the most poignant pictures of the inner struggles of a servant of God to be found in all the Bible. Jeremiah feels that all he preaches is, "Violence and Destruction." His preaching causes him to suffer depression all day long. "But if I say, I will not speak any more, then there is in my heart as it were a burning fire shut up in my bones, and I am weary with containing it."

Jeremiah was so distressed he wished he had never been born. Nevertheless, he was faithful to his mission for over forty years.

Historical Note About Assyria:

Assyria was having troubles of her own at this same time. Ashurbanipal was the last strong king of Assyria. There had been many revolts through the years, but Assyria had been able to put them down and hold her supremacy over the world of that day. But the end was in sight. Ashurbanipal died in about 633 B.C., while King Josiah was still a child in Judah.

The revolts continued. Assyria was pressed on all sides. Egypt continually strove for independence. To the east, a people called the Medes were growing in strength. Arab tribes from the desert came in to plunder the lands of eastern Palestine and Syria. It was evident that the kings of Assyria could not hold the empire together much longer.

In 625 B.C., shortly after Josiah had begun his first reforms, and Zephaniah and Jeremiah had begun their work, a Chaldean prince named Nabopolassar managed to gain independence for Babylon. Some thirteen years later, in 612 B.C., the Babylonians joined with the Medes and besieged the city of Nineveh. The city fell after only three months, never to be built again. Another decisive battle, at Carchemish, marked the final downfall of Assyria.

All troops had to be called from the provinces to protect Nineveh during these last struggles.

Therefore, the provinces such as Judah were free by default. King Josiah was able to take at least nominal control of most of the land of Canaan. Archaeologists say the city of Megiddo came under his control at this time and became his administrative headquarters for control of the northern section of the land.

We have included a summary of the complete fall of Assyria at this point, but its end did not happen overnight. We will refer back to this information as we proceed with the history of Josiah and his kingdom. At this point, Ashurbanipal has been dead in Nineveh for about eight years; Nabopolassar has rebelled and has set up an independent state in Babylon; Josiah is now a young man and has started purging his land; Zephaniah and Jeremiah have begun their work of prophecy.

The Prophet Nahum
(The Book of Nahum)

Another prophet must be considered before we move forward in our story. Nahum cries out in prophetic exultation — "Nineveh is fallen!" There is no mention of Judah's need for repentance. It is a joyful message to the people of Judah, not just because an enemy is falling, but as an assurance that God is just and is avenging the wickedness of Assyria.

The exact date of Nahum is not known. He mentions the destruction of the Egyptian city of Thebes (or No-Amon) as an accomplished fact, which places the book after 663 B.C. when the Assyrians destroyed that city. The fall of Nineveh was in 612 B.C., so the book was written somewhere between these two dates. We are placing it here in the early days of Josiah, making the date between 640 and 620.

The little book can be easily outlined. The first chapter is a triumphant song over the impending fall of Nineveh. The second chapter describes the destruction that is to come. And the third chapter tells of the guilt of the city.

Doom of Nineveh is Decreed by God (chapter 1):

Chapter 1 presents the two-fold nature of God. "Behold the goodness and the severity of God" (Rom. 11:22). God is jealous, an avenging God who never lets His enemies go unpunished. Yet, it is not an unreasonable, quick flaring up of temper. The Lord is slow to wrath, but the judgment will surely come. Nothing is too hard for the all-powerful God. His way is in the whirlwind and in the storm. The clouds are to God as the clouds of dust a man stirs up as he walks along. The rich lands of Bashan, Carmel, and Lebanon would dry up if the Lord so willed. The mountains and hills quake before Him. "Who can stand before His indignation?"

Yet this same God is a stronghold in the time of trouble to those who trust in Him. He is good. He will destroy His enemies as in an overwhelming flood. Assyria's whole history was one of rebellion to God, therefore they would be cut down. God had used Assyria to punish Judah for her wickedness, but now the time has come for Assyria to be punished, and God assures Judah it will be done. There will not even be descendants of Assyria to bear her name.

Look, Judah! There comes one over the mountains, bringing the good news about the fall of Nineveh. Gather together and celebrate your feast days — because your enemy is defeated!

Siege and Destruction of Nineveh — Decreed by God (chapter 2):

"Nineveh, guard the fortress; watch the road; brace yourselves; marshal all your strength, for destruction is coming. The shields of his soldiers are red; the warriors are clad in scarlet. The metal on the chariots flashes on the day they are made ready; the spears of pine are brandished. The chariots storm through the streets, rushing back and forth through the squares. They look like flaming torches; they dart about like lightning."

Destruction is everywhere. The people of Nineveh cry, "Stop! Stop!" — but none will listen. Instead they plunder the silver and plunder the gold. The city is pillaged, plundered, stripped! Hearts melt, knees give way, bodies tremble, and every face grows pale. Where now is the cruelty of Assyria? They were the lion who devoured others, and now their turn has come. The Lord says, "I am against you, O Nineveh!"

Nineveh's Sins and her Inevitable Doom (chapter 3):

But the punishment was deserved. God had not acted unjustly. Nineveh was a city full of blood, of lies, of plunder, and victims. Therefore, the crack of whips, the clatter of wheels, the galloping of horses, and jolting of chariots will be heard. There will be many casualties, piles of dead, bodies without number, people stumbling over corpses — all because of the wanton lust of a harlot — a wicked city who had been known for her cruelty. Now God was going to strip her naked, and let all the nations see her filthiness. All will flee when her shame is revealed. No one will stay to defend her.

Nineveh's destruction would be no worse than she deserved. The Lord asks, "Are you better than No-Amon (or Thebes)?" Thebes had been the capital city of Egypt from 711 to 663 B.C. It was a powerful city with a huge territory. Yet that powerful city had been cruelly destroyed by Ashurbanipal. The Lord draws a lesson. If you could destroy that powerful rival, are you immune to similar destruction? God answers His own question: "You are not immune! You will be as a drunk person, unable to control your actions. Your strongholds will be as easily shaken loose as ripe fruit on a tree. Your people will be seized by panic and will be like defenseless women. In order to avoid complete destruction, you will throw open your gates in surrender to your enemies."

Therefore, O Nineveh, prepare for battle. Draw water for a siege; strengthen your defenses; because the battle is coming. The fire will devour you. Gather a large army — but, though there are many, they will flee in the heat of the battle. The merchants, the crowned, the captains — all shall flee. All are dead — never to rise again. The city is destroyed and will never be rebuilt. All that hear the report will clap their hands in joy and mockery. There will be none to pity, because all nations have been harassed by wicked Assyria.

Josiah Commands that the Temple be Repaired
(2 Kings 22:3-7; 2 Chron. 34:8-13):

In the eighteenth year of his reign, having cleansed the land and the temple of the trappings of idolatry, Josiah sent Shaphan the son of Azaliah, Maaseiah the governor of the city, and Joah the chronicler to repair the house of Jehovah. They went to Hilkiah the high priest and took the money which had been collected, and delivered it to the workmen.

This money had been collected from those even of Manasseh, Ephraim, and all the remnant of Israel as well as from Judah. Yet this was the money brought into the house of God which had been taken up by the Levites, the keepers of the threshold. Therefore, some people from the north (the very poor Israelites left, plus the mixed race living in the territory) were coming to the temple of Jehovah. This is one of the passages that lets us know that Josiah must have exercised a great deal of control over old Israel, now that Assyria was declining fast. Josiah had the de facto rule over virtually the whole land of Israel by this time.

The workers repaired and restored the temple, purchasing dressed stone, timber for joists, and beams for the buildings. All this was needed because the kings of Judah had allowed the temple to fall into ruin. The workers did their work faithfully.

Book of the Law Found
(2 Kings 22:8-13; 2 Chron. 34:14-21):

When Hilkiah went in to bring out the money from the house of God, he found "the book of the law of Jehovah given by Moses" (literally "by the hand of Moses"). Hilkiah told Shaphan the scribe, "I have found the Book of the Law in the temple of the Lord."

The book of the law would be the portion we call the Pentateuch — that is, Genesis through Deuteronomy. Some have speculated that this was the copy of the law written by Moses himself. The Bible tells that when Moses finished recording the law he prepared a copy of it to be placed with the ark of the covenant. "And it came to pass, when Moses had made an end of writing the words of this law in a book, until they were finished, that Moses commanded the Levites, that bare the ark of the covenant of Jehovah, saying, 'Take this book of the law, and put it by the side of the ark of the covenant of Jehovah your God, that it may be there for a witness against thee'" (Deut. 31:24-26). The expression, "by the hand of Moses," could mean this was the very copy written by Moses, but not necessarily. Even a copy of the original would have been viewed as having been given by the hand of Moses, because it was the substance of the material written that was important, not whose handwriting it was.

When the ark of the covenant was put into the new temple in Solomon's day, the only things with it were the two tables of stone which Moses received in the mount with Jehovah (1 Kings 8:9). This copy of the law that was found was a scroll, not the tables of stone. The copy of the complete law, which Moses left as a witness, must have been lost at some time. It is not surprising that such a thing happened, because the ark of God had already been misused by the days of Solomon. Since that time, there have been several rulers who despised God's word and completely neglected the temple (for example, Jehoram, Athaliah, Ahaz, and Manasseh). We shudder to think what may have been done to the ark during this time.

Shaphan took the scroll with him when he went to the king to report the progress of the repair work on the temple. Shaphan reported that the money had been given to the workmen as ordered, and that the work was moving forward. Then he said, "Hilkiah the priest has given me a book he found." And he opened it and began reading from it.

Surely, in view of the reforms Josiah had initiated, and in the light of the strong support of such men as Jeremiah, Zephaniah, Hilkiah, and Shaphan, we must conclude that they already knew something of the law of God. It is equally clear, however, that Josiah had <u>never</u> heard the passage which was read to him from the law. We are not told what passage was read, nor how much was read, but try reading Deuteronomy 28:15-68 or Leviticus 26:14-45, imagining yourself to be a conscientious young king of

Judah.

When Josiah heard the words of the law, he rent his clothes in distress. He was terrified! He knew that Judah's cup of wickedness had overflowed! Were these terrible consequences described in the law about to begin? He desperately wanted to know.

Josiah commanded Hilkiah, Shaphan, Shaphan's son Ahikam, Abdon, and Asaiah the king's servant, saying, "Go; inquire of Jehovah for me and for those left in Israel and in Judah, concerning the words of the book that has been found, for great is the wrath of Jehovah that is about to be poured out upon us because our fathers have not kept the words of this book."

Ahikam was a supporter of Jeremiah (Jer. 26:24), and the father of Gedaliah who was appointed governor of the captives Nebuchadnezzar left in Judah in 586 B.C. (2 Kings 25:22; Jer. 39:14).

Josiah's men went to Huldah, a prophetess who was living in the lower city (second quarter) of Jerusalem. They asked her according to Josiah's orders.

She replied, "This is what Jehovah says: Tell the man who sent you that the Lord says, 'Behold I am going to bring calamity upon this place, and upon its inhabitants, even all the curses that are written in the book which has been read before the king of Judah. I will do this because they have forsaken me and have burned incense unto other gods, that they might provoke me to anger. Therefore my wrath will be poured out upon this place, and it shall not be quenched.'

"But also tell the king of Judah who sent you," Huldah continued, "that God says, 'Concerning these words you have heard, because your heart was tender, you humbled yourself before God when you heard His words against this place and against its inhabitants: you humbled yourself and rent your clothes, and wept before me, I also have heard you. Behold, I will gather you to your fathers, and you will go to your grave in peace. Your eyes will not see all the calamity which I will bring upon this place and upon its inhabitants.'"

Josiah's messengers returned and gave him the news. Though Josiah dreaded the calamities that would fall upon Judah, he was glad that, because of his seeking the Lord, he would be spared. Josiah therefore redoubled his efforts to serve the Lord and to try to turn the hearts of his people back to Jehovah.

Covenant Renewed with Jehovah
(2 Kings 23:1-3; 2 Chron. 34:29-32):

Josiah commanded the elders of Judah to come together. Then he and all the leaders and the people, small and great, went up to the temple and renewed their covenant with God.

This was the fourth time the covenant had been renewed since the kingdom divided. It was done in the days of Asa (2 Chron. 15:12); in the days of Jehoiada when the child Joash was made king (2 Kings 11:17); in the days of Hezekiah (2 Chron. 29:10); and now in Josiah's day.

Josiah read the book of the law that had been found in the hearing of all the people. Then he renewed his covenant with God — promising to "follow the Lord and keep his commands, regulations and decrees with all his heart and all his soul, and to obey the words of the covenant written in this book." The people joined with him in the pledge, renewing their covenant also.

A Further Description of Josiah's Fight Against Idolatry (2 Kings 23:4-20; 23:24-25; 2 Chron. 34:33):

There had already been an effort on Josiah's part to rid the land of Judah of all its idolatrous objects. Now he goes back out over his land to complete the process. The account given in 2 Kings 23 is a summary of all the things of this nature that Josiah did, including things done before the cleansing and repair of the temple, as well as things done afterward.

The various vessels of Baal and Asherah were burned in the fields of the Kidron. This was probably done northeast of the wall of Jerusalem where the Kidron valley opens out into a wide area. The ashes of the vessels were then taken to Bethel where Jeroboam set up the golden calves to worship many years earlier.

Josiah removed the idolatrous priests who had offered incense in the high places and those who had offered incense to Baal, to the sun, moon, the zodiac, and to all the host of heaven. He brought the Asherah pole out of the house of the Lord, burned it, beat it to dust, and scattered the dust over the graves of those who had worshiped it. The idolaters are here referred to as the "children of the people," meaning those who acted like the children of the surrounding nations instead of the children of God.

Josiah destroyed the houses of the Sodomites. These were the mutilated males who served as "priests" to those who came to practice the licentious worship of the Asherah. The women wove hangings which partitioned off areas where the ritual fornication was practiced. How outrageous that such things were being done in the house where God had chosen to put His name!

The valley of Topheth is thought to have been located just outside the city wall of Jerusalem, where the valley of the son of Hinnon and the valley of the Kidron joined. Here Ahaz and Manasseh had offered their children to Molech, causing them to "pass through the fire" (2 Kings 16:3; 21:6). Josiah defiled the site so that it would no longer be used in such worship.

Josiah took away the horses dedicated to the sun and burned the chariots of the sun with fire. Idolatrous altars made by Ahaz and Manasseh were destroyed. Even the high places Solomon had built for his wives — for Ashtoreth the abomination of the Phoenicians, for Chemosh the abomination of Moab, and for Milcom the abomination of the children of Ammon — Josiah defiled.

Josiah went to Bethel where Jeroboam the son of Nebat had set up the golden calves. He broke down the altar and the high place and burned the Asherah pole. As the king turned, he caught sight of the sepulchers which were in the mount. He had the bones taken out of the sepulchers and burned upon the altar.

Then the king said, "What is that monument there which I see?"

The men of the city replied, "It is the sepulchre of the man of God who foretold that you would burn the bones of the priests upon this altar — the very things you have been doing."

Josiah said, "Let him alone. Let no man move his bones." So they left his bones and the bones of the old prophet of Samaria who had deceived the man of God and caused his death. Thus, in his zeal for the Lord, Josiah fulfilled a prophecy about himself that had been made three hundred years earlier (see 1 Kings 13).

Even among the cities of Samaria Josiah carried out his reforms, destroying altars and high places and killing priests. He also saw to it that the wizards, the teraphim, the idols, and those who had familiar spirits were all put away.

Josiah Keeps the Passover
(2 Kings 23:21-23; 2 Chron. 35:1-19):

In the same year that the temple was repaired, Josiah commanded that the Passover be kept. The Bible says, "There was not kept such a Passover from the days of the judges that judged Israel, nor in all the days of the kings of Israel, nor of the kings of Judah" (2 Kings 23:22). The chronicler says there was no Passover like it from the days of Samuel the prophet (2 Chron. 35:18).

The Passover lamb was killed on the fourteenth day of the first month as the law required (Exod. 12:3, 6). By now the land and the house of God had been purged of idols; the copy of the law had been found; the people had renewed their covenant with the Lord; and the house of God had been repaired. Josiah appointed the priests to their proper duties and encouraged them in their work.

Then Josiah told the Levites, "Put the sacred ark in the temple that Solomon the son of David built. It is not to be carried about on your shoulders."

We have no way of knowing why the ark was not already in the temple or where it had been. Some faithful Levites may have hidden it away for safe-keeping, or it may have been removed at some time to make way for idolatrous items that were put in the temple.

Note, however, that the ark was still in existence at this time. This is the last time the ark of the covenant is mentioned as being in existence. Almost certainly it was taken when the Babylonians destroyed the temple and took all of its wealth to Babylon. There is no way to know what happened to it there, and it is useless to speculate about it.

Josiah himself gave 30,000 lambs and kids and 3,000 bullocks to be used in the Passover celebration. Various leaders gave 2,600 goats and sheep and 300 oxen. The chiefs of the Levites gave 5,000 goats and sheep and 500 oxen. The feast was kept in scrupulous obedience to the law. It seems there was a large number of people from old Israel included in those present for the feast.

This Passover is the last thing told about Josiah before the story of his death, although he lived for a few more years.

Historical Note— Egypt tries to help Assyria:

As we mentioned in an earlier note, a Chaldean named Nabopolassar established his dynasty in Babylon in 625 B.C. He invaded Assyrian territory in 616 B.C. but was unable, at first, to defeat Assyria. Assyria had received help from an unexpected source. The Egyptians had hated the Assyrians, but they saw Babylon rising in power and they feared a vigorous new empire in Mesopotamia. They decided they preferred a weakened Assyria between them and Babylon, and therefore, decided to help Assyria resist the new power.

The Medes joined the Babylonians and took Nineveh in 612 B.C. The Assyrians, propped up by Egypt, moved west to Haran. They were defeated there in 610 B.C. In the summer of 609, the Assyrian king sought to recapture Haran with the help of the new Egyptian king, Pharaoh Necho.

On his way, Necho needed to pass through Josiah's kingdom. Josiah did not want Egypt to help Assyria, so he went out to fight against the Egyptians and was slain in the attempt.

Josiah's Death
(2 Kings 23:29-30; 2 Chron. 35:20-27):

When Pharaoh Necho's army approached Josiah's kingdom, Necho sent ambassadors saying, "There is no problem between you and me. I have not come to fight you today, but against someone else and God has told me to hurry. Do not therefore meddle with God who is with me, lest He destroy you."

Josiah paid no heed. He disguised himself and went out to battle at the valley of Megiddo, and did not listen to the words of Necho from the mouth of God. The Egyptian archers shot Josiah and he commanded his chariot to be driven away. Josiah was mortally wounded and he died. He was buried in the sepulchers of his fathers and all Judah and Jerusalem mourned for him. Jeremiah made a special lamentation for him. It was 609 B.C., and Josiah was only 39 years old.

The Bible gives Josiah the very highest praise. "Like unto him was there no king before him, that turned to Jehovah with all his heart, and with all his soul, and with all his might, according to all the law of Moses; neither after him arose there any like him" (2 Kings 23:25).

Historical Note — Necho Establishes Egyptian Control:

Necho failed in his attempt to help the Assyrians regain Haran. So, instead, he sought to establish the frontier of Egyptian control at Carchemish. He established an Egyptian sphere of influence which reached the Euphrates River. In that way, he temporarily stopped any further Babylonian advances to the west.

Since Pharaoh Necho and his Egyptian forces held control all the way from Egypt to the Euphrates River (look on your map), then he was the one in control enough to be able to interfere in Judah's affairs. He was angry with Judah and with the family of Josiah, so he stepped into their affairs, as the next story shows. Judah was certainly not strong enough militarily to oppose Necho's actions (and, of course, God was no longer with Judah). It was still 609 B.C. when first Jehoahaz and then Jehoiakim became king in Judah.

Jehoahaz (Shallum) — 3 months (wicked)
(2 Kings 23:30-34; 2 Chron. 36:1-4)

When the people of the land saw that Josiah was dead, they made his son Jehoahaz king. He was twenty-three years old. Jehoahaz did that which was evil in God's sight.

Do you remember the prophecy of Huldah? She said judgment was definitely coming upon the land of Judah, but that God would wait until Josiah died. Now Josiah is dead; a wicked king has come to the throne; and the reforms of Josiah evaporate.

After a reign of only three months, Jehoahaz was removed from the throne. Pharaoh Necho of Egypt had him put in chains, brought before him at Riblah in Hamath, and then banished to Egypt. Then Necho imposed an enormous tribute upon Judah — about three and three-fourth tons of silver and about seventy-five pounds of gold. He took Eliakim, Jehoahaz's brother, and made him king. As further proof of his authority over the new king and his country, he changed Eliakim's name to Jehoiakim.

Since Jehoahaz had proven himself to be so wicked, Jeremiah gave this message from the Lord: "Weep ye not for the dead [*Josiah*], neither bemoan him; but weep sore for him that goes away [*Jehoahaz*]; for he shall return no more, nor see his native country. For thus saith Jehovah touching Shallum [*another name for Jehoahaz*] the son of Josiah, king of Judah, who reigned instead of Josiah his father, and who went forth out of this place: he shall not return thither anymore, but in the place whither they have led him captive, there shall he die, and he shall see this land no more" (Jer. 22:10-12). Just as Jeremiah predicted, Jehoahaz died in Egypt, never returning to his homeland.

This is the first time that the lineage of David passes from brother to brother, rather than from father to son. Three sons of Josiah followed him upon the throne: first Jehoahaz, then Jehoiakim, and finally Zedekiah. Jehoiakim was the oldest (2 Kings 24:36); Jehoahaz was next (2 Kings 23:31); and Zedekiah was the youngest (2 Kings 24:18).

The promise to David that his throne would be established and that his seed would reign forever, looked ultimately to the coming of the Messiah, the Christ. Therefore, Jesus was a direct descendant of the kings of Judah (see Matt. 1). But the line becomes somewhat confused at this point. When Jehoahaz was removed by Necho and taken to Egypt where he died, his lineage did not continue. Jehoiakim came to the throne, and he was followed by his son Jehoiachin (also called Jeconiah). Jehoiachin, in turn, surrendered to Babylon, and Zedekiah was set upon the throne as a puppet king. The Jews continued to count Jehoiachin and his heirs as the proper ones in line to rule, and that is the line that Jesus came through (see Matt. 1:11).

But before we continue the history with the story of Jehoiakim, let us look at one more prophet who came on the scene at about this time.

The Prophet Habakkuk
(The Book of Habakkuk)

The dates given for the book of Habakkuk range from about 625 B.C. when Josiah was finishing his reforms in the land, until 605 B.C. when the Babylonians made their first invasion of Judah. Even during the last years of Josiah, there was violence and wickedness on every hand in Judah, just below the surface rituals of service to God (see Jeremiah 3:10). Then, when Josiah died and a wicked king took his place, the hidden wickedness became full blown again. Therefore, the prophet Habakkuk had very perplexing questions in his mind. His book is very different to all the other prophets who came to the people bearing a message from God. Habakkuk, on the other hand, represents the righteous people left in the land, and he goes before Jehovah with a question for Him to answer.

God's Judgment Upon Judah, the Wicked People of God, Through the Chaldeans (1:1-2:3):
The message of the prophet is very clear. First there is the mourning and genuine sorrow in Habakkuk's heart as he sees the evil about him in the nation of Judah. Therefore, his first question to God: "How long shall I cry, and you will not hear?" How can God be indifferent to the sin in Judah? There is perverseness, violence, and strife on every hand. Does not the righteous God rule in the heavens? Why? O God, why?

God gives His answer: "I am not indifferent; I am working a work that you would not believe if it were told. I am raising up the Chaldeans [*Babylonians*] to punish my people. They are a cruel nation. They will march through the land and possess houses that do not belong to them. The army is powerful and swift. They shall come for violence. Kings and princes will mean nothing to them; they will scoff at them. They are guilty men who have made power their god."

God's answer raises another great question in Habakkuk's mind, though. He is glad to know that Jehovah is not oblivious to Judah's wickedness, but Jehovah is pure. How can He allow those as wicked as the Chaldeans to swallow up those who are more righteous than they? Judah was wicked, as the prophet knew, but they were not as wicked as Babylon. O Lord, will Babylon not be stopped somewhere? Will they continually slay nations?

Habakkuk says, "I will stand at my watch. I will station myself on the wall and wait to see what the Lord will answer."

The Lord gives His answer in chapter 2. He tells Habakkuk to write the vision so plainly that all may see it and be warned to run. Judgment will indeed come to this wicked nation. It may tarry and not come as soon as man thinks it should — but wait for it. It will surely come when God has completed His purpose. The soul that is lifted up cannot live; but, "the just shall live by his faith." This is a glorious promise. God is just in His dealings with both the righteous and the unrighteous.

God's Judgment Upon the Chaldeans, the Ungodly World Power (2:4-20):

God's description of the Chaldeans is *not* flattering. The Chaldean is arrogant and greedy. He is wicked. The Chaldeans were planting the seeds of their own destruction. That is always the way of evil wherever it may be found. Judah had made judgment inevitable by her own sin. Now the tool of that judgment was not important. It might be from a wicked nation, or a righteous nation; from a big nation, or a small one — it did not matter. But if that conquering nation were sowing seeds of wickedness itself, then it too was sowing seeds of its own destruction.

Babylon was the nation under consideration in this little book, but the principles expressed are universal principles. A nation will stand as long it upholds decency and justice in its dealings with its citizens. But, as it becomes more and more oppressive and wicked, it is building more and more toward destruction from within, making it susceptible to attacks from within or without. Only in righteousness and justice is there life, whether in an individual or a nation.

Beginning in 2:6, God pronounces five woes upon the wicked, destructive attitude found in Babylon. "Woe to him who increases that which is not his." A nation can overrun the world for a time, but then the oppressed people will rise up against it and plunder the plunderer. It is inevitable.

"Woe to him who covets an evil covetousness to his house." Woe to the one who makes his own nation rich by coveting and taking the wealth of another nation. The very property so taken will testify against the nation in the day of judgment.

"Woe to him who builds a town with the blood of battles." Will people so captured weary themselves defending the city? The Lord of hosts will come in judgment and the whole world will be filled with the knowledge of His glory.

"Woe to him who gives drink to his neighbor so that he may see his neighbor's shame." Now it is your turn! The shame, the reproach, the destruction you have meted out to others will return upon you!

"Woe to the one who builds idols and puts his trust in them." What value is an idol? A man carved it; it is his own creation; yet the man puts his trust in it. Can it give guidance? It has no power. "But the Lord is in His holy temple; let all the earth keep silence before Him."

155

So, Habakkuk has his answer. God is aware of Judah's wickedness and plans to chastise the nation. He plans to use the violence and aggression and greed of the Babylonians to do so, but He will not ignore the wickedness of the Babylonians. He will judge them as He will judge all wickedness.

Prayer for Compassion in the Midst of Judgment (3:1-19):
The last chapter of the book is a powerful, poetic description of the power of God who came from Teman, from Mount Paran to meet His people. Full of power and brightness, He drove asunder the nations and scattered the mountains. Jehovah passed and the mountains saw the Lord and were afraid. The Lord marched through the land and threshed the nations. Why? Was it merely because of His anger? The prophet answers by saying, "You came out to deliver your people, to save your anointed one." God punishes the wicked for the salvation of His people. He has always done what is best and good for His people.

Habakkuk knew that judgment was coming, so he prayed that God remember mercy in His wrath. Habakkuk expresses his own dread for the coming day by saying, "I heard what the Lord said, and I trembled. I must wait for the invasion and calamity to come. I can do nothing to avoid it, or turn it away. But though the fig tree shall not flourish, nor fruit be on the vine; though there be no olives, and though the fields yield no food; though the flock be cut off from the fold, and there be no herd in the stalls, yet I will rejoice in the Lord. I will take joy in the God of my salvation. Jehovah, the Lord, is my strength, and He makes my feet like the feet of a deer, and enables me to tread upon the heights." This is the faith we all must imitate.

Jehoiakim (Eliakim) — 11 years (wicked)
(2 Kings 23:36-24:6; 2 Chron. 36:5-8)

As we have mentioned, when Pharaoh Necho removed Jehoahaz from the throne, he placed Eliakim the son of Josiah in his place in Judah and changed his name to Jehoiakim. Necho demanded an enormous tribute from Jehoiakim, who had to tax his people heavily in order to pay it. Jehoiakim was very wicked. It was still 609 B.C.

At the beginning of Jehoiakim's reign, Jeremiah was commanded to go preach in the court of the Lord's house to those who came to worship (Jer. 26). God's hope was: "Perhaps they will listen and each will turn from his evil way. Then I will relent and not bring on them the disaster I was planning because of the evil they have done."

Jeremiah was told to say, "Thus says Jehovah: 'If you will not listen to me, to walk in my law, which I have set before you, or listen to the words of my servants the prophets, to whom you have not hearkened, then I will make this house like Shiloh, and I will make this city a curse to all the nations of the earth.'"

When Jeremiah finished his prophecy, the priests and false prophets and all the people seized him. They considered his words treason. They said, "You are going to die."

The princes of Judah heard the disturbance, and they came from the king's house to the temple to hear the accusations made against Jeremiah. They also heard Jeremiah's defense. He said, "The Lord sent me to prophesy against this house and against this city. All the things which I have said are true. Now reform your actions and obey God and He will relent and not bring the disaster upon you. But as for me, do whatever you think is good and right. I am in your hands. Be assured, however, that if you kill me, you will bring the guilt of innocent blood upon this city and only increase the judgment against it."

The princes argued with the priests and prophets about whether Jeremiah should be killed. Then some elders of Judah stepped forward and cited the example of Micah the prophet who prophesied during the days of Hezekiah. He prophesied that Zion should be plowed as a field and Jerusalem should become heaps, yet Hezekiah and the people of that day did not put him to death. Instead, they repented and God relented and did not bring the predicted disaster at that time. "We are about to bring a terrible disaster upon ourselves!" the elders said.

Therefore, Jeremiah was spared. But another prophet was not so fortunate. A man named Uriah prophesied at this same time and he, too, prophesied against Jerusalem and Judah. Jehoiakim and his officials determined to kill him, so he fled to Egypt in fear. Jehoiakim sent men to Egypt to bring Uriah back, and when they had done so, the prophet was killed and buried in the graves of the common people.

Nevertheless, this time, the princes, particularly Ahikam the son of Shaphan, would not allow Jeremiah to be put to death.

The First Invasion: The Beginning of Captivity
(2 Kings 23:34-24:6; 2 Chron. 36:4-8):

The time has come for the fall of Judah. Therefore the historians recording the history in both 2 Kings and 2 Chronicles merely summarize the invasions and the captives taken. We learn more details from the prophets Jeremiah, Daniel, and Ezekiel who all lived at this time. There are also Babylonian records that have been found that tell of this same period. We will attempt to combine the information in the historical summaries, in the prophets, and in the Babylonian records and set it forth as clearly as possible.

Remember that the story was simpler when it involved the story of God's people alone. At that time we considered other nations only as they, in turn, touched God's people. If Judah were still faithful to God, then the story would continue that same way at this point. God could protect His people against any enemy — no matter how strong that enemy was. But Judah is not faithful. God has warned and warned, and now the time has come for Judah to be punished. Therefore, the history of other nations becomes totally intertwined with the history of Judah. We cannot understand Judah's history without understanding a little about what is happening on the world scene.

First, let us look at the summaries the inspired historians give about King Jehoiakim. After telling that Pharaoh Necho deposed Jehoahaz and placed Jehoiakim upon the throne, and telling that Jehoiakim had to pay Necho tribute, the historian tells us that Jehoiakim was extremely wicked. That means we can expect the predicted destruction to come swiftly.

Sure enough, the very next fact we are told is that Nebuchadnezzar, king of Babylon, invaded the land. Jehoiakim paid him tribute for three years and then rebelled. As a result, raiders from the Chaldeans, Syrians, Moabites, and Ammonites began to plague Judah. At some point, Nebuchadnezzar had Jehoiakim himself bound with bronze shackles to be taken to Babylon. Vessels were taken from the temple at this time and were carried to Babylon. The historian tells us that all these things were brought upon Judah at the Lord's command, because of the wickedness in the land — the wickedness that had become too full for God to ignore in the days of King Manasseh who had filled Jerusalem with innocent blood. Jehoiakim reigned a total of eleven years — years filled with "detestable" acts.

In a moment we will look at additional information we learn about Jehoiakim in the prophets. Next, however, let us look at the world scene. What is happening to Egypt and Babylon to bring about the changes in allegiance required of Jehoiakim?

Historical Note — Babylon Gains Control:
Things continued as they were until 605, with Necho of Egypt in Carchemish, holding control all the way to the Euphrates River, and the young kingdom of Babylon gathering its strength. Then the crown prince of Babylon, Nebuchadnezzar, launched a surprise attack on Necho's forces at Carchemish. He pursued them all the way to the border of Egypt.

No one knows what else he might have done at that point, because he received word that his father had died. Taking only a few men, Nebuchadnezzar sped straight across the desert back to Babylon (look on your map) to take the throne of his father. He left his army to come through the various governments of Palestine, accepting the allegiance of the peoples. Jehoiakim submitted at that time and became Babylon's vassal (2 Kings 24:1).

Daniel: In the First Group of Captives
(Dan. 1:1-7):
It was customary to take some of the best and brightest young men from captive nations to seal the allegiance given. It was at this time Daniel and his friends Shadrach, Meshach, and Abednego were taken to Babylon as captives.

Daniel says he was taken captive in the third year of Jehoiakim (Dan. 1:1-3). Yet according to all available records, Nebuchadnezzar did not come into Judah until after he defeated Necho at Carchemish in the fourth year of Jehoiakim (Jer. 46:2). The fourth year of Jehoiakim (605 B.C.) was the first year of Nebuchadnezzar (Jer. 25:1). Probably Daniel refers to the time when Nebuchadnezzar set out on his expedition. He then smote Necho at the beginning of the fourth year of Jehoiakim. That means Daniel and his friends were actually taken early in that fourth year of Jehoiakim, although the Babylonian campaign had begun in Jehoiakim's third year.

In the Babylonian campaign which started in King Jehoiakim's third year, the Babylonian soldiers besieged the city of Jerusalem. The Lord delivered Jehoiakim into their hands, and the Babylonians took what they chose. They demanded tribute from Jehoiakim, took valuable articles from the temple itself, and took the best of the young men from the city. The articles from the temple of Jehovah were placed in the temples of the Babylonian gods. It was 606/605 B.C. The Babylonian captivity had begun.

Nebuchadnezzar ordered Ashpenaz, the chief of his eunuchs, to select the very finest of the young men from the Israelites. The ones chosen were from the royal family and the nobility. They were young men with no physical defects, handsome, and with an aptitude for all kinds of learning. These young men were to be trained in all the learning of the Chaldeans so that they might someday serve in the palace of the king. The training was scheduled to last three years.

Among the young men chosen, there were four friends: Daniel, Hananiah, Mishael, and Azariah. The Babylonians gave them new names and started their training. Daniel was named Belteshazzar; Hananiah was named Shadrach; Mishael was named Meshach; and Azariah was named Abednego.

Do you remember the prophecy Isaiah told King Hezekiah when he showed his Babylonian guests all his wealth? Isaiah told him: "The time will surely come when everything in your palace, and all that your fathers have stored up until this day, will be carried to Babylon. Nothing will be left, says the Lord. And some of your descendants, your own flesh and blood, that will be born to you, will be taken away, and they will become eunuchs in the palace of the king of Babylon" (2 Kings 20:17-18). Everything has not yet been taken from Jerusalem, but the first of the treasures are in Babylon, and Hezekiah's own descendants, the seed royal, are serving as young eunuchs, being trained to serve in the palace of the king. God's promises come true — whether for good or for evil!

We believe that, to avoid confusion, we will wait to study the stories of Daniel and his three friends until the book on the captivity, return, and years of silence. Do not forget that there are events happening in the lives of the captives who have been taken to Babylon, as well as the stirring events taking place in Judah and Jerusalem. In that book, we will drop back in our history to fit the stories of Daniel into their proper setting.

Take a new map:

Take a new map of Bible Lands, and draw in the empire of Babylon. When you have copied the map shown, you will have drawn the empire as it was at its largest, and it is not yet at its full strength at this point in history, but it soon will be. Note where the tiny, sick kingdom of Judah is crumbling. Compare the map of Babylon with the map of Assyria. Babylon never became as large an empire as Assyria, because it was a very short-lived empire. Assyria lasted a few hundred years, while Babylon lasted less than one hundred years.

Jeremiah Predicts the Captivity and its Length
(Jeremiah 25:1-14):

It was in the same year of the battle at Carchemish that Jeremiah warned the people of Judah again of their impending doom, and told the length of their captivity. It was in the fourth year of King Jehoiakim and in the first year of King Nebuchadnezzar of Babylon. The time was 606/605 B.C.

Jeremiah spoke to all the people of Judah and Jerusalem: "For twenty-three years — since the thirteenth year of Josiah until now — I have been telling you the word of the Lord. Other prophets have done the same. We have warned you over and over, but you have not listened. We have said, 'Turn now, each of you, from your evil ways and *you can stay in the land that the Lord gave to you and to your forefathers*. Turn away from your false gods and do not provoke the Lord to anger and He will not harm you. But you have not listened! Therefore God has summoned all the peoples of the north and is bringing His servant Nebuchadnezzar against the land and its inhabitants. God will completely destroy this nation and her neighbors, and will make them an object of horror and scorn, and an everlasting ruin. God will banish the inhabitants of the land from the sounds of joy and gladness. The whole country will become a desolate wasteland, and you will serve the king of

Babylon for *seventy years.*"

> *The destruction and captivity of the land of Judah had been predicted many times by now, and also the promise of the return of a remnant had been made many times. But this is the first time there has been a mention of a specific time involved. Jeremiah says the people of Judah will serve the king of Babylon seventy years. Even at this point, the severity of that service to the king was dependent upon the actions of the people of Judah. The first invasion of the Babylonians came in the same year Jeremiah made this statement. Jehoiakim submitted, a few captives were taken, and a few treasures were taken from the temple. If the people had repented, then they could have served the Babylonian king from their own homeland and could have been spared further tragedy. As you study the period of the captivity, watch for the fulfillment of this prophesy of Jeremiah. Watch even the time factor.*

Jeremiah's prophecy was not complete when he told of the captivity of Judah. He continued by saying: "But when the seventy years are fulfilled, God will punish the king of Babylon and his nation. They will be made desolate forever. They themselves will be enslaved by many nations and great kings. They will be repaid for all their evil deeds." Later, Jeremiah even foretells that the Medes will be God's instrument by which He will punish Babylon (Jer. 51:11). In the next book of this series, we will watch the history unfold until this prophecy is fulfilled also.

Example of the Rechabites (Jeremiah 35:1-19):
> *The precise year of Jehoiakim's reign in which this story occurred is not given. Since, however, the army of Nebuchadnezzar was near Jerusalem (35:11), it was almost certainly the fourth year of Jehoiakim, the year of Nebuchadnezzar's first invasion.*

Jehovah told Jeremiah, "Go to the Rechabites and bring them to the house of Jehovah, into one of the chambers and give them wine to drink."

As instructed, Jeremiah went to Jaazaniah, the son of Jeremiah [*not the prophet*], and took him, his brethren, his sons, and the whole house of the Rechabites and brought them to the house of God, into the chamber of the sons of Hanan. He set before them bowls of wine and cups, and said, "Have some wine."

To Jeremiah's surprise, however, they replied, "We will drink no wine, because our ancestor, Jonadab the son of Rechab, commanded us saying, 'You shall drink no wine, neither you nor your sons for ever; neither shall you build houses, nor sow seed, nor plant vineyards, nor have any; but all your days you will dwell in tents so that you may live many days in the land in which you visit.' And we have obeyed the voice of Jonadab our father. We have drunk no wine. We have built no houses, nor planted vineyards or fields, but we have dwelt in tents. The only reason why we are in the city of Jerusalem now is for fear of the army of the Chaldeans."

Jehovah brought His lesson. He told Jeremiah to tell the men of Judah: "Will you not pay attention to what I say? The words which Jonadab spoke to his children, they obey to this day. But I have spoken to you time and again, and you have not listened. Since the sons of Jonadab the Rechabite have done as their father commanded, and you have not, I tell you that I will bring upon Judah and the inhabitants of Jerusalem all the calamities that I have threatened them with."

Jeremiah also told the house of the Rechabites, "The Lord says that because you have obeyed the voice of your father, Jonadab the son of Rechab shall not lack a man to stand before me for ever."

The story of Jonadab the Rechabite goes back about 250 years to the day when Jehu was destroying the house of Ahab. As Jehu was heading for Samaria, he met Jonadab [or Jehonadab] and invited him into his chariot to see his zeal for Jehovah. Jonadab assisted Jehu in handing out the vestments to the worshipers of Baal which marked them for destruction (2 Kings 10:15-23).

One time Jonadab told his children not to drink wine, etc., and for 250 years they had scrupulously obeyed his word. Jehovah wished His children were as obedient.

Jehoiakim Burns the Scroll of Jeremiah
(Jeremiah 36:1-32):

In that same year, the fourth year of Jehoiakim, God commanded Jeremiah to take a scroll and write all the words He had spoken against Israel and Judah and against all the nations. All the messages of Jeremiah that he had spoken since the thirteenth year of Josiah were to be recorded. Jeremiah dictated the words and his scribe Baruch wrote them on the scroll.

The portion written would be approximately the part we summarized in the first 20 chapters. Imagine those predictions being made about the kingdom you were personally responsible for, and then think how any right thinking person should have responded when he heard it read.

God said, "Perhaps when the people of Judah hear about every disaster I plan to inflict on them, each of them will turn from his wicked way; then I will forgive their wickedness and their sin." [*Do you see God's mercy? He still wanted to save His people.*]

Jeremiah told Baruch, "I am restricted; I cannot go to the Lord's temple. Therefore you go to the temple on a day of fasting and read the scroll of the word of the Lord to the people. Read it to all who come, and perhaps they will listen." It had taken time for the scroll to be written. By now it was the ninth month of the fifth year of Jehoiakim. The first captives had been gone for more than a year by now.

A special fast had been proclaimed. This was not the fast commanded by the law in connection with the day of atonement because that fast was in the seventh month — *approximately October of our year* (Lev. 16:29-34). This was in the ninth month (*December*).

Baruch went and read the law as he had been commanded. A man named Micaiah heard the reading and he told the princes of Judah about it. They sent word to Baruch saying, "Bring the scroll from which you have read to the people, and come to us." Baruch went, and they said, "Sit down now, and read it to us."

They were all afraid when they heard the words. They said, "We must tell the king all these words." But they feared for Baruch's life, so they asked him, "How did you write these words? Did Jeremiah dictate them to you?" Baruch assured them that was true.

The princes said, "Go and hide, you and Jeremiah. Do not let anyone know where you are." So Baruch left, and the princes went in before King Jehoiakim. But before they went, they took the precaution of hiding the scroll.

After they told the king what they had heard, he sent Jehudi to fetch the scroll, and then had him read it aloud. It was winter, and there was a fire burning in a brazier. As Jehudi would read three or four columns of the scroll, the king cut that portion off with his penknife and threw it into the fire. The process continued until the whole scroll was burned.

Three of the men who had brought word about the scroll — Elnathan, Delaiah, and Gemariah — protested and urged the king not to burn the scroll. The others, the kings's attendants, paid no attention. They were not afraid, nor did they tear their clothes over what the king did. Jehoiakim commanded that Baruch and Jeremiah be arrested, but they could not be found. The Lord had hidden them.

Jehovah then commanded that another scroll be written. The Lord sent a direct message about Jehoiakim saying, "He will have no one to sit on the throne of David; his body will be thrown out and exposed to the heat by day and the frost by night. I will punish him and his children and his attendants for their wickedness; I will bring on them, and those living in Jerusalem, and the people of Judah every disaster I pronounced against them, because they have not listened."

Therefore, Jeremiah took a new scroll and gave it to Baruch, and dictated the words which had been written before; and many other words were added.

Jehoiakim's Last Days
(2 Kings 24:1-6; Jer. 22:18-19):

As we noted in the summary the inspired historians give about Jehoiakim, the text says that he served Nebuchadnezzar three years and then rebelled against him (2 Kings 24:1). This fits the Babylonian record. It was in 601 B.C. that Nebuchadnezzar came back to finish his struggle against Egypt. Instead, Necho's forces severely defeated Babylon. Nebuchadnezzar's army was so badly defeated he had to go home and spend the next eighteen months rebuilding his forces.

If our timing is correct, likely Jehoiakim's rebellion was connected with this episode, probably when he saw Babylon defeated. Since Nebuchadnezzar was tied up elsewhere with other business, he did not come back immediately to force Jehoiakim into submission. Jehoiakim's circumstances as king certainly were not improved by his rebellion, however, because he suffered raids from all sides — from the Chaldeans, the Syrians, the Moabites, and the Ammonites. There is no definite information available on the subject, but it may well be that Nebuchadnezzar was encouraging these raids. The matter was brought about, however, by the Lord to continue the process of Judah's destruction for her sins.

At some point, Jehoiakim was bound in shackles to be taken to Babylon (2 Chron. 36:6). Yet from all other accounts there is no evidence that he was ever actually taken captive. He ruled for eleven years in Jerusalem and died before Nebuchadnezzar's army reached the city again. It must be that he was bound either when Nebuchadnezzar's men first came into Jerusalem demanding submission in 605, or during one of the later raids that began in about 601/600. Jehoiakim must have feverishly pledged his allegiance in order to spare himself, and was released to rule a little longer. The inspired historian does not give enough information for us to know all details.

No details are given about Jehoiakim's death, but Jeremiah said: "Regarding Jehoiakim the son of Josiah king of Judah, they shall not mourn for him saying, 'Oh my brother!' or 'Oh our ruler!' or 'Oh his glory!' He will be buried like a donkey, drawn and cast forth beyond the gates of Jerusalem" (Jer. 22:18-19). We have already noted another prophecy of Jeremiah that said, "His dead body will be cast out in the day to the heat, and in the night to frost" (Jer. 36:30). This indicates Jehoiakim was slain during one of the skirmishes with one of the raiding parties mentioned above, and was not given a proper burial.

Historical Note — Babylon comes again:
Nebuchadnezzar and his army set out again for Jerusalem in late 598 B.C. From the Babylonian chronicles we learn that Nebuchadnezzar mustered his troops about three months before Jerusalem was taken in early 597 B.C. Some have said that Nebuchadnezzar headed for Jerusalem to punish Jehoiakim for his rebellion, but that by the time he reached Jerusalem, Jehoiakim had died, and Jehoiachin his son had taken the throne. It is more likely that Jehoiakim's death was the occasion Nebuchadnezzar took to go down and reassert his control over Judah.

Jehoiachin (Coniah, Jeconiah) — 3 months (wicked)
(2 Kings 24:8-15; 25:27-30; 2 Chron. 36:9-10)

It is easy to see from the few verses devoted to Jehoiachin's life that not much is given about him. He was only eighteen years old when he followed his father Jehoiakim upon the throne and he ruled for only three months and ten days. For that brief time he followed in the ways of his father. Even the knowledge that Nebuchadnezzar was on his way, and the siege of Jerusalem itself, did nothing to bring about a reformation of his character.

Chronological Note:
2 Kings 24:8 gives Jehoiachin's age as eighteen years old when he became king. 2 Chronicles 36:9 gives it as eight years old. There were other child kings, so it would be possible that he was only eight years old, and his advisers were the ones who made the decisions. It specifically mentions his mother surrendering at the same time the young king surrendered, which might suggest she was in a position of adviser. But eighteen seems to fit the story better because his wives are mentioned (2 Kings 24:15), and he is said to have done "that which is evil in the sight of the Lord" (2 Kings 24:9).

It was too late to save Jerusalem. God said through Jeremiah, "Even if you, Coniah," *[another name for Jehoiachin]* "were a signet ring on my right hand, I would still pull you off. I will hand you over to those who seek your life, to those you fear — to Nebuchadnezzar king of Babylon and to the Babylonians. I will hurl you and the mother who gave you birth into another country, where neither of you was born, and there you both will die. You will never come back to the land you long to return to... This is what the Lord says: 'Record this man as if he were childless, a man who will not prosper in his lifetime, for none of his offspring will prosper, none will sit on the throne of David, or rule anymore in Judah'" (Jer. 22:24-30).

Note about David's Line — The Branch (Jer. 23:5ff):

God's word through Jeremiah is quite specific here that no descendant of Jehoiachin will ever reign in Jerusalem. That statement is a death blow to the doctrine taught by many religious groups today that Jesus, a direct descendant of Jehoiachin, will yet return to earth and rule in the physical city of Jerusalem. Jeremiah is emphatic in saying that will not happen.

Yet, only a few verses later, in Jeremiah 23:5-6, Jeremiah does predict a ruler, a king, to be raised up from the house of David. This will be a king who will reign wisely and do what is just and right in the land. In his day Judah will be saved and Israel will live in safety. The name of that ruler will be "The Lord Our Righteousness." The imagery is that of a tree that was cut down (the house of David), but from that tree, a shoot, or new branch, will grow out to be a King, the Lord Our Righteousness.

When the angel appeared to Mary he told her the child she would bear would be given the "throne of his father David: And he shall reign over the house of Jacob for ever; and of his kingdom there shall be no end" (Luke 1:32-33). On the day of Pentecost Peter declared that Jesus arose from the dead and returned to heaven to be seated upon the throne of David — to reign in heaven for ever (Acts 2:29-36).

The officers of Nebuchadnezzar advanced on Jerusalem and laid siege to it. Nebuchadnezzar himself came up to the city while his officers were besieging it. The city was not destroyed at this time because Jehoiachin and all his officers surrendered.

Jehoiachin was taken prisoner. All the treasures were taken from the temple and from the palace, including all the gold articles that Solomon had made for the temple. In addition, all the officers, fighting men, craftsmen, and artisans of the city were taken into exile — a total of 10,000. The king's mother, his wives, his officials, and the leading men of the city were taken. A special force of 7,000 fighting men described as "strong and fit for war" and a thousand craftsmen and artisans were taken, either in addition to the ones already mentioned, or perhaps this description is only a breakdown of the 10,000 mentioned above. Only the poorest of the people were left in the land.

The prophet Ezekiel was among these captives. He describes himself as one of the captives, and he usually dates the events in his book by what year it was in terms of the captivity of Jehoiachin (see Ezek. 1:2; 8:1; 20:1; 40:1). We will look at Ezekiel and his work more closely later, in the book dealing directly with the period of the captivity and return. Ezekiel, like Daniel, was starting his work in Babylon while these last events were taking place in Jerusalem. We feel that it will be less confusing in the study if we finish the events in Jerusalem before going to Babylon to look at the events taking place there.

Historical Note:

From comparing the Bible records and the Babylonian records, we can construct an exact chronology of this invasion. According to the Babylonian records, King Nebuchadnezzar mustered his troops and set out for Judah in his seventh year (598 B.C.). King Jehoiakim died in Jerusalem just about the time Nebuchadnezzar began mustering his troops in Babylon. These exact dates are given in the Babylonian Chronicles.

The Bible gives the date as the eighth year of Nebuchadnezzar (2 Kings 24:12), but there is no conflict between it and the Babylonian Chronicle, because the Bible also says that the captives were carried away to Babylon "at the return of the year," or as we would say, at the beginning of the new year (2 Chron. 36:10). About fifteen days after the city of Jerusalem was captured, the captives were led away.

The month Adar gave way to the month Nisan and a new year had begun — the eighth year of Nebuchadnezzar.

Jehoiachin's Release from Prison
(2 Kings 25:27-30):

In the thirty-seventh year of his exile, Jehoiachin was released from prison. A man named Evil-Merodach had come to the throne in Babylon. He released Jehoiachin on the twenty-seventh day of the twelfth month. From that time forward, Jehoiachin was given a place of honor higher than the other captive kings. He put aside his prison clothes and ate at the king's table regularly.

Jehoiachin was the one the Jews counted as the rightful heir to the throne. Just as Jeremiah had predicted, there was never another man of his descendants to reign upon the throne in Jerusalem, but Jesus was born as a direct descendant of Jehoiachin (Matt. 1:11-12).

Zedekiah (Mattaniah) — 11 years (wicked)
(2 Kings 24:17-25:7; 2 Chron. 36:10-21)

Nebuchadnezzar appointed Mattaniah, a third son of Josiah and uncle to Jehoiachin, as the successor to Jehoiachin. Nebuchadnezzar changed his name to Zedekiah. Zedekiah had the same mother as Jehoahaz who was deposed and banished to Egypt by Necho (see 2 Kings 23:31; 24:18). Zedekiah was twenty-one years old when he began to reign and he reigned eleven years. He was a very wicked man. Zedekiah is listed as one of the kings, but he was no more than a puppet under Nebuchadnezzar.

Vision of two Baskets of Figs
(Jeremiah 24:1-10):

Naturally, after the captives were taken from Jerusalem, the ones remaining grieved for those lost. Just at that moment, God spoke to Jeremiah again in a vision. He said, "Jeremiah, what do you see?"

Jeremiah answered, "I see two baskets of figs before the temple of the Lord. One basket is filled with beautiful, just-ripened figs. The other is filled with rotten figs, so poor they cannot be eaten."

Then God said, "The people who have been taken into exile are like the good figs. I have sent them away from this place, but my eyes will watch over them for their good, and I will bring them back to this land. I will build them up and not tear them down. I will plant them and not uproot them. I will give them a heart to know me, to know that I am the Lord. They will be my people, and I will be their God, for they will return to me with all their heart." [*Do you remember the covenant God has wanted with His people all along?*]

God continued, "But like these rotten figs, which are too bad to eat, so will I deal with Zedekiah king of Judah, his officials, and all those left in Jerusalem, whether they remain in the land or go to Egypt. I will make them abhorred and an offense to all the kingdoms of the earth. They will be a reproach and a byword, an object of ridicule and cursing no matter where they go. I will send the sword, famine, and plague against them until they are destroyed from the land I gave to them and their fathers."

God was telling Jeremiah that he was grieving for the wrong group. God had caused the best of the people to be taken captive so that He could spare them and bring them back as a remnant. Grieve for those left in the land because tragedy is still ahead for them. They are not worth saving!

Message of Jeremiah to the Captives
(Jeremiah 29:1-32):

After the Babylonians had carried away Jehoiachin (Jeconiah), the queen-mother, the eunuchs, the princes of Judah, and the artisans of the land, Jeremiah wrote them a letter and sent it by the hand of Elasah the son of Shaphan and Gemariah the son of Hilkiah whom Zedekiah was sending on business to Nebuchadnezzar. They were to deliver Jeremiah's letter to the captives.

The Shaphan and Hilkiah who are mentioned often in the book of Jeremiah are the men who served under King Josiah — Shaphan the scribe and Hilkiah the priest who found the book of the law in the temple and read it to the young king. They were very good men and it seems these sons were good men too, although at least one wicked son of Shaphan (Jaazaniah — Ezek. 8:11) is also mentioned.

The letter said:

Thus says the Lord: Build houses for yourselves and plan to live in them. Plant gardens and eat their fruit. Get married and have sons and daughters, and then take wives for your sons, and husbands for your daughters, and multiply. Do not let your number go down.

Seek the peace of the city to which you have been carried. Pray to the Lord for it, because if the city enjoys peace, you will have peace.

Do not listen to the false prophets among you. They prophesy falsely in my name, but I have not sent them, saith the Lord.

Jehovah says, "After seventy years have been accomplished for Babylon, I will visit you and will cause you to come back unto this place. For I am thinking thoughts of peace for you and not evil. If you will call upon me and seek for me, I will be available and I will come and bring an end to your captivity. I will gather you from the nations, and I will bring you back to the place from which I caused you to be carried away.

Chronological Note:

Jeremiah first gave the figure of seventy years for the length of the captivity right after the first captives were taken in 605 B.C. (see Jer. 25:1, 11-12). Now, here after the second group was taken in 597 B.C., the figure of seventy years is given again as the length of the captivity. Finally, after the city of Jerusalem was destroyed in 586 B.C., the historian records that the land lay desolate until the seventy years were completed (2 Chron. 36:21).

Even though the figure is given at three different times, it is counted from the days when the first captives were taken until the first captives returned (605 to 536/5 B.C.). It seems the seventy year figure referred to the length of time Babylon would stay in power as the captive force. Nebuchadnezzar began his reign in the same year Daniel and others were taken captive. As soon as Babylon was captured by the Medes and Persians, the new ruler gave the decree allowing captive people to go home — thus the end of the captivity.

Promise of a Better Day; A New Covenant (Jeremiah 30-31):

Captivity had become horribly real to God's people by now. It was clear that Jehovah was doing what He had said He would do. Chastisement had begun. Now God saw a need to comfort His people, to tell them that there would be deliverance. So God says of Judah's captors, "I will break his yoke from off your neck." He said that His people would serve Him (30:8-9).

This deliverance, however, would not come until chastisement was accomplished, because Judah's sins were many. Nevertheless the day would come when the Lord would bring His people home, and they would be His people, and He would be their God (30:11-17, 22).

In the day of restoration, the Lord promises He will make a new covenant with the house of Israel and with the house of Judah. It will not be like the covenant He made with them when they were come up out of Egypt (see Exod. 19-24). They had broken that covenant. With His new covenant, Jehovah will put His law in the innermost parts of His people, and He will write His law in their hearts, and He will be their God, and they will be His people. No more will those in the kingdom of God have to teach one another to "know the Lord," for they will all know the Lord. And the Lord said, "I will forgive their iniquity, and their sin will I remember no more" (31:31-34).

Conflict Between Jeremiah and Hananiah
(Jeremiah 27:1-28:17):

Nowhere else do we see the conflict between the prophets of God and the false prophets as vividly as we do in the book of Jeremiah.

God told Jeremiah to make a wooden yoke and wear it around his neck. Then he was to tell Judah and all her surrounding neighbors that God had placed the yoke of Babylon upon them, and that if they would submit, then they could remain in their own land and prosper.

Do you see God's mercy continuing, even for this wicked remnant still left in the land? God has already told Jeremiah what will happen to the group, because God could foresee their continued rebellion, but God is still giving them a chance to lessen the punishment before them.

Jeremiah went out before the people with his yoke around his neck, and he gave everyone the message from God. He told them that God had given the king of Babylon power over even the beasts of the field and the birds of the air. "Now, please submit to him. If you submit you will be allowed to stay in your land and prosper, but if you do not submit, God will punish the nation with the sword, famine and plague. Why listen to your false prophets who tell you to rebel? Why cause your city to be destroyed?"

Jeremiah took his message to every class of people — to the common man, to the king, and to the priests. The false prophets were saying no more treasures would be taken from the city, but Jeremiah tells the priests that if they do not submit, every remaining treasure in the city will be taken to Babylon and "they will remain there until God comes to get them to bring them back."

A false prophet, Hananiah, heard Jeremiah's message. He came before the people and said, "This is what God truly says: 'I will break the yoke of Babylon. Within two years all the articles that have been taken from the house of the Lord will be returned. Jehoiachin and all the other exiles who have been taken to Babylon will return to Judah.'"

Jeremiah answered, "Amen! May the Lord do so! May the Lord fulfill everything you have said! But from the earliest times, the way one recognizes a prophet from God is by whether his word comes true."

Hananiah walked over to Jeremiah and broke the yoke on his neck and repeated his prophecy that within two years the captivity would be over.

Jehovah then spoke to Jeremiah saying, "Tell Hananiah that the yoke of wood will be replaced by a yoke of iron because I have put the yoke of the king of Babylon upon the necks of all these nations, and they will serve him."

Jeremiah told Hananiah, "The Lord has not sent you. You prophesy lies. Therefore the Lord says you will die this year because you have spoken rebellion against Jehovah."

Two months later Hananiah was dead!

The Fall of Jerusalem
(2 Kings 24:20b-25:21; 2 Chron. 36:13-21):

Zedekiah served King Nebuchadnezzar for nine years and then rebelled, depending, as usual, upon the Egyptians to assist him. Soon the Babylonian army was laying siege to Jerusalem. It was the ninth year and the tenth month of Zedekiah (Jer. 39:1).

In Babylon, Ezekiel was informed by Jehovah that the army of Babylon was drawing near Jerusalem. God said, "Son of man, write down the name of the day, this very day, because today the king of Babylon has reached Jerusalem" (Ezek. 24:1-2).

Jeremiah and the fall of Jerusalem:

As we have already seen, there is a wealth of information in Jeremiah regarding the history of Judah in its last days. We will see that this is also true even during the siege of Jerusalem itself.

Jeremiah was threatened with death (26:8); he was imprisoned on different occasions (20:1-6; 32:2-3; 37:16; 38:4-13). The feelings of the people ran especially high during the siege as Jeremiah preached: "He that abides in this city shall die by the sword, and by the famine, and by the plague; but he that goes out and surrenders to the Chaldeans that besiege you, he shall live... For God has set His face upon this city for calamity, and not for good... It shall be given into the hand of the king of Babylon, and he shall burn it with fire" (21:9-10).

Zedekiah was a weak king. Occasionally he had a glimmer of interest in what God planned to do. He sent Pashhur the priest to Jeremiah to inquire of Jehovah. Zedekiah remembered the stories of the wonderful deliverance God had wrought in the days of Asa against Zerah the Ethiopian (2 Chron. 14:9-15) and in the days of Hezekiah against Sennacherib the Assyrian (2 Kings 18:13-19:37). Zedekiah's desperate wish was: "Perhaps the Lord will deal with us according to all His wondrous works, that the king of Babylon will leave us" (Jer. 21:2). Instead God said, "No. Instead I will make your weapons ineffective, and I will be fighting on the Chaldeans' side" (Jer. 21:3-7).

Fairly early in the siege, before Jeremiah was imprisoned, an Egyptian army came up to fight the Chaldeans. This raised hope in Jerusalem that the siege was broken, because, when the Chaldeans heard of the approach of the Egyptian army, they pulled away from Jerusalem (Jer. 37:5).

Through Jeremiah, however, God said: "Thus shall you say to the king of Judah who sent you to inquire of me: 'Behold, Pharaoh's army, which has come forth to help you, will return to their own land. And the Chaldeans will come back and fight against this city; and they will take it and burn it with fire. Do not deceive yourselves saying the Chaldeans will surely leave, *because they will not leave.* Even if you had smitten the entire army of the Chaldeans, and all they had left were wounded men, they would get up out of their tents and burn this city with fire'" (Jer. 37:6-10).

In the midst of the siege, God told Zedekiah that he would see Nebuchadnezzar's eyes with his eyes and speak to him face to face and that he would be taken to Babylon where he would die in peace (Jer. 32:4; 34:1-7). About this same time, God told Ezekiel in Babylon that the prince in Jerusalem (Zedekiah) would be brought to Babylon, but that he would not "see" the land, and that he would die there (Ezek. 12:13).

Later in a secret conversation with Jeremiah, Zedekiah was urged to surrender to the king of Babylon. Jeremiah said, "Thus saith the Lord, 'If you surrender to the king of Babylon, your life will be spared and this city will not be burned down; you and your family will live. But if you will not surrender, this city will be handed over to the Babylonians and they will burn it down; you yourself will not escape from their hands'" (Jer. 38:17-18).

Zedekiah was afraid to take Jeremiah's advice. Do you see how he could have yet lightened the calamity upon his city? We marvel at the refusal of these men to listen to the word of the Lord!

Jeremiah In the Dungeon (Jeremiah 38:1-28):

Even during the siege, Jeremiah begged the people: "The one who remains in this city will die by the sword, by famine, and by the plague. But he who surrenders to the Chaldeans will live another day." This infuriated some of the leaders, and they begged Zedekiah to kill Jeremiah, because his words were weakening the people's resolve.

Zedekiah gave them permission to do as they wished, and they cast Jeremiah into the dungeon of Malchijah. They lowered Jeremiah into the dungeon with ropes. There was no water in the dungeon, but the bottom was a bog, a mire, and Jeremiah sank into the mire — a terrifying experience to be sure!

Ebed-melech, an Ethiopian eunuch in the king's house, heard what they had done to Jeremiah, and he came to the king and said, "My lord the king, these men have done evil in putting Jeremiah into the dungeon. He will certainly die where he is because there is no more bread."

Zekekiah therefore commanded Ebed-melech to take thirty men and go rescue Jeremiah. Ebed-melech promptly went with the men and got rags and worn-out garments from the house of the king. They lowered the rags to Jeremiah, and Ebed-melech said, "Put these rags and worn-out garments under your arms to pad against the ropes." Jeremiah did so, and was pulled up out of the dungeon. During the rest of the siege, Jeremiah was kept in the court of the guard.

Do you see how weak a ruler Zedekiah was? He was afraid to listen to Jeremiah and surrender to the king of Babylon, but he would give in to whatever demands his officials made. If some wanted

Jeremiah killed, he gave them permission to do so. If another came and told him Jeremiah ought to be rescued, he gave permission for him to do so.

Zedekiah wanted to know what was really going to happen. Jeremiah said, "Will you kill me if I tell you?" Zedekiah swore secretly to Jehovah that he would not. Jeremiah told him, even here at this last minute, that if he surerendered to the king of Babylon that he would live, and Jerusalem would not be burned.

Nevertheless, Zedekiah was afraid and would not do as the Lord spoke through Jeremiah.

It was too late for the captivity of the people to be averted, but if the city itself could be spared, they would have a home to come to.

The Siege Continues:

The Babylonians made a breach in the city in the ninth day of the fourth month of the eleventh year of Zedekiah. The princes of the king of Babylon came into the city and sat in the middle gate. Instead of submitting to Nebuchadnezzar as Jeremiah had said, Zedekiah fled with the men of war, heading to the Jordan River. The Chaldeans pursued and overtook them in the plains of Jericho. Zedekiah was taken to Riblah to Nebuchadnezzar who passed sentence upon him. He killed Zedekiah's sons as Zedekiah watched, and then put Zedekiah's eyes out. He was then bound in fetters and taken to Babylon (Jer. 39; 2 Kings 25:1-7).

Thus both prophecies were fulfilled. Jeremiah had said Zedekiah would see the king of Babylon, and Ezekiel had said he would be taken to Babylon, would not "see" it.

Many people were slain. Many were carried away captive. All the vessels of the temple, and the treasures of the temple, and of the king, and his princes were carried away to Babylon. The temple was burned down; the palace and every important house in the city was burned; the city wall was broken down and destroyed. The bronze pillars, the bronze altar, and all the movable stands of bronze were broken into pieces that could be carried to Babylon. Only the very poor of the people who had nothing were left (Jer. 39; 2 Kings 25:8-17).

Nebuchadnezzar had given command regarding Jeremiah: "Take him and look well to him. Do him no harm and do as he says." Jeremiah was given the option of going to Babylon as an honored man of the captivity, or staying in Judah. He decided to stay (Jer. 39:11-14; 40:1-6).

Thus Jerusalem is fallen. There is no more Judah. We can weep with Jeremiah as we behold Jerusalem burned and battered, an empty pile of rubble with no sounds but the wind sighing through her empty streets and the lonely cry of a bird.

Jeremiah writes: "How lonely is the city which once was full of people! She has become as a widow, she who was great among the nations. She weeps sore in the night, and her tears run down her cheeks" (Lam. 1:1-2a). The book of Lamentations is Jeremiah's poetic expression of grief for Jerusalem.

The chronicler states that Judah's captivity was because of her sins. She committed all the abominations of the nations. Her people polluted the house of the Lord which He sanctified in

Jerusalem. They totally ignored His prophets, mocking and scoffing at them, until the wrath of the Lord arose against His people, *till there was no remedy* (2 Chron. 36:14-16). What a fearsome, awful thought — that men can sin to the point of no return, where wrath is inevitable. Let us take heed!

Gedaliah is Appointed Governor
(2 Kings 25:22-26; Jeremiah 40:5-44:30):

Gedaliah was the son of Ahikam, the grandson of Shaphan who served in the days of King Josiah (2 Kings 22:14; Jer. 26:24). He was appointed governor by Nebuchadnezzar, to govern the people left in Judah. He set up headquarters in the city of Mizpah since Jerusalem was a pile of rubble.

When the Babylonians were gone, the Jewish captains of the forces that were in the fields returned [*in other words, Jewish officers who had fled from Jerusalem, almost certainly before the siege*]. They found that Nebuchadnezzar had made Gedaliah governor. They went to him, and he spoke to them saying, "Serve the king of Babylon, and it will be well with you. I will dwell at Mizpah and stand before the Chaldeans, but you go out into the fields and gather your wine, your summer fruits, and your oil, and live in the cities that you have taken." One of the captains was a man named Ishmael.

Other officers and people soon came back from among the Moabites, Ammonites, and Edomites, where they had been hiding from the Babylonians. Though there was so much devastation in the land, things appeared to be returning to normal for this tiny group.

After a time, some of the later group of officers went to Gedaliah and said, "Did you know that Baalis the king of Ammon has sent Ishmael to kill you?" But Gedaliah did not believe them.

These later officers were led by a man named Johanan. He went back to Gedaliah privately, and begged him to let him kill Ishmael, but again Gedaliah refused to believe him. He said, "You are speaking falsely of Ishmael."

No more than two months after Gedaliah became governor, Ishmael rose up and killed him, his aides, and the Chaldeans Nebuchadnezzar had left there. He also treacherously killed seventy out of eighty men on their way to worship. He filled a pit with the slain. Then he gathered together all the king's daughters and all the people at Mizpah which the Chaldeans had committed to the care of Gedaliah, and started toward the land of Ammon.

Johanan heard what was happening, so he gathered men together and they went to fight against Ishmael. The captives were recovered, but Ishmael and eight of his men escaped.

Johanan, his men, and the captives moved to a place near Bethlehem, in order to flee to Egypt. They were afraid to stay in the land because they were afraid the Chaldeans would take revenge for the death of the governor they had appointed.

All the captains came to Jeremiah and said, "Hear our supplication and pray to Jehovah for us that He will show us the way in which we should go, and the thing we should do." Jeremiah agreed to pray to God, and they swore solemnly that whatever God said, they would obey the voice of the Lord. That sounded really good.

Judah Alone

Ten days later, God gave His answer to Jeremiah, and Jeremiah called the people together to hear the message from God:

If you stay in the land, I will build you up and not tear you down; I will plant you and not uproot you, for I am grieved over the disaster that has come upon you. Do not fear the king of Babylon, for I am with you and will deliver you out of his hands.

However, if you do not obey me and stay in this land, then be assured that the sword and famine will follow you to Egypt, and you will die there. Not one will escape the disaster I will send upon you there. As my wrath has been poured out upon Jerusalem, so will my wrath be poured out upon you in Egypt. You will be an object of cursings and horror, of condemnation and reproach; you will never see this place again.

But when the people heard the message, they said "No! We will go to the land of Egypt." Jeremiah pled with the people to listen to God. He warned them it would be a fatal mistake if they disobeyed God and went into Egypt.

But the leaders of the people, including Johanan, said, "You are lying. The Lord our God has not sent you. Baruch [*Jeremiah's scribe*] has set you against us to deliver us into the hands of the Chaldeans." So they took all the people and went to Egypt. They compelled Jeremiah and Baruch to go with them.

The Bible does not tell the final end of Jeremiah, but apparently he died in Egypt. There he continued to testify to his people that they should not worship idols, but they said, "We will not listen to what you say is the word of the Lord. We are going to do as we please. Nothing has gone right for us since we stopped worshiping idols, so we are going to worship her again" — for they had vowed to worship the queen of heaven.

God told them through Jeremiah that He would cut them off completely. How sad to think of Jeremiah seeing his people worship their idols until the day he died.

****

How sad! All of God's people have been taken into captivity. The only people left in the land are the ones brought in by the king of Assyria over a hundred years before. They have mingled with the very poor Israelites who had been left at that time. There are still a very few of the neighboring people left in their territories, even though they are under the complete control of the king of Babylon. Therefore, there are a few Moabites, Ammonites, Edomites, Philistines, and Phoenicians left — though they have no power. But God's people are gone! The beautiful promised land is left desolate. Why? Is it God's fault? Read the little book of Lamentations again and grieve with Jeremiah over the land.

How doth the city sit solitary, that was full of people!
She is become as a widow, that was great among the nations!...
Among all her lovers she hath none to comfort her:
All her friends have dealt treacherously with her;
they are become her enemies...

For Jehovah hath afflicted her for the multitude of her transgressions...

Maps

CANAAN
TRIBAL TERRITORIES
OF ISRAEL

Scale of Miles
0   10   20   30   40

Mediterranean Sea

Sidon

Damascus •

Tyre

Abel-beth-
maacah   • Laish

Kanah

Beth-anath

Kadesh•

Beth-shemesh

MANASSEH

Waters of
Merom

ASHER

Hazor

NAPHTALI

Chinnereth

Sea of
Chinnereth

Rimmon

Golan •

ZEBULUN

Gath-hepher

• Deberath   Yarmuk R.

Jokneam •

Chesulloth

Dor

Megiddo

ISSACHAR

Ramoth-gilead •

Shihor-libnath

Taanach •

Bethshan •

Jahesh-gilead

Ibleam •

• Mahanaim

MANASSEH

AMMON

• Shechem•

Kanah

• Taanath-
shiloh

• Succoth

• Penuel

Jabbok R.

Tappuah

• Janoah

Gath-rimmon •

GAD

Joppa

Shiloh

• Ataroth

Gilgal

DAN   EPHRAIM   • Nazareth

Beth-horon

Ekron •

Geba• Ai

Jabneel •

Gezer •   Jericho •

Gibeon •   BENJAMIN

Gilgal

• Abel-shittim

Ashdod •

Kiriath-jearim   Beth-hoglah

Zorah   Jerusalem

Heshbon •   Bezer •

Ashkelon •

JUDAH

REUBEN

Gath •

Eglon •

Dead
Sea

• Gaza

Hebron•

Arnon R.

• Ziklag

SIMEON

M O A B

Way of the Sea

Besor

Beersheba

Hormah

Zered R.

King's Highway

E D O M

173

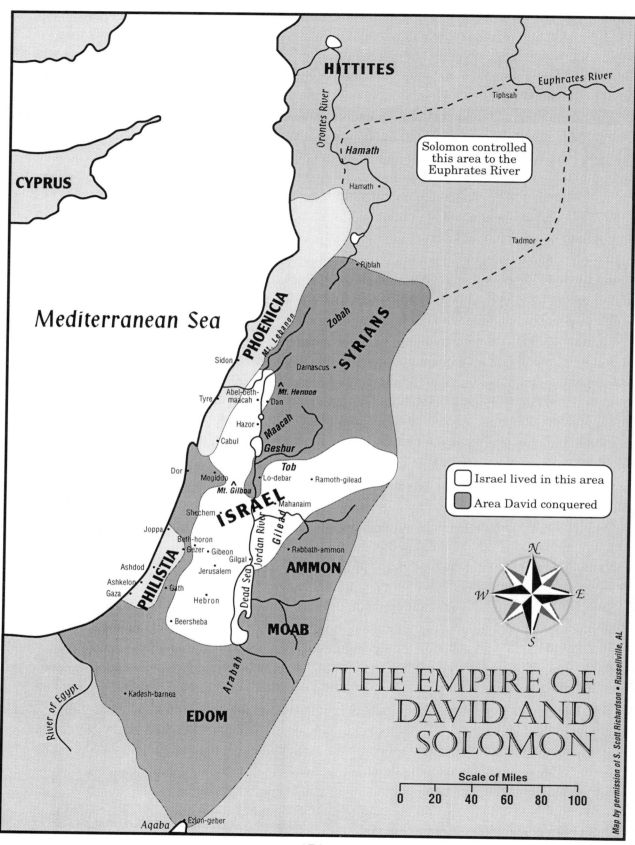

HITTITES

Euphrates River

Orontes River

Tiphsah

Hamath

Solomon controlled this area to the Euphrates River

CYPRUS

Hamath

Tadmor

Riblah

Mediterranean Sea

PHOENICIA

Zobah

SYRIANS

Mt. Lebanon

Sidon

Damascus

Abel-beth-maacah

Mt. Hermon

Tyre

Dan

Hazor

Maacah

Cabul

Geshur

Tob

Dor

Lo-debar

Ramoth-gilead

Megiddo

Mt. Gilboa

ISRAEL

Israel lived in this area

Mahanaim

Area David conquered

Shechem

Joppa

Gilead

Jordan River

Beth-horon

Gezer

Gibeon

Rabbath-ammon

Ashdod

Gilgal

AMMON

Ashkelon

Jerusalem

Gaza

PHILISTIA

Gath

Dead Sea

Hebron

Beersheba

MOAB

N

W   E

S

Arabah

THE EMPIRE OF DAVID AND SOLOMON

River of Egypt

Kadesh-barnea

EDOM

Map by permission of S. Scott Richardson • Russellville, AL

Scale of Miles

0   20   40   60   80   100

Aqaba

Ezion-geber

174

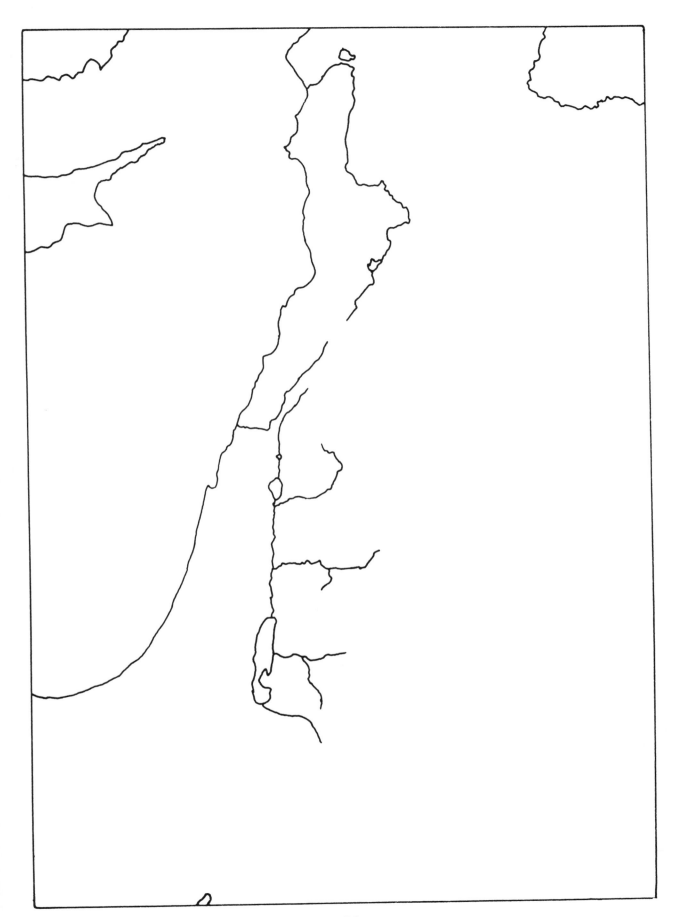

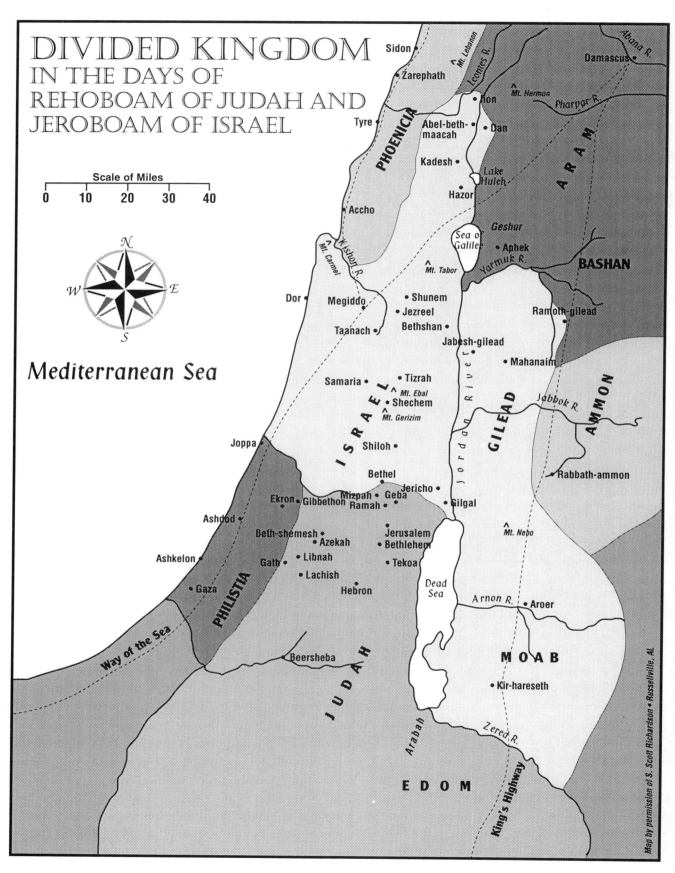

DIVIDED KINGDOM
IN THE DAYS OF
REHOBOAM OF JUDAH AND
JEROBOAM OF ISRAEL

Scale of Miles

0   10   20   30   40

Mediterranean Sea

Sidon
Zarephath
Tyre
PHOENICIA
Accho
Dor
Megiddo
Taanach

Mt. Lebanon
Leontes R.
Ijon
Abel-beth-maacah
Dan
Kadesh
Lake Huleh
Hazor
Mt. Herman

Damascus
Abana R.
Pharpar R.
ARAM

Geshur
Sea of Galilee
Aphek
Yarmuk R.
BASHAN

Shunem
Jezreel
Bethshan
Jabesh-gilead
Mt. Tabor

Ramoth-gilead

Samaria
ISRAEL
Mt. Ebal
Shechem
Mt. Gerizim
Tizrah

Jordan River
GILEAD
Mahanaim
Jabbok R.
AMMON

Joppa
Shiloh
Bethel
Mizpah Geba
Ekron Gibbethon Ramah
Jericho
Gilgal
Rabbath-ammon

Ashdod
Beth-shemesh Azekah
Jerusalem
Bethlehem
Mt. Nebo

Ashkelon
Gath Libnah
Lachish
Tekoa
Hebron

Gaza
PHILISTIA
Dead Sea
Arnon R. Aroer

Way of the Sea

Beersheba

JUDAH

MOAB
Kir-hareseth

Arabah
Zered R.

EDOM

King's Highway

Map by permission of S. Scott Richardson • Russellville, AL

176

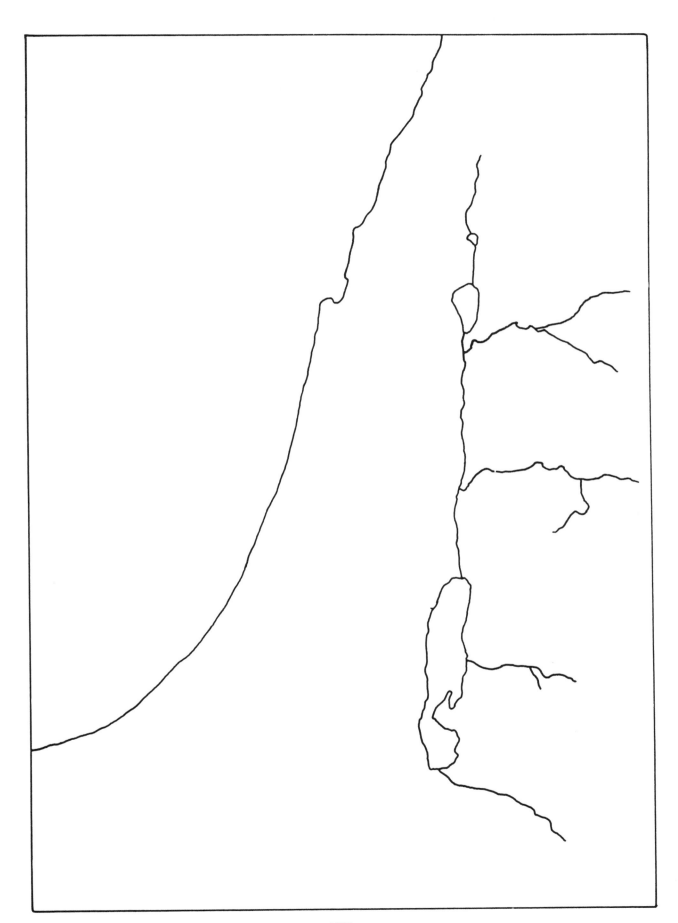

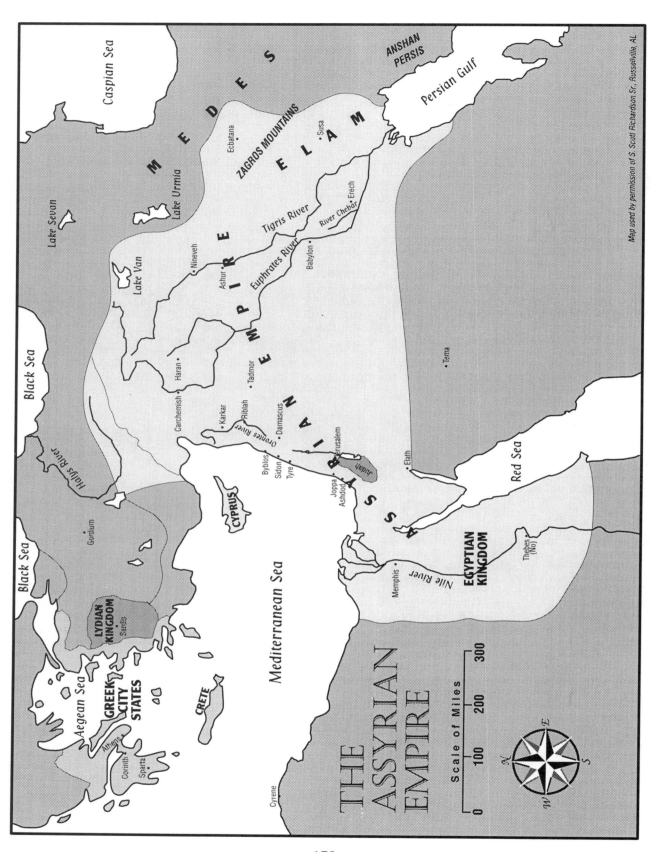

THE ASSYRIAN EMPIRE

Scale of Miles

0 100 200 300

Caspian Sea

ANSHAN
PERSIS

Persian Gulf

M E D E S

ZAGROS MOUNTAINS

• Ecbatana

E L A M

• Susa

Tigris River

Erech •

River Chebar

E M P I R E

• Nineveh

• Ashur

Euphrates River

Babylon •

Lake Urmia

Lake Van

Black Sea

Lake Sevan

• Haran

• Carchemish

• Tadmor

• Karkar

• Riblah

Orontes River

• Damascus

• Tema

Byblos •
Sidon •
Tyre •

• Jerusalem

Judah

A S S Y R I A N

• Elath

Red Sea

Joppa •
Ashdod •

Halys River

Gordium •

CYPRUS

Mediterranean Sea

LYDIAN
KINGDOM

• Sardis

EGYPTIAN
KINGDOM

Nile River

Memphis •

Thebes
(No) •

Black Sea

Aegean Sea

GREEK
CITY
STATES

CRETE

Athens •

Corinth •
Sparta •

Cyrene •

178

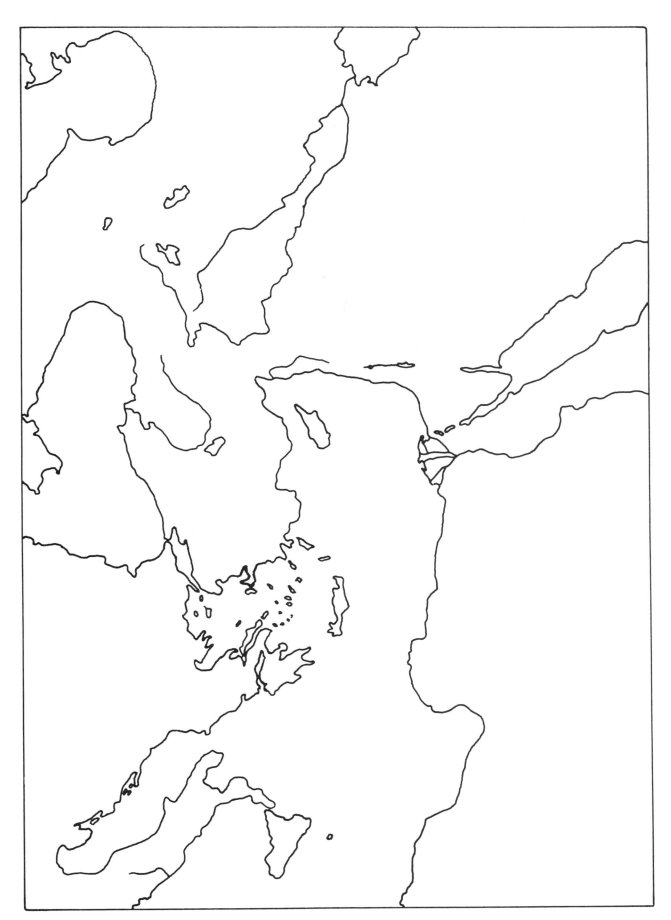

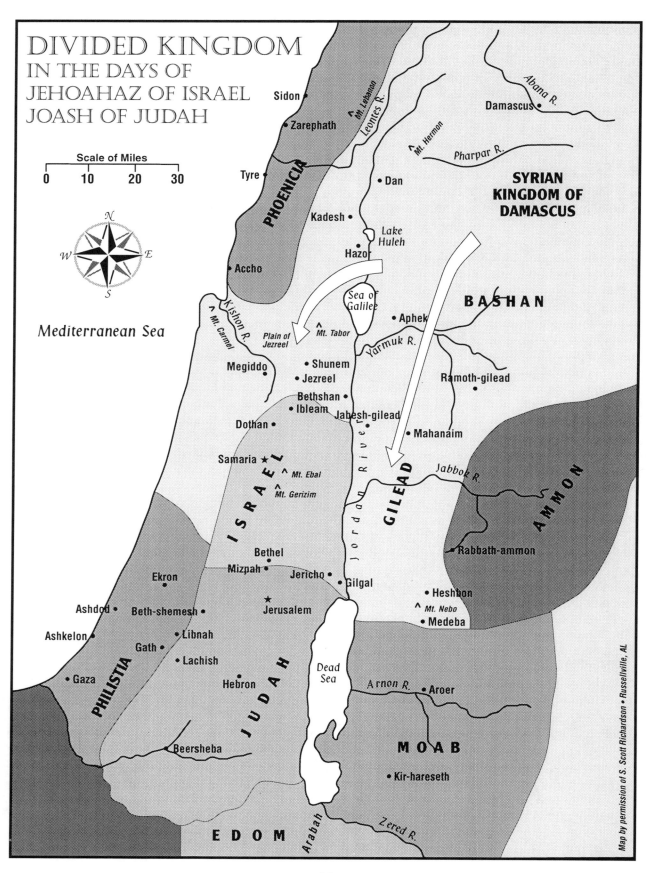

DIVIDED KINGDOM
IN THE DAYS OF
JEHOAHAZ OF ISRAEL
JOASH OF JUDAH

Scale of Miles

0   10   20   30

N
W   E
S

Mediterranean Sea

Sidon
Zarephath

PHOENICIA

Tyre

Leontes R.
Mt. Lebanon

Abana R.
Damascus

Mt. Hermon
Pharpar R.

Dan

**SYRIAN
KINGDOM OF
DAMASCUS**

Kadesh

Lake
Huleh

Hazor

Accho

Sea of
Galilee

BASHAN

Aphek

Kishon R.
Mt. Carmel

Plain of
Jezreel

Mt. Tabor

Yarmuk R.

Megiddo

Shunem
Jezreel

Ramoth-gilead

Bethshan
Ibleam

Jabesh-gilead

Dothan

Mahanaim

Samaria ★

Mt. Ebal

Mt. Gerizim

Jordan River

GILEAD

Jabbok R.

AMMON

Bethel

Mizpah

Jericho

Gilgal

Rabbath-ammon

Ekron

★
Jerusalem

Heshbon

Mt. Nebo

Medeba

Ashdod

Beth-shemesh

Ashkelon

Libnah

Gath

Lachish

PHILISTIA

J U D A H

Dead
Sea

Arnon R.   Aroer

Gaza

Hebron

Beersheba

M O A B

Kir-hareseth

E D O M

Arabah

Zered R.

Map by permission of S. Scott Richardson • Russellville, AL

180

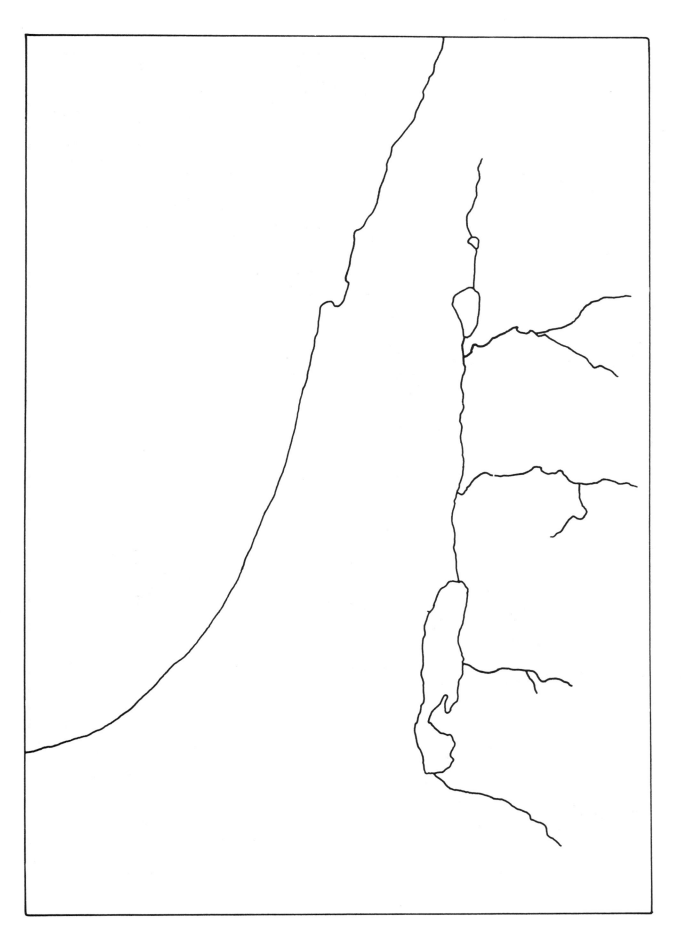

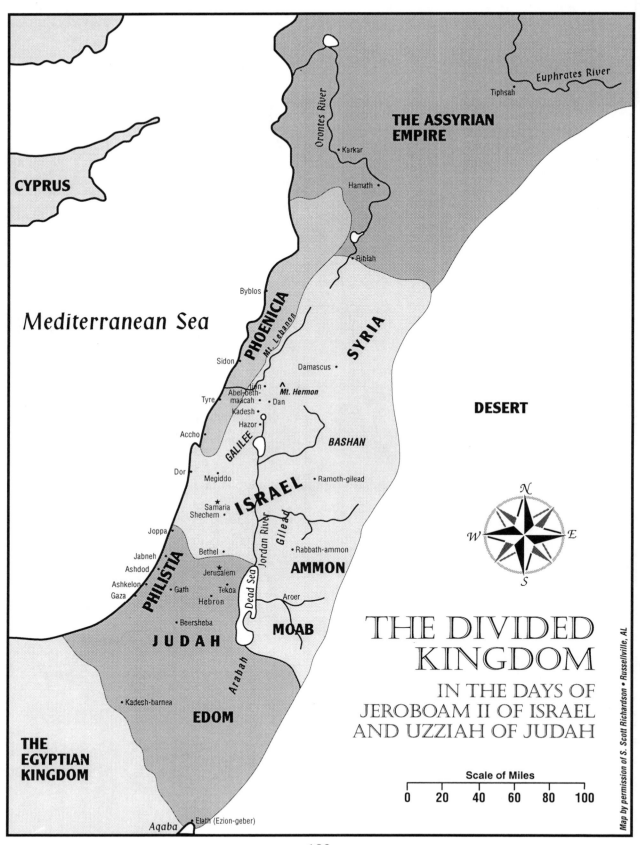

CYPRUS

Mediterranean Sea

THE ASSYRIAN EMPIRE

Euphrates River

Tiphsah

Orontes River

Karkar

Hamath

Riblah

Byblos

PHOENICIA

SYRIA

Mt. Lebanon

Sidon

Damascus

DESERT

Abel-beth-maacah
Ijon
Tyre
Dan
Mt. Hermon

Kadesh

Hazor

BASHAN

Accho

GALILEE

Dor

Megiddo

Ramoth-gilead

ISRAEL

Samaria
Shechem

Gilead

Joppa

Jordan River

Jabneh

Bethel

Rabbath-ammon

Ashdod

Jerusalem

AMMON

Ashkelon
Gaza

Gath

Tekoa

Hebron

Aroer

PHILISTIA

Dead Sea

Beersheba

MOAB

JUDAH

Arabah

Kadesh-barnea

EDOM

THE EGYPTIAN KINGDOM

Aqaba
Elath (Ezion-geber)

N
W   E
S

THE DIVIDED KINGDOM

IN THE DAYS OF JEROBOAM II OF ISRAEL AND UZZIAH OF JUDAH

Map by permission of S. Scott Richardson • Russellville, AL

Scale of Miles

0   20   40   60   80   100

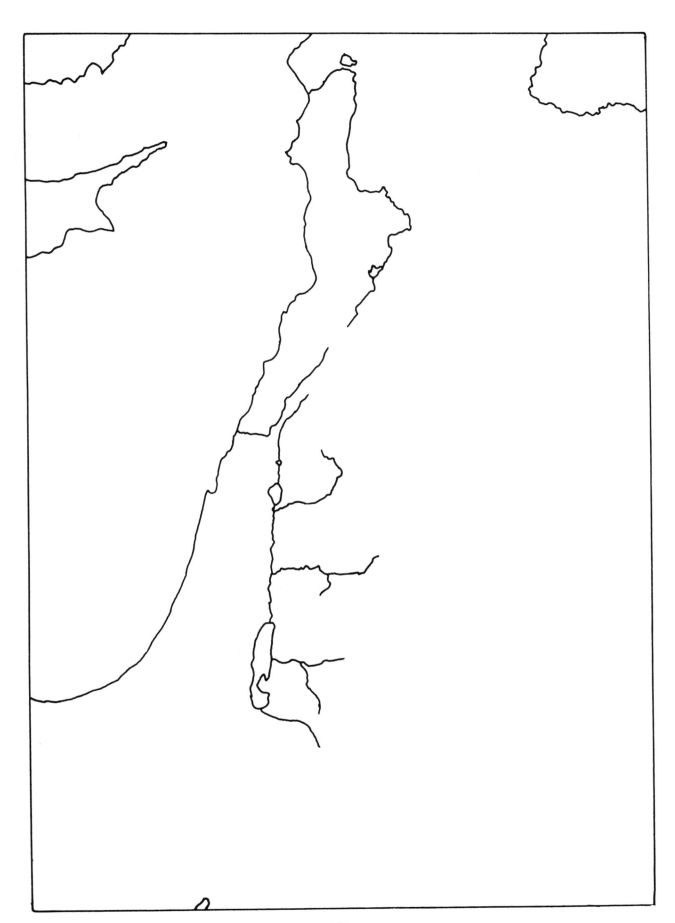

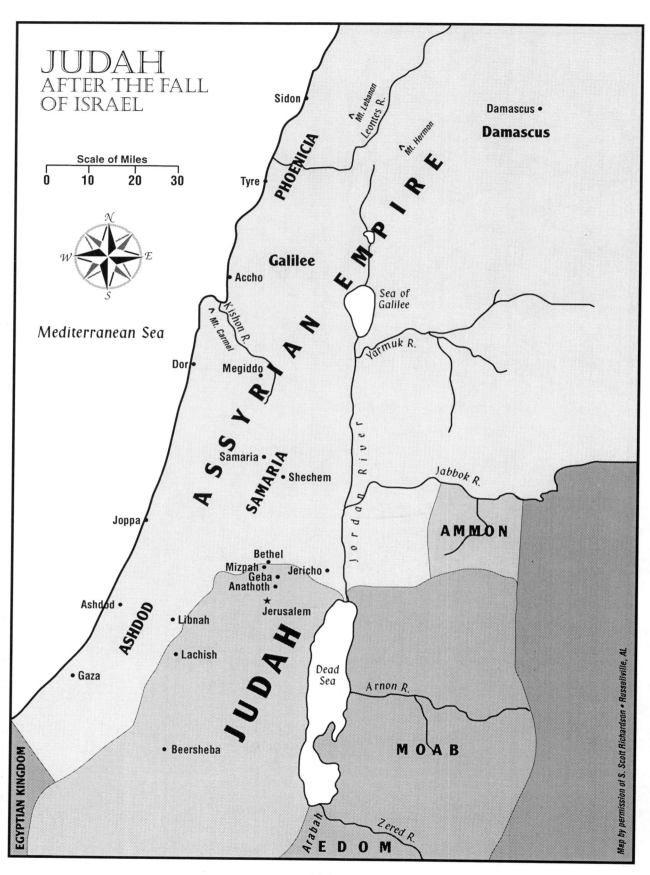

JUDAH
AFTER THE FALL
OF ISRAEL

Scale of Miles
0   10   20   30

Mediterranean Sea

Sidon •

Damascus •
Damascus

PHOENICIA

Mt. Lebanon

Leontes R.

Mt. Hermon

Tyre •

Galilee

• Accho

Sea of Galilee

Kishon R.

Mt. Carmel

Yarmuk R.

Dor •

Megiddo •

A S S Y R I A N   E M P I R E

Samaria •

SAMARIA

• Shechem

Jabbok R.

Joppa •

Jordan River

AMMON

Bethel •
Mizpah •   • Jericho •
Geba •
Anathoth •

★
Jerusalem

Ashdod •

ASHDOD

• Libnah

• Lachish

Dead Sea

Arnon R.

• Gaza

J U D A H

• Beersheba

M O A B

EGYPTIAN KINGDOM

Arabah   *Zered R.*

E D O M

Map by permission of S. Scott Richardson • Russellville, AL

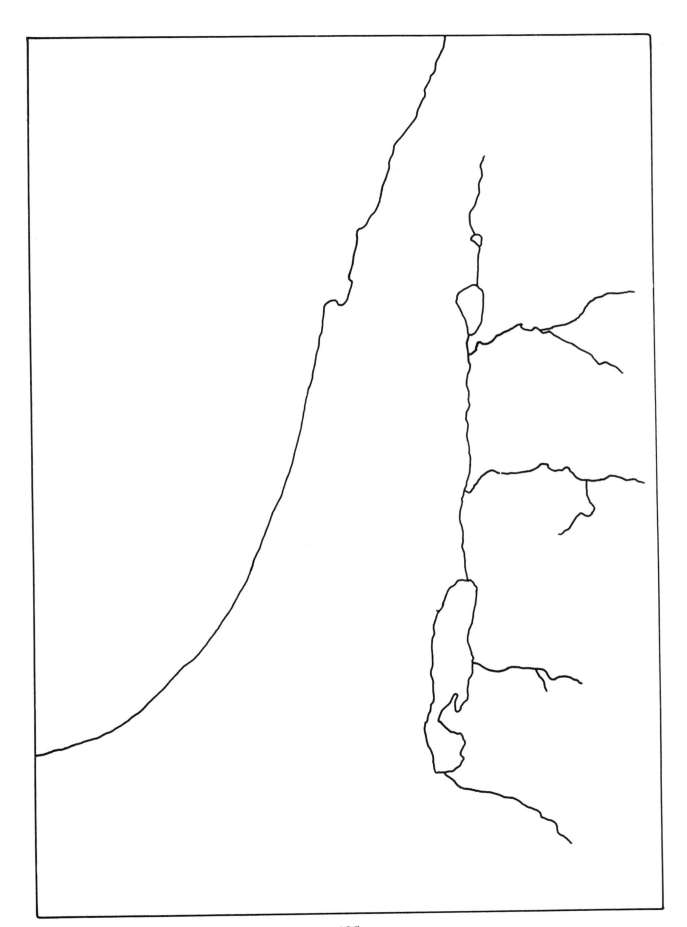

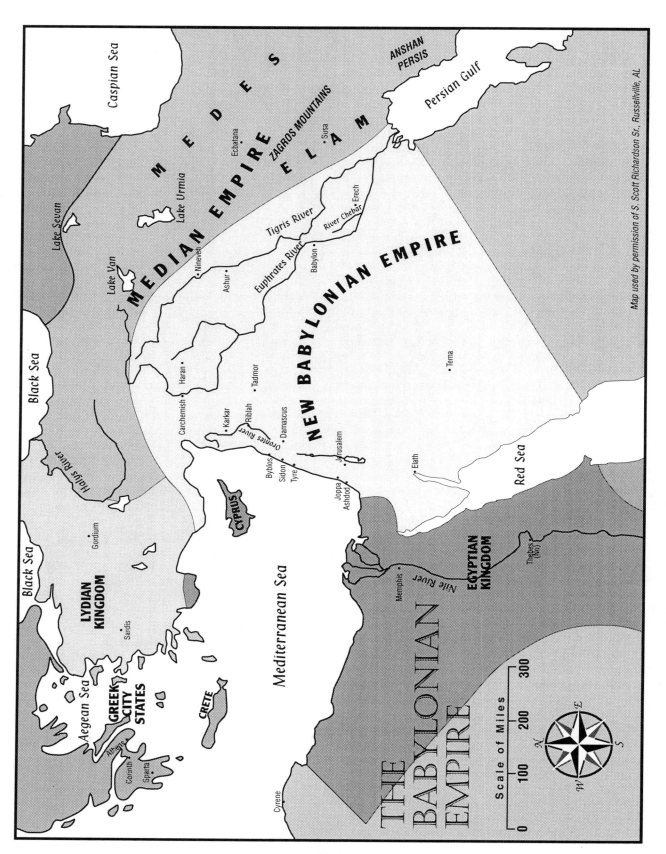

THE BABYLONIAN EMPIRE

Scale of Miles

0   100   200   300

Map used by permission of S. Scott Richardson Sr., Russellville, AL

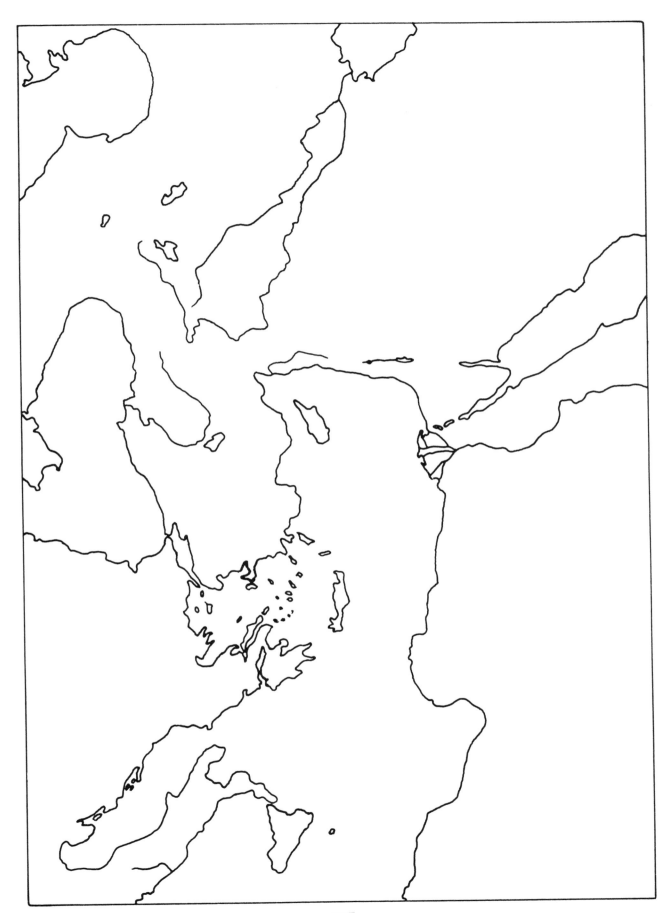

Bibliography

Bruce, F. F. *Israel and the Nations*. Grand Rapids: William B. Eerdmans Publishing Company, 1969.

Clare, Israel Smith. *Standard History of the World*, Vol. 1. Cincinnati: Standard Historical Society, 1928.

Crockett, William Day. *A Harmony of the Books of Samuel, Kings, and Chronicles*. Grand Rapids: Baker Book House, 1951.

Gardner, Joseph L. (ed.). *Reader's Digest Atlas of the Bible*, Pleasantville, N. Y.: The Reader's Digest Association, Inc., 1981.

Hailey, Homer. *A Commentary of Isaiah*. Grand Rapids: Baker Book House, 1985.

Hailey, Homer. *The Minor Prophets*. Grand Rapids: Baker Book House, 1972.

Keil, Carl, and Delitzsch, Franz. *Biblical Commentary on the Old Testament*, Vols. II, IV, V. Reprint. Grand Rapids: Associated Publishers and Authors, Inc., n.d.

Keyes, Nelson Beecher. *Story of the Bible World*. Maplewood, N. J.: C. S. Hammond & Company, 1959.

Oates, Joan. *Babylon*. London: Thames and Hudson Ltd., 1979.

Pfeiffer, Charles. *Baker's Bible Atlas*. Revised ed. Grand Rapids: Baker Book House, 1969.

Pfeiffer, Charles. *The Divided Kingdom*. Grand Rapids: Baker Book House, 1967.

Stancliff, Leon D. *The Biblical Prophets in Outlined Notes*. Nashville: Gospel Advocate Company, 1976.

Thomas, D. Winton, (ed.). *Documents From Old Testament Times*. New York: Harper & Row, 1961.

Waldron, Bob and Sandra. *History and Geography of the Bible Story*. Fairmont, Indiana: Guardian of Truth Foundation, 1984.

Young, Edward J. *The Book of Isaiah*. Grand Rapids: William B. Eerdmans Publishing Company, 1965.